ICONIC SPACES

The Dark Theology of Samuel Beckett's Drama

SANDRA WYNANDS

University of Notre Dame Press
Notre Dame, Indiana

Copyright © 2007 by University of Notre Dame
Notre Dame, Indiana 46556
www.undpress.nd.edu
All Rights Reserved

Designed by Wendy McMillen
Set in 10.5/14 Bell MT by EM Studio
Printed on 55# Nature's Recycle paper in the U.S.A. by Versa Press

Library of Congress Cataloging-in-Publication Data

Wynands, Sandra, 1970–
Iconic spaces : the dark theology of Samuel Beckett's drama /
Sandra Wynands.
    p. cm.
Includes bibliographical references and index.
ISBN-13: 978-0-268-04410-7 (pbk. : alk. paper)
ISBN-10: 0-268-04410-4 (pbk. : alk. paper)
1. Beckett, Samuel, 1906–1989—Criticism and interpretation.
2. Beckett, Samuel, 1906-1989—Religion. 3. Theology in literature.
4. Spiritual life in literature.   I. Title.
PR6003.E282Z975   2007
848'.91409—dc22

2007020101

Contents

Acknowledgments

There are many people without whom this book would not have taken shape. Kevin Hart, in particular, extended his exceptional generosity to me. His encompassing view of literature, philosophy, theology, and art has enabled me to look far beyond the small world I could have seen by myself. He accompanied me on every step of the way to completion and publication of this book and my gratitude is immense but necessarily inadequate. Without Sheila Rabillard's conviction that I could contribute something worthwhile to the much-ploughed field of Beckett scholarship this book would not have grown beyond its embryonic stage. I would like to thank the English Department at the University of Victoria, Canada, for an intellectual home while I wrote these pages and the members of All Saints of Alaska Orthodox Church in Victoria for a spiritual one and for the most heartfelt commitment to community I have ever experienced. In particular my thanks go to Stephen Scobie, Smaro Kamboureli, Patrick Grant, Christopher Keep, Thomas Cleary, Colleen Donnelly, Lori Emerson, Denise Fidia, Fr. John Hainsworth, and Laura Coward.

A slightly different version of chapter 1 previously appeared in *Religion and Literature* (37.3). I thank the editors there and at Notre Dame University Press. Special thanks go to Barbara Hanrahan, the director of the press, and to Gerald Bruns. My two anonymous readers for Notre Dame University Press offered generous reviews that went far beyond the call of duty.

My deep gratitude goes to my husband, Raphael Foshay, for years of love, friendship, and a shared intellectual and spiritual path, and to my parents for their love and confidence. My parents Willi and Siegrid Wynands are the most loyal supporters of my work, despite the language barrier between them and the fruits of their commitment. My thanks to all of you for your countless gifts.

Abbreviations

D	*Disjecta*
E	*Endgame*
F	*Film*
ISIS	*Ill Seen Ill Said*
M	*Murphy (The Trilogy)*
Mo	*Molloy (The Trilogy)*
MP	*Le Monde et Le Pantalon*
P	*Proust*
SP	*Collected Shorter Plays*
"TD"	"Three Dialogues"
U	*The Unnamable (The Trilogy)*
W	*Watt*
WG	*Waiting for Godot*
WW	*Worstward Ho*

Chapter 1

Introduction

While staying at his mother's house in Ireland just after the end of World War II, Samuel Beckett decisively closed an early chapter of his writing career. He had what is often touted in Beckett criticism as a "revelation," which at the very least was a radical insight that would guide his writing for the rest of his career and, indeed, would lead his development into the inimitable writer he became. During his stay in Foxrock, Beckett came to realize "that Joyce had gone as far as one could in the direction of knowing more, [being] in control of one's material. He was always adding to it; you only have to look at his proofs to see that. I saw that my own way was in impoverishment, in lack of knowledge and in taking away, in subtracting rather than adding."[1] Beckett undoubtedly began to come into his own when he stopped producing mere carbon copies of Joycean texts. He began to write in French, which as a second, consciously learned language made it easier for him to cut through the "terribly arbitrary materiality of the word surface" (*D* 53) in an attempt to make language conscious through a process of reduction. Beckett took the dictum "less is more" seriously.

1

It may be dangerous to make too much of a single and singular insight such as this one; to be sure, there were other important turning points in Beckett's career. One of these was the impasse he encountered after completing *The Unnamable*, which left him floundering for quite a long while. Then a modified approach opened up new vistas of radically pared down, almost static prose such as one finds in *Worstward Ho* and the other works of the second trilogy, the so-called closed space novels. Yet even this change depended on—or was a variant pursuit of—the revelation at Foxrock. The shift in direction after *The Unnamable* did not solve Beckett's dilemma; rather, it enabled him fully to articulate it in increasingly radical experiments until he found himself driven to distraction by his own uncompromising nature. In a letter, he described his work on the novel *Worstward Ho:* "Struggling with impossible prose. English. With loathing."[2] This idiosyncratic staccato message is part of a letter to his American producer Alan Schneider. Somewhat humorously the letter adopts the same style that dominates *Worstward Ho* throughout. Beckett here is obsessively engaged in a project that is by definition endless.

At Foxrock, Beckett realized that his work was motivated not by fullness, but by the infinite circumscription of an unfathomable emptiness. In many ways, including its fragmentation of plot, its mélange of discursive snippets, its long stream-of-consciousness passages, Joyce's *Ulysses* is doubtless a typically "decentered" modernist text, but as an artistic whole it is masterminded by Joyce. It is well known that it is possible to cross-reference *Ulysses* and to end up with a minute chronology of Bloomsday, and, in fact, with a minute portrait of Dublin. In this sense the centrality of consciousness reigns supreme in the book. Beckett's project is in some ways more radical because he asks whether or not it is mistaken to assume that the process of writing can ever be "complete." If writing, as Beckett proposes, is a self-contradictory process that cannot be unified or totalized, it is a mistake to approach it through the covert ego-identity of authorial consciousness, even if that hides behind the wholeness of a work of art.

This decentering of consciousness is in many ways part of a process that reaches as far back as the sixteenth century, when Giordano Bruno's radical Copernicanism challenged the firmly entrenched dogmatic idea that God is the ubiquitous center of the universe. In what was a time thoroughly characterized by Aristotelian thought, Bruno returned to Neoplatonist ideas. He took seriously the understanding that God has his center everywhere and his circumference nowhere: if that is the case, Bruno conjectured, it must be possible for each soul, for each consciousness, to see God from any point whatsoever. In fact, the world would cease to be a *uni*verse and be seen instead as more of a "multiverse." While this realization could increase human appreciation of the infinite glory of God, at the same time it ushered in a gravitational shift from divine to human.

A series of substitutions begins with Petrarch and continues through the Renaissance and Enlightenment in which human consciousness begins to take the place of a centered conception of God. No true decentering occurs. Instead the center merely shifts to a secular context. Thus during the Renaissance human love, love of an idealized woman, can lead to the pinnacle of religious experience. Idealized objects of love such as Dante's Beatrice or Petrarch's Laura begin to personify the Platonic idea of beauty. In Descartes, finally, human consciousness in the form of the cogito becomes the only source of certainty. Consciousness becomes a self-grounding principle, with the result that the divine runs the danger of being reduced to anthropomorphic proportions: secularization dismisses the sacred and at the same time the sacralization of the secular ensures that the boundaries between the secular and the sacred become blurred.[3] The divine assumes human proportions and, mutatis mutandis, the human is given near-divine status. Another cycle repeats itself: now the centrality of human consciousness must be questioned, but the process can lead to utter nihilism just as much as it can facilitate an attempt to see infinite divine transcendence for what it is.

So dislodging the centrality of human consciousness, as Beckett does in *The Unnamable* and numerous shorter texts—works in which it becomes impossible to say who, if anyone, is speaking—to a certain extent means dislodging the anthropomorphic God, or more generally the God of the positive religions. But this does not equal the outright atheism of a Sartrean existentialism, which was dominating the intellectual scene in mid-twentieth-century Paris. Beckett's position, sometimes described as an atheism, is subtler (if one can indeed still call it atheistic), and there were figures other than Sartre on Beckett's intellectual horizon in the 1940s and 1950s who were much more important to his own artistic obsessions.

One of these figures is Maurice Blanchot. Blanchot himself and his immediate circle spent a good part of their intellectual lives in the shadow of existentialism. The work, for example, of his lifelong friend Emmanuel Lévinas was merely tolerated by *Les Tempes Modernes*. Blanchot's work, much like Beckett's, deliberately undertakes to separate God and the sacred from the conceptions of the positive religions. Like Beckett, Blanchot calls himself an atheist and at the same time is aware that the statement "I am an atheist" cannot legitimately be made: "the 'I' and God are homologous."[4] Blanchot lends new credence to the truism that the profession of atheism is as much a profession of belief as that of the believer.

In *Faux Pas* Blanchot memorably advances his own formulation of the dilemma in which the contradictory impulse of writing lands the writer. "The writer," Blanchot says, "finds himself in the increasingly ludicrous condition of having nothing to write, of having no means with which to write it, and of being constrained by the utter necessity of always writing it. Having nothing to express must be taken in the most literal manner."[5] Beckett gives very similar expression to the problem and in all likelihood the convergence with his formulation in the "Three Dialogues" is not coincidental: too close is the resemblance, too obvious the influence. There Beckett postulates that in the process of writing there is "nothing to express, nothing with which to express, nothing from which to express, no power to express, no desire to express, together with the obligation to express" ("TD" 139). Until correspondence between Beckett and Blanchot or some other indication of direct influence surfaces, there is no way of knowing whether this convergence was a deliberate act on Beckett's part or a coincidence born of the fact that sharing a very narrow preoccupation with a particular question might result in very similar formulations. In any case, Beckett aligns himself much more closely with the man in the shadows of existentialist Paris.

For Blanchot, as for Beckett, the process of writing is inherently aporetic: it involves the approach to a point that can never be reached and never be known discursively. This point is brought into "existence," if such a word can aptly adumbrate its elusive nature, by the process of writing and yet writing can never "own" it nor fully define it. At the same time the elusive point is its only "purpose": it draws its energy from nowhere else. In a chapter titled "Encountering the Imaginary," Blanchot describes this contradictory dynamic:

> Narrative is the movement toward a point—one that is not only unknown, ignored, and foreign, but such that it seems, even before and outside of this movement, to have no kind of reality; yet one that is so imperious that it is from that point alone that the narrative draws its attraction, in such a way that it cannot even "begin" before having reached it; but it is only the narrative and the unforeseeable movement of the narrative that provide the space where the point becomes real, powerful and alluring.[6]

In the "Three Dialogues" Beckett tries to come to theoretical terms with the possibility of an art that defines itself outside the quest for and the chase after this elusive point. This does not mean that Beckett is uncertain whether the process of writing is an aporia or not: the artistic "pursuit" never loses its aporetic nature for Beckett and he would always embrace Blanchot's formulation. The question rather becomes whether the aporia of art is driven by a quest for what the artist knows to be an unattainable resolution of the aporia, or whether its defining feature is a simple embrace of the aporia that the artist should not even try to resolve. Indeed, Beckett argues in the "Three Dialogues," the quest might impose a linearity on the artistic endeavor that is quite foreign to its aporetic nature.

Perplexingly for those accustomed to reading Beckett in the light of existentialist atheism and the Theater of the Absurd, the aporia of writing as it is performatively enacted in Beckett's texts bears the same mark of irreducibility as does the divine in the texts of negative theology. The negative theologian cannot hope ever to capture God conceptually, and indeed the verbal acrobatics apophaticism enacts indicates that this cannot and must not be negative theology's aim. And yet, despite this parallel, Beckett the self-professed atheist could not be called a "religious" person by any stretch of the imagination. "I have no religious feeling," he said to Tom Driver. "Once I had a religious emotion. It was at my first communion. No more."[7] Beckett, it is safe to say, does not affirm the presence of God. His writing attests rather to God's absence. The "God" his characters appeal to refuses to reveal himself and to fulfill their petitions, and the world his characters inhabit lacks any indication of bearing divine meaning or being guided by divine will. Beckett's people go around in circles, unable to free themselves from their self-imposed shackles.

Yet what is this absence? Should we unquestioningly take it at face value? Or, differently put, is the absence of God truly an absence? Martin Heidegger reminds us in "The Thing" that "absence is not nothing."[8] The absence of God can be experienced as a presence and Beckett's writing is a testimony to that experience. The absence of presence, or, more accurately, the presence of absence thus turns into an experience of transcendence. Denying God, or denying the God of the positive religions, does not in itself abolish transcendence. For Heidegger, any tradition of thought that proclaims the absence of God must still contend with the "hidden fullness and wealth of what has been."[9] It builds on that past, inherits its categories, redefines itself in contradistinction from these categories. The task is to be vigilant and to look for the new, displaced ways in which the transcendent henceforth manifests itself: it returns, for instance, as the transcendental ghost of *différance* in Jacques Derrida, as well as in the aporetic conception of writing in Beckett and Blanchot. Indeed, for Heidegger it is the poet's role to keep a space open for the return of God.

Blanchot's idea of the "Outside" is another such transcendental ghost that manifests covertly a form of transcendence that takes its lead from negative rather than positive theology. It is worth dwelling on this idea for a while insofar as it helps us understand Beckett's conception of writing. Writing has to pass through the "Outside" of language, a neutral, empty space detached from author as well as reader, and therefore from all interiority of authorial intention as well as its expression in the work of art. The Outside approaches in the paradoxical movement of drawing near to what withdraws. Therefore it is not really "outside" at all. That is, it is not in opposition to something else outside itself. Properly speaking, then, what Blanchot calls the "Outside" is inside and outside at the same time.

Understanding writing in this way allows us to see it as an iconic space: like the icon, writing through the Outside does not renounce the realm of representation but situates itself squarely in it. Yet at the same time it upsets the logic of representation because it functions by its own. This is a nonmimetic logic that aims to make the divine experientially present in the realm of representation. The painted icon uses techniques such as reverse perspective in ways similar to the manner in which negative theology employs aporia: to indicate an order that will not bow to the laws of representation and to the reifying human gaze. Instead the image will exert its own gaze. The icon confronts the viewer directly; it threatens to burst out of the frame instead of collecting the image tidily within it. Beckett's prose and his stage images converge in a kind of iconic point zero, where the inevitable metonymy of aporetic discourse tips over into the metaphor of visual iconicity.

Yet it needs to be said again that Beckett's existentialist critics have a point: Beckett does not profess God's presence in the same way an icon does. Beckett does not affirm God, but an absence or emptiness of God. This is an iconic emptiness, however, and I contend that it is structurally indistinguishable from the conceptual emptiness of God in negative theology. But how can this parallel be a legitimate move given Beckett's atheism? The answer is that confessional declarations of loyalty are wholly inadequate here. Reconsider what "atheism" means. Popular wisdom has it that atheism and theism are really not very different from one another. They are two sides of the same coin: both are based on faith or belief, the content of which the two positions merely configure differently. But there is more truth to the common sense of this picture: atheism will not be a genuine alternative to theism as long as it configures itself as the coin's reverse. For as long as it does so, it effectively buys into the same principles as the theism of the positive religions, namely those of presence. Jean-Luc Nancy points out that to this day atheism has not managed to substitute for the positivist God anything other than another figure, instance, or idea of supreme meaning: "of an end, of a good, of a parousia," that is to say, of presence, and, as we have seen earlier, especially the presence of the human being, particularly human consciousness.[10]

"Absence" as it occurs in Beckett, then, must not be seen in opposition to presence. It is neither a presence nor an absence, but rather both presence and absence: a point that withdraws as one approaches and whose only claim to "existence" is this aporetic movement. In order to be genuinely different from positive theism, atheism must resist the temptation to substitute another presence for God. This "deconstructed" atheism begins to converge with negative theology, putting a postmodern spin on Bruno's suspicion of the unity of opposites.

Negative theology tries to "deconstruct" theology, so that we may speak of God unhampered by such metaphysical categories as "being" and "existence," which pertain exclusively to the relative, human realm. Its aim is to guard the absolute transcendence of God, to whom no humanly conceivable categories like being, affirmation, or negation— presence or absence—can apply. The question whether there is or is no God is deflected and becomes a performative "event," an experience of the nonconceptual performed in and by language in the process of writing.

The Outside provides Blanchot with an imaginary complex that enables him to consider God or the sacred detached from the positive religions—and this Beckett wants to do at all costs. As an Irishman he is acutely aware of the political aberrations of organized religion. During his formative childhood years Beckett experienced the positive religions largely as instruments of power driven by ideology. Dublin was caught up in violent turmoil following the Easter uprising of 1916 and Beckett was there to witness it: in Foxrock, safely on the margins of the troubles in Dublin, his father took him to the top of a hill from which the flames that raged in the city could be clearly seen. Only nine years old at the time and still attending primary school at Earlsfort House in Dublin, Beckett was but vaguely aware of the political conflicts shaking his country. Nevertheless, the experience on the hill in Foxrock stayed with him for many years to come and he continued to think of it with "fear and horror."[11] The school Beckett attended after completing his primary education was a prestigious Protestant institution, Portora, in what was to become Northern Ireland. After the nation was partitioned during his second year at Portora, the military consequences of misguided religion accompanied him at the end of each term when he had to pass armed British border patrols on his way into Ireland.[12]

In a landmark interview conducted by Tom Driver in the early 1960s, Beckett speaks with derision of the customs of popular Catholicism in Ireland: "When you pass a church on an Irish bus, all the hands flurry in the sign of the cross. One day the dogs of Ireland will do that too and perhaps also the pigs."[13] There was never a tendency in Beckett to reconcile himself with the manifestations of organized religion, which he continued to view as hypocritical, superficial, or unthinking. Yet he recognized that the fundamental religious impulse is everywhere present. Thus, while he refused to stage this transcendence in classical terms, it does not disappear entirely; it merely manifests itself differently, in a displaced fashion. This moment of displacement of the sacred pervades the literary and cultural milieu of the time: it is recognizable in Blanchot's Outside; Georges Bataille celebrates it in the irreducibility of excess and frenzied expenditure: laughter, festival, sacrifice, religion, sexuality, violence, death, as well as God are all manifestations of the sacred for Bataille. And the displaced sacred recurs in yet a different guise in the quasi-transcendental status of Derrida's *différance*.

■   The voluminous and insightful body of Beckett criticism has for the most part objectified and domesticated the role of religion and the sacred in Beckett's work, and as a result it has failed to grasp the full extent of the challenge his writing presents for the reader's understanding of literature and the religious. In the early days of grappling with the religious dimension in Beckett's work, and from then on with surprising persistence, scholars have focused on his resistance to domesticated forms of religion—whether institutional, political, or emotional—as if Beckett's engagement with the religious stopped there. Not shedding their own blinkers, critics of religion often situate it as diametrically opposed to the courage of existential enquiry. Believers are seen to seek solace in false security. But it is dangerous not to question one's own ideas of religion and to assume Beckett to do the same. As a result, engagement with religion and with Beckett's work does not take place at the most fundamental level, but at the level of concept.

As part of the attempt to uncover the religious dimension in Beckett's work, one often finds appeals to episodes or tendencies in Beckett's life itself or to his characters. A character's derision at the surface forms of religious convention, for example, is easily assumed to be consistent with the values Beckett as a person stands for. Beckett the author does not graduate from his position as a disgruntled lapsed Protestant obsessively pontificating on the hopelessness of human existence in a spirit of

wallowing negativity. Yet in character coherence (as the centered analyzing subject's counterpart), plot content (which implies a container
and something contained within it), or narrative linearity (and its teleological trajectory), objectification has already occurred. Beckett thoroughly questions each of these literary conventions. Why should a critic
hang on to them in the face of abundant rhetorical strategies that undermine them? Even Mary Bryden's landmark study *Samuel Beckett and the
Idea of God*, which handles religion evenly and strives for neutrality, refuses to address the *idea* of God or our lack thereof. Instead, it uncovers
a fascinating array of religious or theological allusions at the phenotypic
level and argues positions Beckett's text may take toward them. However, in the depths of Beckett's theology of transdecendence these positions fall before rigorous self-deconstruction.

Beckett's work emphasizes metaphor and remains incomprehensible at the mimetic level. As a result allegorical readings proliferate fruitfully. The odd one has reached notoriety: Godot stands for God? . . .
Against any indication to the contrary Didi and Gogo become believers.
Allegorical readings fully account for the antimimetic nature of Beckett's work, but a danger lurks in them, too. Allegory is built on one-to-
one correspondence of the literal and the allegorical levels, and a conceptual frame is once again imposed on wild writing that tries to free
itself from such constraints. Attempts to read Beckett in the light of the
work of a specific philosophical system can easily fall into the same reductive trap. In trailblazing explorations during the late 1980s and early
1990s, such scholars as Thomas Trezise, Steven Connor, and Carla Locatelli alerted others to the striking affinities between Beckett's work
and Derrida's thought, providing the first informed accounts of Beckett's writing in the light of something other than existentialist philosophy. (The latter still exercises its grip on Beckett studies—so much
so that even Shira Wolosky's 1995 study of Beckett, Eliot, and Celan,
which clearly appreciates the role of negative theology in Beckett's work,
assumes the values that inform negative theology to enter Beckett's
work only in an inverted fashion.) Yet when a particular theorist's
thought is "applied" to literature, that which fails to defer to the specificity of the reading must fall by the wayside.

This book is an attempt to talk about Beckett's works not as books—
not as the prestigious cultural objects with intellectual clout and market

value, their "knowledge" neatly packaged between the covers—and to take seriously the interminable challenge of writing they bring to life for the reader. Beckett makes the insistent demand on his reader to throw conceptuality overboard and to confront in the interminable process of writing that which refuses to yield to the power of the concept: an "Outside" of language, brought into being through literature and nonetheless never captured by it. Negative theology, when practiced rigorously, deconstructs its own concepts of God in order to guard his absolute transcendence, including the dualism implicit in the concept of absolute transcendence. Literary apophaticism, which understands writing as a spiritual vocation, cultivates extreme self-referentiality in order to avoid the traps of objectification and reification that arise from the analytic conventions of plot, character, narrative, and so on.

Hence I do not intend to offer interpretations of Beckett's texts. Rather, I intend to uncover the fundamental apophatic impulse in Beckett's work that makes any postulation of objectifiable "content" impossible. By way of this apophatic impulse his writing appeals to what by definition exceeds conceptualization. In other words, I intend to approach the impulse to conceptualize, which drives the majority of Beckett's commentators, in the way late Beckett approaches early Beckett: deconstructively.

Beckett's earlier and most famous work for the theater, especially *Waiting for Godot* and the more severe *Endgame*, is in retrospect also his most "conventional" (although it must have hardly seemed so for those who walked out of the early performances in shock). It is conventional because it holds on to a skeletal framework of character and plot: Didi, Gogo, Hamm, and Clov are distinct personalities, and although hardly anything "happens" in the play, the plot of *Godot* unmistakably consists of two tramps waiting beneath a tree. The daring austerity of the late work is embryonically present, but Beckett has not yet completed the leap into a type of writing that systematically and categorically empties itself of all positive conventions traditionally used in the production and analysis of the literary text. It is not difficult to demonstrate that earlier Beckett is preoccupied with the same undecidabilities, but late Beckettian prose and drama performs them more radically and self-referentially in the depths of text and image, not at the surface level of plot, which has long since ceased to exist in late Beckett.

Driving the plot of *Endgame*, for instance, is a dichotomy of form and formlessness. Hamm is tirelessly at work on the project of situating himself firmly in a narrative space-time continuum ("it's time for my story" [*E* 34]), while Clov works equally tirelessly at undermining his every effort. The peculiar symbiosis of their relationship derives precisely from this aporia: psychologically the two are in a destructive deadlock (Hamm is dependent on Clov and Clov is unable to define his existence independently of Hamm), but formally they perform a play on the verge of the breakdown of the spatiotemporal narrative (that is, the book in the Blanchotian sense), which Hamm tries to uphold and on which he builds his power. Its demise is the precondition for Blanchotian writing. Hamm needs the certainty of knowing precisely what and where he is. Anxiously he inquires whether it is time for his pain killer (*E* 14). Evidently the emphasis is not so much on the sedative effects of the medication, which could be obtained without further delay, but on knowing precisely what time of day it is. Likewise, he asks for his chair to be put precisely in the center of the room (*E* 23), a position of unrivaled clarity from which he may survey the entirety of his kingdom. Clov, however, puts him up against the wall rather than in the center, and later tells him point blank that there is no more pain killer (*E* 46). Hamm's world is on the verge of chaos; it has run out of the fixed reference points on which it depends. The rudimentary plot structure of *Endgame* supports such allegory; for Beckett's late work it is wholly inadequate.

It is no accident that the anecdote about the tailor, who takes more than three months to finish a pair of trousers and drives the customer to exasperation in the process, occurs in *Endgame*.[14] The anecdote allegorically sets the theme for the play and for Beckett's entire body of work: what is the relationship between representation and the real, between art and what we call reality? Which of the two do we valorize, and which may we call the real? Beckett asks us to radically rethink these categories. The late texts programmatically empty themselves, and any attempts to force them into trusted models of literary interpretation based on character and plot inevitably return the interpretation to a level of specificity the text has already transcended. It is plausible to read Mouth, the voice in *Not I*, as schizophrenic; the text may support such a reading, but is it useful? To diagnose a personality split decenters the concept of character, but only while presupposing and maintaining its validity. The text of the play, however, cultivates a fragmented, antinarrative mode of presentation, which does not provide sufficient information to reconstruct a coherent plot, and a voice that consistently undermines itself. The text does not offer external, objectified meaning, but performs the radical interiority of writing and the cognitive limits it encounters.

■   For Beckett the "site" of the sacred is at the level of the transcendental. It is at work in language and writing, and, more immediately and idiosyncratically for him, in the visual arts: the apotheosis of art, as it were, is painting. His closest contemporary intellectual soul mate, Blanchot, remains more skeptical of the visual. For Beckett, however, were it not for the fact that the durability of all ontological categories is highly suspect in his work, the visual occupies such a privileged position as to warrant the thesis (defended by Lois Oppenheim) that it claims ontological primacy. One could more accurately say that the visual provides a glimpse of an "ontology without ontology," to adopt the rhetorical figure of Meister Eckhart's preference. Beckett has no doubt that the visual medium is able to achieve what language cannot: its immediacy eludes language. Only the visual, Beckett insinuates time and again, can disclose the immediate presence of phenomena because it skips the mediation of language. Even his prose work strives to approximate as closely as possible the characteristics of the visual, especially its stillness. From this point of view the visual is clearly privileged, but one cannot derive from it ontological certainty.

A Buddhist perspective helps illustrate Beckett's perch between ontological metaphysics and nihilism. It makes it possible to view his concern with emptiness from a spiritually constructive position, as the prerequisite for spiritual enlightenment, and it situates emptiness "outside" the conventional binary opposition of fullness versus emptiness, where emptiness symptomatically is given no more insightful definition than "that which is not full." In Mahayana Buddhism the term for emptiness is *sunyata*. David Loy, who specializes in comparative studies of Western and Eastern philosophy, points out how inadequate the conventional translation of *sunya* as "empty" is. For the implications of the Sanskrit root *su*, from which the term derives, are twofold: it means "'to be swollen,' both like a hollow balloon and like a pregnant woman; therefore the usual English translation 'empty' and 'emptiness' [for *sunya* and *sunyata*] must be supplemented with the notion of 'pregnant with possibilities,'" Loy suggests.[15] Loy finds Mervyn Sprung's translation "absence of being in things" "cumbersome."[16] No doubt it is, but it alerts us to the important fact that *sunyata* does not pertain to the ontological realm. For Buddhism the ontological question does not arise: it is interested solely in the liberation of human beings from suffering and in offering practical help in overcoming the epistemological obstacles that present themselves along the way.

Looking at Beckett's stage images it is difficult not to agree with Beckett that the idea of emptiness can be made most evident visually. Vast expanses of dark empty space unmistakably make their point. The relation of darkness to light, space to matter, and the arrangement of objects in space follow the aesthetic principles of Chinese monochrome ink splash paintings, which, in turn, are products of the Buddhist spirituality that subtends them. Visually as well as linguistically Beckett is a poet of absence (of color), of emptiness (of substance), and of darkness. He is a virtuoso of all conceivable shades of grey, not black. (Again, the tenor is not hopelessness, nihilism, or nothingness.) In all his fascination with the visual and his belief that the visual can yield the truth of phenomena, he does not fall for a metaphysics or a theology of light.

Though not always fully acknowledged, Christianity's roots in Platonism and Neoplatonism has led it to associate God with light. God is the light of truth into which the Christian emerges from the depths of her cave of delusion. The theology of light is pervasive: St. Augustine is not immune from it and neither is St. Thomas Aquinas; St. Bonaventure's idea of the reduction of the arts to theology rests on the reflection of the divine light in creation. Later on this theology of light turns into a metaphysics of light that substitutes for the truth of God the light of human consciousness: the cogito perceives its object on the basis of perspectival Renaissance optics.

Yet theology is no monolith. There are deviations from the near-ubiquitous stronghold of light. "Mystical" thinkers of various traditions have chosen darkness as their preferred image of God. It should go without saying that it is not God who is imagined as dark. Who would know better than the mystics that God can only be represented inadequately?

The image of darkness is no exception. Rather, the human approach to God can only be shrouded in cognitive darkness, since no human being can possibly know God in his fullness.

The "mystical" has somewhat fallen into disrespect. It is a broad and ill-defined term, sometimes wrongly associated with a vague sense of intuition that runs the danger of subtending an identitarian conception of experience. Nonetheless many contemporary theologians, including Michael Sells, Denys Turner, Vladimir Lossky, and Jean-Luc Marion prefer the term "mystical theology" to the misleading and inadequate name "negative theology." For "negative theology" is neither the negation of kataphatic, or "positive," theology (this would keep it locked inside a conceptual binarism) nor does it proceed primarily by negation. It is true that negative theology thinks it can present God's inconceivable nature less inaccurately by taking away rather than ascribing attributes to him. But this strategy does not confine it to the negative side of the equation. Negative theology's primary objective is to guard God's transcendence from the anthropomorphizing tendencies of the conceptual mind. Conceptual thought is best dislodged by paradox, a figure that disobeys the logic of noncontradiction serving binary thought structures. Properly speaking, negative theology *is* that theology of paradox. It does not exist in a vacuum, isolated from positive, or kataphatic theology, but is always braided in with it: negative theology destabilizes the statements kataphatic theology makes by negating them but then, in a third movement, negates its own negation. It is impossible, it implies, to remain in either the affirmative or the negative mode, which makes it necessary to proceed by a "third way." Thinkers who wish to remain true to the third way will hence rate apophatic theology over kataphatic theology—otherwise negative theology would turn into a hermeneutic leading to ever more exact positive knowledge of God.

Jean-Luc Marion is one of the foremost theoreticians of the gift. For him the third way is synonymous with an exit from an economy of exchange. He agrees with Derrida that a genuine gift, be it relative or absolute, can only give itself "outside" such an economy and he develops the idea of the saturated phenomenon to illustrate how such self-giving might be possible. The saturated phenomenon need not be the divine. It can be anything that resists being taken in its entirety from a single vantage point because it gives itself superabundantly. Thus a military battle can be as much of a saturated phenomenon as a beautiful summer day. Its defining characteristic is that it gives itself in excess and overflows the intention the perceiving subject had of it.

According to Edmund Husserl's conception of the "poor" phenomenon, no intuition the subject receives of a phenomenon can ever fulfill the intention. Marion does not doubt that such common phenomena exist, but he contests their ubiquity. In addition, he says, there are other phenomena that give themselves in excess. With great subtlety and rigor Marion demonstrates how the saturated phenomenon as he conceives of it avoids being reabsorbed into the economy. He reconfigures the phenomenological model in terms of pure givenness so that the subject does not constitute the phenomenon; the subject merely receives it.

The idea of a form of excess destabilizing economic order is a recurring motif that has taken various forms in the intellectual debates of the past century. Bataille is no doubt the foremost contributor. In his own ruminations on the sacred he imagines a system based on excess of expenditure without return. A constipated, restricted economy based on accumulation needs to turn to ruthless expenditure as its saving grace. Beckett contributes his own thoughts on economy in "Three Dialogues." There he talks of "an art . . . too proud for the farce of giving and receiving" ("TD" 141). But Beckett's idea of how the economy is to be destabilized is subtler than Bataille's. Anyone who has seen a single Beckett play can attest to the fact that his is not an art of excess in the sense of total theater, for instance. There is no sensory onslaught threatening, and aiming, to overwhelm the spectator with pure all-enveloping spectacle. Excess here must be understood less literally as excess of saturation, which can manifest itself in categories other than quantity. (Marion is content to adopt the Kantian categories in working out the different types of saturation, so a phenomenon can be saturated according to quantity, quality, relation, as well as modality.) Beckett creates minimalist images of extreme concentration that can best be understood as saturated phenomena.

The saturated phenomenon is the master key with which to unlock Beckett's art. Here we have an all-encompassing idea that aims to account for the whole spectrum of phenomenological experience, or rather counter-experience, ranging all the way from the physical sensation of taste to the phenomenon of divine revelation. Marion speaks of "the banality of saturation." Here we can approach divine revelation as well as its displaced counterpart with the same fundamental idea without eliding the difference between them. In an unprecedented way Marion provides the vocabulary for doing so. Diverging from Derrida's position, Marion assumes that what can give itself phenomenologically (and for a Christian there can be no doubt that God can do so) must be describable in phenomenological terms. This does not mean that we can say precisely what counter-experience implies, since counter-experience is by definition that which cannot be assimilated to any previous pattern of experience. It does mean, however, that we can put a phenomenological name to that occurrence.

I begin by asking what the specific conditions of experience are that allow for phenomena of saturation. I do not mean to suggest that there are conditions that bring saturated phenomena into existence. Rather, certain conditions help us perceive saturated phenomena for what they are. *Catastrophe* illustrates this shift toward givenness, which, the play suggests, can only occur by way of nondual perceptual practices. So how can we talk about such experiences of givenness once they have occurred? Here the problem of economy presents itself, which I discuss in relation to the "Three Dialogues." If a saturated phenomenon gives itself "outside" an economy of exchange, how can we talk about it without reentering the economy in the process? Art tries to present what it cannot name or represent, but if art is the adventure of creating an absolutely irreducible discourse—one that presents rather than represents— then its own strategies, but certainly its criticism (the process of writing about art), becomes a negative theology that has to be extremely self-conscious and vigilant. Beckett's work accomplishes both: it creates an irreducible space and it does so by making apparent the process of writing itself. It makes the process of writing its "object," or its topic, and it produces a literature that "embodies" this object and in this sense no longer has an object, just as God cannot be the "object" of negative theology. In this way it becomes the apotheosis of the space of literature as Blanchot conceives of it via the Outside. Hence Beckett's work can only be an embrace of postmodernity, as *Film* makes unmistakably clear: there is no nostalgia for lost unity, but a whole-hearted embrace of nonduality.

This book stages no debate of legitimacy between Beckett's position and a Christian perspective. I do not wish to weigh one against the other and my aim is not to turn Beckett into a closet negative theologian or to prove that he is really a Christian after all. I would not want to be seen as asserting some hypothetical moral superiority of the Christian position—my task is not to judge. Above all, I intend to take Beckett seriously as a thinker of religion and the spiritual life. What I hope the reader will draw from this work is the insight that what Beckett enacts at the level of the transcendental is indistinguishable in form and, to a large extent intent, from negative theology's performative tight-rope act at the level of the transcendent. Beckett's position is symptomatic of a time in history that has renounced classical conceptions of the divine but is haunted by it nonetheless, and as a result seeks God in unusual places. The attempt at an apotheosis of art has occurred at various points throughout literary history—one need only remember *l'art pour l'art*. Unusual is the moral force and spiritual value Beckett finds in art and in literature or the process of writing in particular. Politically motivated power structures cannot hold under the impact of the sacred. Adherents of traditional spiritual traditions have much to learn from the rigor with which Beckett approaches art as spiritual practice. In the end it is up to each reader to affirm God through his or her own act of faith and, surprisingly, to find no contradiction at all with what Beckett affirms differently in his work.

Visuality and Iconicity in Samuel Beckett's *Catastrophe*

Counter to Beckett's usual practice when dedicating a work to an individual, *Catastrophe* is dedicated to someone whom Beckett did not know personally, but who was both an eminent political figure and a fellow artist. Vaclav Havel's imprisonment in "socialist" Czechoslovakia for "subversive" political activities had prompted the work's composition, and its dedication to him is a significant and unusual gesture. *Catastrophe* is most frequently read in a political context. It speaks out against the exploitation of human beings by their fellow humans in institutionalized contexts that disguise and legitimize exploitation—and by so doing it defends human rights with silent eloquence in Beckett's trademark minimalist style. In a single, condensed theatrical image at the end of the play, when the Protagonist raises his head and stares back at the audience, Beckett points toward everyone's complicity with such exploitative structures more effectively and memorably than the evanescent nature of wordy eloquence would have been able to: cruelty does not call for words but for action.¹ Typically, he also thereby avoids the platitudes of polemics that political causes so often generate.

This is precisely the point: how does a deeply philosophical man who does not believe in the unmotivated singularity of horrific events react to the immediacy of a political cause? Bert States points to the first sentence of *Murphy:* "The sun shone, having no alternative, on the nothing new" (*M* 1), a sentence that in many ways summarizes Beckett's artistic sensibility. It echoes, of course, Ecclesiastes 1:9: "What has been is what will be, and what has been done is what will be done; and there is nothing new under the sun." Beckett tends to look for the existence of underlying unchanging structures that prompt atrocities in shifting manifestations throughout the history of humankind (a "human condition," as it were, a term so often used and abused in Beckett criticism). As expected, *Catastrophe* is not a "topical play," analogous to the "topical song"—that is, churned out specifically in response to a particular political event and inevitably losing its bite and becoming unintelligible as soon as the circumstantial data have passed into oblivion.

Even at the level of title (*Play* and *Film* illustrate the pattern) Beckett has a distinct tendency to turn his artistic statements into analyses of constitutive root problems: they transcend the specific and seek the universal. In the same way in which *Film* is a genre-exploration of film, seeking to uncover the visual mechanisms and philosophical assumptions at work in filmmaking and watching, and by extension in Western epistemology in general, *Catastrophe* is about social and perceptual practices that underlie the perpetration of violence. *Catastrophe* "sees" at the base of the violence and humiliation to which the Protagonist is subjected structures of vision and visuality deeply engrained in Western culture, which enable and perpetuate dualistic thought (that is, thought functioning by a logic of noncontradiction). (It is useful to remember that "catastrophe" means "overturning"—maybe of a paradigm or an epistemology.)

This is not to suggest that visual structures are by nature exploitative; Beckett with his great love for the visual arts would be the last to agree with such a proposition. He often traveled great distances, in fact planned trips through entire continents, to stand in front of the paintings he loved and wished to see again. He was a staunch believer in the power of the visual image. To him the image has the advantage of immediacy over words and is therefore more readily able to overwhelm conceptual thought and leave the viewer speechless. In his homage to painter and friend Jack Yeats, Beckett remarks, "In images of such breathless immediacy as these there is no occasion, no time given, no room left, for the lenitive of comment" (*D* 149). In this chapter, I want to suggest that *Catastrophe* criticizes dualistic practices of visuality as they occur predominantly in Western culture, perpetuated by the dominant Western philosophical and theological tradition. *Catastrophe* can then be read to hint at nondual ways of approaching the images shared by Christian and Buddhist negative theologies. I weave my argument through the more widespread political readings of *Catastrophe* to show how such readings link up with a more general critique of representation. Then I look at the power and exploitation that *Catastrophe* sees at work in the representational model of naturalist theater and at the ways in which the play itself destabilizes this model. It is through these destabilizations that the play suggests nondual modes of presentation and perception, which can be illustrated with examples drawn from Buddhist and Christian negative theologies—namely, Ch'an ink-splash paintings and Byzantine iconography.

Negative theologies have a vested interest in nonduality: our thinking about God becomes idolatrous as soon as it turns into a reification that objectifies God into an entity with (anthropomorphic) characteristics and properties. So negative theology will guard against reification of a "reality" that is by nature unobjectifiable. Byzantine icons are a case in point because even on the level of their material objectness they resist our objectifying gaze and dismantle the conventional dualism of observer and object, exerting instead a gaze of their own, but a gaze that does not simply reverse the duality because it cannot be reduced to an essence, a being, an object, or an entity of any kind. At this fundamental level of critique it matters little whether one tries to guard against the reification of a personal God or of our perception of the true nature of reality, so I draw on Christian as well as Buddhist sources without claiming any analogy.

This nondual rethinking of perception goes hand in hand with a rethinking of subjectivity: a constituting subject that objectifies the world of perception is no adequate model. Here Jean-Luc Marion's refiguring of this model in terms of phenomenological givenness becomes important. Marion turns the Husserlian standard of the "poor phenomenon," according to which no given intuition can fulfill our intention of a phenomenon, on its head. He does not doubt that there are poor phenomena or common phenomena, which also mostly remain partially unfulfilled by intuition although adequation is at least theoretically possible, but he refuses to accept them as the norm. Instead, he says, there are also phenomena that give themselves in excess of any intention, overflowing the intention and thus frustrating every attempt on the part of the subject to constitute them as phenomena. These he calls "saturated phenomena." Under their sway the subject turns into what Marion calls "the gifted"—a receiver of a phenomenon that gives itself of its own accord. Finally, Marion's analysis of the saturated phenomenon links up with Beckett's criticism of an art of expression: the work of art as phenomenological intuition does not need to be measured against a previous intention to assess whether it adequately measures up to it and expresses it. It can give itself regardless of intention, its concentrated, minimalist form overflowing any intention. Beckett's ideal of expressionless art appears in a new light: it is no art utterly reduced in sensuous stimulus, but rather an art of reduction to givenness.

■ It is, of course, no accident that Beckett should locate his reflections on the visual paradigm in the arts, more particularly, in a theater: a fictional as well as an actual one. For one thing, it saves the play from degenerating into mere finger-pointing. Instead of finding wrong with specific "alien" social practices such as politics or science, Beckett instead locates the "enemy" in the artists' own ranks, within each individual. Appropriately, Havel's reply to Beckett, which came in the form of a naturalist play titled *Mistake*, is about prisoners building within the prison walls a social order based on the same principles that oppressed them outside and thus it obviously picks up on the same thought: individuals are the victims of their own practices, not of an outside force. Moreover, simply to say that science and politics are based on dualistic thought and exploitation would not only have been stating the obvious, it would also have been uncharacteristically reductive.

As it is, the unavoidable undercurrent of the play is that art shares with science its basic assumptions, its fundamental dualism and hence its exploitative nature. The Director in *Catastrophe* does not tire of concocting ever new, ever more degrading poses for his Protagonist, whose shivering, half-naked, deformed body is exposed on a pedestal to the voyeuristic gaze of the theater audience for its entertainment and intellectual stimulation. As is often the case, the overeager assistant, keen to earn her laurels and to make her way ahead by hook or by crook (and, in this case, by unbearable sycophancy), is willing even to overstep the rules of the game as they are: more than once the Director has to call her back from imposing a further humiliation on the Protagonist and admonishes her merely to "[s]ay it" (*SP* 297)—to stay confined to representation in language instead of insisting on the real thing.

Such an analysis of the dynamics of theatrical production has to have consequences for, or will conceivably even spring from, Beckett's reflections on his own directorial work in the theater. Beckett had the reputation for being a perfectionist who would not let things rest until he had produced an image on stage that corresponded to his own vision in minute detail, and he often pushed actors to the end of their tethers in trying to make them conform to this vision. The circumstances in which *Not I*, for instance, came into being gives special relevance to the questions *Catastrophe* raises. *Not I*, being kenotic, is far from trying to conceive of a conceptual image, of catastrophe or otherwise. But even though it does not set out to produce a representation of (human) misery for a theater audience's "entertainment," the apparatus into which the actress's body has to be strapped for the duration of the play nonetheless inflicts very real physical pain and emotional distress. Both Jessica Tandy, who premiered the role in New York, and Billie Whitelaw reported their discomfort. Whitelaw stated that she would never do the play again, for fear of losing her sanity.[2] For her, playing Mouth was "a terrible inner scream, like falling backwards into hell,"[3] and, according to Linda Ben-Zvi, she was taken aback at her interlocutors' obvious insensitivity to her pain when friends suggested after watching *Not I* in the theater that it was impossible to tell whether the mouth was real or recorded.[4]

In *Catastrophe*, then, Beckett "links the theme of human victimization to the paradox of theatre preparing unpleasant subjects for the pleasure of an audience," Bert States summarizes.[5] Here an old dilemma is encountered, one that Theodor Adorno famously expressed in his well-known statement, directed at Paul Celan, that writing poetry after Auschwitz was barbaric.[6] A representation of Holocaust atrocities can never give adequate expression to the inconceivable and inexpressible horror that was a daily reality in the concentration camps. By the mere fact of being a representation it will fall short of life itself, which knows no curtain and no suspension of disbelief. In fact, by making the atrocities part of an (inevitably) aestheticized representation, the artist robs them of their singularity by repeating them (in an aesthetic realm) and in the process bestows on them a certain legitimation: the cruelty and the pain are no longer unspeakable, and what can be signified in language is at least in principle repeatable because it falls within the limits of human conception. The degree of critical distance with which an artist approaches his or her topic does not change this basic mechanism.

Beckett, too, has an inherent mistrust of language and its capacity to express concepts or authorial intention. His equally strong beliefs in language's inadequacy and yet also in what he calls the artist's "obligation to express," and, finally, his conviction that expression itself needs to be overcome (cf. "Three Dialogues") will become relevant later on. For the moment, suffice it to note his acute awareness of the failure of language to render the experience of reality *adequately*—a problem that has a strong moral dimension when that experience is one of calamity, cruelty, catastrophe: "If you really get down to the disaster, the slightest eloquence becomes unbearable. Whatever is said is so far from experience. . . . There is a danger of rising up into rhetoric. Speak it even and pride comes. Words are a form of complacency."[7] Again, according to Beckett, the fictional director and his assistant, as much as the real one and the real audience, take part in the complacent legitimation of violence à la Adorno.

Yet Beckett's critique of representation in *Catastrophe* is more far-reaching than this because it is not concerned exclusively with the representation *of* violence. Rather, the play seems to suggest that there is a gap between experience and its representation that makes the artist himself or herself a likely perpetrator of violence, because representation *itself* is violence. Beckett locates the core of the issue in the exploitative gaze that is enabled by the dualistic split inherent in representation itself. The structures of enframing and instrumentality this split brings with it are violence: the Holocaust, the world wars, and environmental destruction all bear witness to it. Vision as an epistemological tool has claimed an exalted position in Western metaphysics. It is the least "embodied" of the senses. For Hegel, for example, sight, together with hearing, is one of the "theoretical senses," which enables a relation of what is externally present to rational intelligence.[8] Hegel thinks that the other senses, by contrast, present objects in their specific sensuous individuality, which appeals to desire rather than rationality.

David Levin surmises "that the thrust of Heidegger's critique of metaphysics brings forth serious questions regarding the complicity of vision—vision elevated to the position of paradigm for knowledge and rationality—in the historical domination of our 'universal' metaphysics."[9] One might conclude that every effort to deconstruct metaphysics has to contend to some extent with visuality, as Beckett has clearly understood. To illustrate the predatory tendency of vision, Paul Virilio evokes a photo-report in a fashion magazine in which "an elegantly attired 'beauty queen' is filmed running through the ruin of Sarajevo among stoved-in cars, imitating the fatal flight of the town's inhabitants as snipers open fire on them. The sight line of the fashion photographer then becomes completely indistinguishable from that of the assassin lying in wait. It is his solitary excitement we are invited to share."[10] And Levin concludes, as if in conversation with Virilio, and as the perfect summary of *Catastrophe:* "Observation has become cruelty. Obsessed with the picture, the image, we take part, whether willingly or unwillingly, in the production of suffering."[11] Thus, it is of secondary importance that the Director and the Assistant in *Catastrophe* want explicitly to construct an image of misery—this is, as it were, merely as far as Beckett is willing to go in order to make a (polemical) point. In fact, *any* image they could construct would participate in an economy of violence.

Later in his career Beckett completely abandons representational models of adequation. For him the aim cannot be an adequation between intention and intuition, or a *Vorstellung* and the thing itself. Such a model will always be based on a dualism between signification and fulfillment. Instead, Beckett turns away from mimetic models and models of adequation to an art of *Darstellung,* or immediate sense presentation. The

Jena Romantics were still sustained by a belief in the unity and power of the imagination that would be capable of rendering, *darstellen*, the artist's vision once it had been freed from the chains of mimetic representation. This is a trust Beckett, as a postmodern, can no longer have. In this radical turn toward *Darstellung* he tries to avoid the expression of any previous interiority of *Vorstellung*. Or, inversely, he tries to avoid the process of measuring the work of art against a preceding intention. Instead, it is to give itself in and of itself as a saturated phenomenon: the truth of the artwork is not measured in terms of (at best) adequation to an intention, but overflows it. Beckett begins to create saturated phenomena of the theater.

■ *Catastrophe* links the inherent dualism of representation to the visual as the ground of our acts of knowing. Especially during the Renaissance and the Enlightenment the visual advanced from being the most eminent sense among several, which it had been through most of Western history, to become the very paradigm of truth. We are now hardly aware of the extent to which the visual paradigm has infiltrated everyday language: visual metaphors abound. And at least since Plato's famous cave allegory the visual paradigm is, moreover, linked most directly to the dualist structures of representation. It is true, as Martin Jay points out, that in the cave allegory visuality figures prominently as a source of deception rather than illumination, and one will have to conclude that "Greek culture was not as univocally inclined towards celebrating vision as may appear at first glance."[12] Jay suggests, however, that nevertheless "it must still be acknowledged that Hellenic thought did on the whole privilege the visual over any other sense. Even in its negative guises, its power was evident."[13]

Greek culture was dominated by a metaphysics of light, which would become a full-fledged mysticism of light in the Middle Ages and onward. In *On the Reduction of the Arts to Theology*, for example, St. Bonaventure equates light with truth and knowledge: God is the source of all light and, therefore, truth. His light radiates throughout the world and creation participates in truth to the extent that it reflects the light.[14] The crucial moment in the history of visuality in the Western world is, of course, the development of perspective in visual representation during the Italian Renaissance—"one of the most fateful innovations in Western culture."[15] With the help of the rules laid out in Alberti's *De Pittura*, three-dimensional, rationalized space could be translated to a two-dimensional surface. For this analytical gaze—that of Beckett's director and assistant—to be possible, the visible has to become the object of *ratio:* an object to be manipulated, not the divine allegory of the Middle Ages in which everything is charged with meaning and human beings intimately involved in a narrative unfolding all around them. The observer must perceive herself as a distinct and separate subject looking at an object from a single fixed point of view replacing the multiple vantage points one associates with the Middle Ages, so that it becomes possible to render the picture internally consistent. As a result, perspectivalism not only renders a given object from one specific vantage point but also prescribes this vantage point for the viewer as well. Thus, Jay tells us, any act of viewing will involve two symmetrical pyramids, or rather "a mirror intersecting one pyramid, which then reflected that pyramid's apex back in the other direction."[16] One apex is the viewer's eye, the other the point of convergence of the flight lines in the picture while the picture itself acts as the mirror. Especially the painted perspectival flats that were used in stage design in the nineteenth century (and that provoked Adolphe Appia's scorn because of their tendency to clash with the actual three-dimensionality of the actors and real objects on stage) reveal the extent to which theater conformed to the regime of the monocular apex: the invisible fourth wall of the proscenium becomes the mirror.

The structure of the inverted pyramid becomes especially important with Descartes, who "tacitly adopted the position of the perspectivalist painter using a camera obscura."[17] In this way he is able to posit the radical split between self-reflexive subject and independent object, the bifurcation that ushers in modernity. Because the subject is certain only of its own existence as a self-referential entity, the outside world must inevitably be envisioned as a separate phenomenon altogether, of which the subject can nonetheless gain true knowledge: in fact, the cogito's self-certainty and self-identity are the only possible foundations of truth. This establishes the most fateful dualism in Western philosophy and it also elevates the scientific gaze and the narcissistic mirror image inherent in identitarian reflexivity to the prominent epistemological paradigm of Western modernity.

In *Catastrophe* Beckett points out to an excessively self-conscious audience the extent to which the exploitative gaze of voyeurism operates. Yet instead of focusing on Beckett's critique of the visual paradigm in theater directly, as Sartrean analyses in particular will do, coming to it through the back door of representation emphasizes how *Catastrophe*'s critique of representation reaches all the way back to Plato. Western theories of the theater and of art in general find their most fundamental and most devastating reference point in Plato's critique of mimesis, and even in such movements as the so-called Theater of the Real, which aim deliberately at overcoming mimetic constraints, theater does not so much overcome its limitations as meet them: "face to face with its double, *the thing* it can never be."[18] For however much theater may try to overcome representation, it cannot overcome the difference between the staged act and life itself. A real chair in the context of a performance will always be a chair playing a chair. Even shamanistic ritual, invoked frequently over the past twenty years or so as a way of tapping into some primordial, universal source of energy that makes theater immediately experiential, is defined by the fact that it occurs in a controlled environment removed from the unpredictability of life itself. This enables the shaman to channel supernatural or cosmic energy toward specific ends.

Hence, with a provocative critique like *Catastrophe*, it seems that Beckett's aim cannot be to urge audiences and theater practitioners to *overcome* representation. Any such attempt achieves nothing because it establishes a dualism between itself and what it set out to overcome. Perhaps, then, it is not a matter of overcoming so much as bringing a different, nondual awareness to the old. Nonduality is not representation's Other. Rather, it is the nature of nonduality not to be framed in terms of a polarized opposition with respect to other terms, otherwise it would not be nondual. This means that the nonconceptuality of any nondual nonconcept, such as the Buddhist *sunyata*, has to be rigorous: it cannot be thought of as something that operates outside of conceptuality or language since this very movement would imply reification. As Masao Abe puts it, simply and succinctly: "Shunyata is entirely unobjectifiable and unconceptualizable. . . . Accordingly, if Shunyata is conceived *somewhere outside* one's self-existence it is not true Shunyata any longer because Shunyata conceived outside one's existence turns into *something* represented and called by oneself 'Shunyata.'"[19]

For the same reason, it is impossible to say whether something, for example language, is by nature either dual or nondual. One cannot call language inherently dualist (because it consists of the dualist building blocks of subject and predicate) and then want to catapult oneself somewhere outside language where nonconcepts no longer run the risk of being sucked back into logocentric thought. At the same time it is equally logocentric to postulate as the logical alternative to remain within language's system of differences (as Derrida does). Such a solution does not avoid reification, as it sets out to do, but rather stays with a valorization of difference: having successfully deconstructed identity, it then fails to deconstruct its opposite.[20]

Language is both dual and nondual, and shows itself conceptually or nonconceptually, according to the way it is grasped. The Buddhist philosopher Nagarjuna uses the example of a snake ineptly handled to illustrate this point: rightly grasped the snake (of language) will be harmless, while it can be lethal when approached with a dualist everyday mind. Nagarjuna calls incurable those who will turn even nonduality— *sunyata*—into a concept. From the Buddhist perspective mind at the relative, conceptual, representational level is thus confronted with two truths: "that of a personal everyday world and a higher one which surpasses it,"[21] where the higher truth is *sunya*—empty. But this emptiness is not to be taken in the sense of European nihilism, but rather as mind emptied of limiting conceptualizations so it may become open for what at the relative level would be called the "impossible."

This higher truth is not situated elsewhere, in some transcendent realm beyond this world, but rather is within it, and unfolds, as it were, as soon as we stop looking for the transcendent or for the groundbreaking paradigm shift that changes everything. Otherwise our very efforts to "solve the problem" are precisely what maintains the problem. There are "two truths," then, only from the conceptual, representational point of view. The higher one precisely undoes the opposition, but it cannot be known purely discursively. "Perhaps this is what we always sought," Loy summarizes provocatively: "not to become real, but to realize that we don't need to become real."[22] Nagarjuna's seventh-century commentator

Candrakirti glosses this point thus: "The very coming to rest, the non-functioning of perceptions as signs of all named things, is itself *nirvana*."[23] The core of the problem, then, is once again linked to structures of visuality: linguistic signs objectify appearances into self-existing things of which a person's ego-identity is one. As soon as this process ceases the disconcerting paradox of our awareness of our own mortality disappears also. In a sense we are mortal only as long as we perceive ourselves as caught in a space-time continuum, which irreversibly carries us toward death.[24]

More than any other medium of representation, the theater depends on dualist structures of visuality. Theatrical performance is defined by an audience looking at actors in a more or less scenic presentation that unfolds before them. At the height of the naturalist proscenium stage, during the first half of the twentieth century (admittedly an atypical chapter in theater history), actors were even expected not to acknowledge the audience's existence at all—a practice that intensifies the impression of being involved in a voyeuristic activity complete with the power dynamic inherent in it: staring through the ubiquitous translucent fourth wall into the privacy of somebody else's living room, objectifying what one sees there. This dynamic must be broken in order to push the play, and representation, beyond its frame. Theatrical experiments other than the naturalist grant the actor far greater agency in reacting to the audience's gaze. But given that, despite its stylization, *Catastrophe* more than any other of Beckett's plays functions within a semblance of naturalism (and evokes it even while transgressing it), it does not seem polemical to compare the play with what is otherwise Beckett's diametrical opposite.

The destabilization of this one-sidedness occurs when the Protagonist returns the audience's gaze. Like Sartre's voyeur who hears the rustling of the bush behind him, the audience is suddenly thrown back on itself and becomes aware—in the few stubborn cases when the penny has not yet dropped—of its own exploitative collaboration with the Director and Assistant. Most importantly, though, the play's fictional frame of reference is broken and switches from the fictional setting of the theatrical rehearsal to the actual act of performance, from the representation to the real.[25] Or rather, from the (fictional) real of rehearsal (involving actors playing actors) to the actual performance (with characters in a Beckett play): the play within the play is the real (rehearsal rather than play) and the live performance is, in fact, a representation—an intriguing chiasmus. *Catastrophe* enters into a cycle of intricate self-referential feedback that makes an unambiguous position impossible. The spectator of Beckett's play finds herself in a double bind: to clap one's hands at the end of his play to a certain extent means to applaud the very exploitation that the fictional audience (whose canned expressions of "transports of joy" are presented to the real audience like a mirror) applauded like a flock of mindless sheep. For while *Catastrophe*'s point is precisely the critique of this mechanism, the play's final moments point out that it does not escape it itself. The Protagonist's very act of resistance, the real catastrophe that transgresses the rules of theatrical etiquette and happens outside of the fictional director's control, is what is staged for the real audience night after night, thus being sucked back into the economy of exploitation.

Yet this is true only to a limited extent because the Protagonist's stare also produces for the real audience in the theater a kind of Brechtian alienation effect, so that from this moment on the awakened, cigar-smoking, critically distanced audience is acutely aware of the play's—any play's—two levels of reality, the fictional and the actual, the real and the image.[26] As a result, the spectator of *Catastrophe* sees at the moment of the play's climax simultaneously the character in the fictional Director's play, Beckett's play, and the actor on stage—whom she meets on a par, as in a Brechtian *Lehrstück*. In this moment of insight, when the actor momentarily steps out of his role to face the audience in the real theater, the relationship between the actor/character in Beckett's play and the spectator is one of equality and reciprocity in which both, together with the playwright, assure one another of their common understanding.

Further self-referential instabilities open up when one reminds oneself of the extent to which *Catastrophe* plays with the assumptions of naturalism. After all, naturalism as a theatrical movement arose as a reaction to conventions of representation that were perceived as artificial, stilted, or foreign to the theatrical medium. Naturalism aimed to break through petrified structures of representation and to produce life itself. The everyday existence of physical beings was to be put on stage. What naturalism ended up producing on stage was, of course, not life, but a representation thereof. At least the beginning of *Catastrophe* is situated squarely within the naturalist tradition, although the stylized, repetitive idiom ("I make a note") already signals some ironic distance from it. *Catastrophe* puts on stage the stuff that life in the theater is made of: a rehearsal. It offers a voyeuristic peek behind the scenes of theatrical illusion. It shows that illusion in the making; in other words, it shows not the illusion but life. It is part of the game of confusion *Catastrophe* plays with the spectator that in this logic even the "bare stage" (*SP* 297), so unlikely in naturalism, can be seen as a naturalistic rendering of an avant-garde play in the process of being staged. In fact, *Catastrophe* takes naturalism at its word by incorporating as "actors" a real theater audience and a real theater, not adding the fourth wall but rather removing the remaining three: it is more real than naturalism ever was, although it does precisely what naturalism set out to do, and in this gesture oversteps the conventions of its model. The confusions that arise from conflations of the real and the fictional situate *Catastrophe* beyond the confines of naturalist convention. By the end of the play, *Catastrophe* has moved from a realistic context ("Rehearsal. Final touches to the last scene." [*SP* 297]) to an abstract space that finds the stage in complete darkness save an illuminated bodiless head floating in space. But while the play thwarts precisely the expectation of showing the real thing—namely, the finished artistic product (a naturalist play)—by showing a rehearsal it still shows the finished product: a new play by acclaimed Nobel Prize winning genius Samuel Beckett. Thus in the final analysis the audience is free to reinstate what Derrida calls "transcendental signifieds" against Beckett's explicit intention.

All these mechanisms contribute to a process of destabilization completed in the Protagonist's return of the gaze that makes any stable one-sided viewing impossible. Instead, what is instigated is, as Barbara Freedman puts it, a "fractured reciprocity, whereby beholder and beheld reverse position in a way that renders a steady position of spectatorship impossible."[27] For Freedman, the deflection of the gaze is an important strategy in disrupting frames of representation.

Innovative approaches to solving the problem of representation can be seen at work in various genres. It is worth dwelling on two seemingly disparate examples from the realm of the visual arts, Byzantine iconography and Buddhist ink-splash painting, because they link up directly with the return of the gaze and hence are relevant to the structures of visuality Beckett explores in *Catastrophe*. Finally, the two examples will emerge as not at all disparate.

Byzantine iconography faces the difficulty of "presenting" for the believer's veneration an image of the transcendent divinity that stays clear of the pitfalls of idolatry. In other words, the icon must not be a mere representation lest it situate the divine in the realm of what is humanly conceivable, and the Eastern Church insists above all on the unknowability of God. Iconography solves this problem by what modernity has come to call "reverse perspective," but which is in fact the only possible and logical perspective from the Byzantine point of view. Byzantine icons lack depth: there is no simulated third dimension in the form of flight lines converging in the back of the picture. Instead, the viewer is confronted with a wall of gold or, more modestly, ocher that deflects the human gaze. Jean Paris gives voice to the radical conclusion that follows: "If there is no depth in Byzantine mosaics, if the divine space prevents our intrusion by opposing a dazzling wall of gold to our own 'regard,' as a supernatural frontier which reveals and at the same time forbids the absolute infinity of the Being, clearly the third dimension is not to be found in the background of the image, but *in front* of it, protruding straightforward as the very Regard of Transcendence itself: *we are the third dimension, we are the picture*."[28]

This radical reversal is emphasized by the gaze of Christ or the *theotokos* that is directed at the viewer. In their purest form even depictions of the *theotokos* with the child show both looking not at each other, but at the viewer, with the *theotokos* standing upright and Christ visible in her belly or suspended in space in front of her, depending on how one wants to read the image. On the other hand, depictions that are influenced by the secular space of the Italian Renaissance—that is, by our human-centered relation to the image—tend to humanize the iconic space by seating the *theotokos* and emotionalizing the setting by having her exchange loving glances with her child.[29] The icon generally known as the "Mother of God of the Sign" is a pure representative of the first style, while the "Mother of God of Tenderness," and even the Vladimir Icon of Constantinople are examples of the second. The Vladimir Icon is still a fully theological space, but its style enters an entirely new phase in the sentimentalized perspectival paintings of the Virgin and Child by Andrea Solario and Raphael, Paris points out.[30]

In Byzantine iconography, then, the image does the looking. The unknowable God, infinitely beyond human conception and not to be constituted by a transcendental ego that is in Western culture virtually synonymous with the monocular eye/I, gazes upon his creation, literally his image and likeness: the congregation in church. To emphasize this point, icons that depict biblical scenes sometimes have flight lines that converge on the viewer rather than away from her—a practice that has a profoundly destabilizing effect on the viewing experience. The image resists being seen, as it were, by persistently coming at the viewer instead of presenting itself complacently for consumption. Or else, multiple perspectives or viewpoints clash in the same image, producing a similarly confusing effect for the viewer by giving her no stable position from which to survey the scene in its entirety.

The Byzantine icon thus constitutes an intriguing parallel to the situation on Beckett's stage at the end of *Catastrophe*. In both cases the gaze emanates from what would conventionally be called the "image," destabilizing the distinction between reality and its representation. Both do so from a space that does not comply with the usual Western viewing habits. Like the icon, Beckett's play has moved from a naturalist presentation that conforms to the parameters of Enlightenment vision to an abstract space presenting "a face freed from its moorings, floating as visual emblem in the stage's obscurity," given to impenetrable surrounding darkness.[31] Both appeal to dimensions other than the conventional three, which are manifested by stretching representation to its limits.

Along the lines of the Brechtian alienation effect, the Protagonist turns from being a fictional character to being a human being acting in a play at the moment the representational logic of the play is disrupted and the character stares back at the audience. The play then takes full advantage of an ambivalent coexistence of the real and the fictional in any theatrical space. The two always exist simultaneously in the theater and the Protagonist's stare simply allows the real to emerge momentarily from behind the image. At this very moment the image becomes iconic in Jean-Luc Marion's typology of saturated phenomena.

Marion develops an ascending typology of saturated phenomena that starts with the event, continues with the idol, the flesh, the icon, and culminates in a super-phenomenon, the phenomenon of revelation. Each one is saturated according to one of the Kantian categories and the phenomenon of revelation is saturated in all categories at once. The event is saturated according to quantity (since it is impossible to take in its entirety from any single vantage point), the idol according to quality (it bedazzles), the flesh according to relation (it is a kind of "auto-affective" phenomenon, since in sensation there is no difference between, say, what is heard and the hearing), and, finally, the icon is saturated according to modality (since the I no longer defines its possibility or existence).

The second and fourth phenomena are especially interesting because, like the stage image in *Catastrophe*, one can flip over into the other. According to the typology a painting or, in the case of Beckett's play, the stage image is an idol because it keeps "to itself," as it were, all its concentrated visuality, all the bedazzlement it generates. The icon's glory, however, comes from outside it: the real glory is the saintly prototype that cannot be represented, but rather is presented in the icon. The idol, on the contrary, also presents, but it presents nothing other than itself.

So at the moment when the ambivalence between the imaginary and the real comes fully into play in *Catastrophe*, or when the actor emerges perceivably from behind the mask of character, the image moves from being idolatrous to being iconic. Differently put, it moves from giving itself as visual spectacle to exerting its own gaze and offering no spectacle whatsoever: the icon "tolerates no gaze."[32] Marion includes the face of the Other among the saturated phenomena he characterizes as iconic, although he is careful to point out that what is implied here is not solely or even primarily an ethical obligation to the Other à la Lévinas. The latter foregrounds the boundlessness of one's ethical obligation to the Other absolutely, and only from the absoluteness of that pre-phenomenal relationship does he derive a mechanism that brings God to mind.[33] For Marion, on the other hand, any icon, whether human or wooden, is automatically in continuity with the divine. As he says in *God without Being*, "[W]hat characterizes the icon painted on wood does not come from the hand of a man but from the infinite depth that crosses it . . . . The essential in the icon—the intention that envisages—comes to it from elsewhere."[34] The icon will always try to make the invisible visible, and it will do so according to a logic that is not mimetic.

The icon does not attempt to represent Christ or the saints. Its austere lines and aesthetic asceticism leave no question about that. It aims rather higher: it wants to present divinity. "The icon steps outside the mimetic logic of the image by what it accomplishes entirely in its reference to a prototype."[35] St. Theodore the Studite, one of the foremost defenders of icons of the ninth century, is able to clarify precisely what Marion means by this. For St. Theodore the icon and the divine or saintly prototype to which it refers do not belong to two different orders, such as image and original would in the logic of mimesis, but to the order of related things. An icon is different from its prototype in quantity, but not in quality:

> The prototype and the image belong to the category of related things, like the double and the half. For the prototype always implies the image of which it is the prototype, and the double always implies the half in relation to which it is called double. For there would not be a prototype if there were no image; there would not even be any double, if some half were not understood. But since these things exist simultaneously, they are understood and subsist together. Therefore, since no time intervenes between them, the one does not have a different veneration from the other, but both have one and the same.[36]

There would be no image without the prototype, but also, more surprisingly, no prototype without the image. There is no original and copy; rather, the "image" and "original" are simultaneous. The two are in a categorial relationship of interdependence; one cannot exist without the other, thus one does not precede the other in a relationship of ontological primacy, although the two are in ontological interdependence.

Now we can say more about what attracts Beckett to the theater especially in his late art, when he turns toward the theater for what prose can only realize imperfectly. Like the painting or the icon, and unlike language, which inevitably moves along a temporal axis, the theatrical image is able to give itself all at once. This is especially true of Beckett's late stage images, which literally become paintings strangely disturbed by minimal motion: action is reduced to a minimum. In other words, the visual more easily reaches the critical threshold of phenomenal saturation than prose does. At the same time, however, the theater foregrounds in a more immediately experiential manner the same ambivalence that

Maurice Blanchot takes to characterize the space of literature in general. Theater, like the Byzantine icon, always gives the real and the imaginary at the same time because the physicality of the actor, or the phenomenological givenness of a chair as chair, rather than as stage prop, never recedes entirely behind the fictional context of the play. The difference is that the icon presupposes the divine prototype whereas the space of literature, in the manifestation it takes with Beckett, does not—although it does not deny it either. Rather, it achieves a similarly irreducible iconicity in the horizontal realm of the text.

So it is an iconic structure that Beckett looks for in his endeavors to create an expressionless art, an art that is "[t]he expression that there is nothing to express, nothing from which to express, no power to express, no desire to express, together with the obligation to express" ("TD" 139). As we established earlier, it is not enough to situate oneself in some hypothetical space outside expression. What is needed is an iconic space that is both inside and outside, and does not adhere to the binary logic of representation.

The most pervasive characteristic of Beckett's art is probably his frustration, and fascination, with the limits of language, with representation and the Ineffable. In an early German letter to a publisher who tried to win Beckett's multilingual talents for a translation of *Ringelnatz* into English, Beckett wrote as a damper to Axel Kaun's enthusiasm: "Es wird mir tatsächlich immer schwieriger, ja sinnloser ein offizielles Englisch zu schreiben. Und immer mehr wie ein Schleier kommt mir meine Sprache vor, den man zerreissen muss, um an die dahinterliegeden Dinge (oder das dahinterliegende Nichts) zu kommen. [I find it increasingly difficult, indeed increasingly pointless, to write an official English. My own language seems to me more and more like a veil that needs to be torn in order to get at the things (or the Nothingness) behind it.]" (*D* 52. Translation mine.) What Beckett keeps of this attitude throughout his writing life is the hope reflected here of a transcendent elsewhere that will reveal things for what they are (be that a plenitude or nothing at all—he won't commit himself); what he questions is the method of arriving there by any mode of adequation. Beckett's skepticism works both ways, in the form of mistrust of mimesis and of *Vorstellung*. In order to be freed from the dualist shackles of representation one must retain the Romantic belief in *Darstellung*, to be sure, but once the *Darstellung* "returns" to the artist as phenomenological intuition, the criterion of its truth must not be whether it conforms to a preceding *Vorstellung* of it. It must no longer be the subject that "assembles" what it finds to conform to its *Vorstellung.* It is an art of radical presentation that calls for a fundamentally different conception of subjectivity, since the traditional centered, self-grounded subject or transcendental ego is markedly unfit either to create or to receive such art. Indeed, it calls for a nondual way of creating art and inhabiting the world. The example of Chinese ink-splash painting will clarify the implications.

A relatively recent article by Junko Matoba explicitly links *sunyata* to Beckett's visual style in his late drama. Matoba isolates darkness and decentering as the most important characteristics in Japanese mono-chrome painting and identifies the darkened area on Beckett's stage with the empty white space in Japanese ink paintings, and thereby with *sunyata.* But in her conclusion she remains both loyal to dualism and to the established currents of Beckett criticism. She concludes: "The religious notion of nothing in Yohaku [the empty white space in Japanese ink painting] is positive, whereas Beckett's is a 'dung-heap' accumulated from an agnostic stance for neither the positive nor the negative."[37]

Norman Bryson, in a short essay titled "The Gaze in the Expanded Field," offers a much more compelling account of the philosophical implications of Ch'an ink-splash paintings that will elucidate at greater depth why the parallels with Beckett's art are so compelling. Bryson establishes first of all that in order to overcome representation in painting the object needs to be lifted out of the frame. The frame fixes the point of view from which the object is depicted, prescribes a point of view for the viewer, and at the same time wants to evoke the impression of showing the object in its entirety, when this is clearly impossible: a cube can never be shown fully on a canvas, and yet we state without hesitation that we are in fact seeing a cube. Instead, Bryson suggests, the object needs to be placed "on the expanded field of blankness or *sunyata*" so that "[t]he object opens out *omnidirectionally* on to the universal surround, against which it defines itself negatively and diacritically."[38] He finds this "expanded field" at work in Ch'an painting, a discipline that arises directly from its practitioners' (normally monks) full immersion in the "concept" of *sunyata.* Bryson specifically discusses a landscape by Sesshu, whom Matoba also uses as an example, and who worked in

China in the second half of the fifteenth century: "When we look at things, we do see only a tangent, and not the full radiation of light emitted omnidirectionally. Ch'an does not dispute that. What Ch'an does dispute is that the profile which thus appears can be identified with the object itself. . . . What the image needs to include is the fact of the object's remainder, the other views which pass out from the object to all those uncountable places where the viewer is not."[39] The image includes this by virtue of *sunyata* (which "inhabits" the empty space in the painting) and does so in the following way. The paintings, produced by accomplished Buddhist monks, emerge from a practice of meditation and an integrated way of life the "aim" of which is to transcend the dualism of the everyday perception of the world in favor of a nondual one. Through a regime of concentration, contemplation, and meditation meant to help one detach herself from self and thought, the practitioner attunes herself to a universal orderedness, so that a merging takes place between the meditating subject and the outside world. The meditation practice is intended to tire the conceptual mind, especially through the use of koans, contradictory "riddles" without solution, that make the mind spin between the conceptual possibilities until it comes to rest and lets go of habitual binary thought patterns. Nagarjuna might be the most rigorous logician among mystics: according to him an assertion has four possible forms: "(1) that it is; (2) that it is not; (3) that it both-is-and-is-not; (4) that it neither-is-nor-is-not."[40] This fourfold pattern exhausts the ontological implications of the verb "to be." The "result" of this process (though, as with Derrida, one must be careful not to reify it into a "method") is *sunyata*.

Consequently, when the practitioner flings ink onto the canvas, what emerges is not the result of random chance, nor obviously the intention of the artist, but a manifestation of that universal order: the picture is witness to the practitioner's own being in the world that is in turn tuned to the universal order. Thus the artist's intuition in creation is not merely a function of individual subjectivity. Artists commonly describe such moments of creation as inspired by God and in which they were merely the executive organs: a widespread metaphor in Western culture to describe the nondual moment, David Loy suggests.[41] Bryson evocatively summarizes the process thus: "The flinging of ink marks the surrender of the fixed form of the image to the global configuration of force that subtends it. *Eidos* is scattered to the four winds. The image is made to float on the forces which lie outside the frame; it is *thrown*, as one throws dice. What breaks into the image is the rest of the universe, everything outside the frame."[42] Life itself enters into the picture, but not because it is the more authentic cousin of representation and hence to be preferred to the weak copy, but because life *is* the image; as Loy put it, *nirvana is samsara.*

With Chinese ink-splash paintings and also with Byzantine iconography (which allows for artistic individuality only within the narrow historical bounds of the type) we have found examples of artistic production that go beyond subject-centered models of artistic expression. So what happens to the audience in Beckett's plays; or, more narrowly put, what happens to the "subject" once the artist has created and the work of art comes flooding back as intuition? Jean-Luc Marion rethinks the post-Husserlian subject as "the gifted"—a "receiver" who does not constitute the phenomenon, but rather submits to its givenness, "lights up as on a control panel,"[43] as Marion says, when the phenomenal information hits it, and turns it into manifestation. Likewise, he refigures the Husserlian standard of the "poor" phenomenon. He does not doubt that there are such phenomena whose intuition can never fulfill the subject's intention, but intention is no longer the defining moment of phenomenological cognition. It is givenness, and he can therefore allow for other phenomena as well, namely phenomena that exceed intention: "saturated phenomena" or "paradoxes," as Marion also calls them, that send the receiver into endless hermeneutic loops of trying, unsuccessfully, to constitute the phenomenon.

Beckett spent hours in front of the *Decollation of St. John the Baptist* in the cathedral in Valetta trying to come to terms with the saturation of visibility in Caravaggio's painting. Eventually the painting inspired the stage image for *Not I*. Marion argues that the saturation of visibility in painting comes about because the visual presents itself entirely two-dimensionally, "without any remainder of appresentation."[44] We do not worry about visualizing those sides of depicted objects that are not shown because we have enough on our hands with what is, Marion muses with reference to Caravaggio's *The Conversion of St. Paul*. And he has an evocative description of its effect on the viewer: "I am not wondering about the largely hidden anatomy of the animal, or about the silhouette of the manservant, almost vanished, moreover in the shadow. I am not even enquiring about the identity of the light (or of the voice) that calls him: I am overwhelmed, the luminous lake flooding all at once the side opposed to the flash of lightning, which seems to have struck in front of the painting, thus behind my back."[45]

Here, no doubt, the subject does not constitute any object, but the phenomenon overwhelms the subject with its visual saturation. If phenomena are not constituted by subjects they cannot be objectified in opposition to subjects, the iconic Protagonist points out at the end of *Catastrophe*. Together with the constituting subject the objectifying gaze that torments the Protagonist also disappears: no violence can be implicit in the gaze of a receiver of phenomenal intuition who understands himself as the recipient of a gift. The iconicity of Chinese ink-splash painting and Byzantine iconography, as we see them through the filter of Beckett's *Catastrophe*, reveal patterns of visuality that demand of the "observer," or rather the gifted, a way of conducting herself differently in the world: the framework of *Ge-stell* will not do, since the visual refuses to allow itself to be objectified into *Zuhandenheit*.

"Three Dialogues" and the Economy of Art

> [I]f it is not almost everything, it is anything but nothing—
>
> or, if it's nothing, it's a nothing which *counts*,
>
> which in my view counts a lot.
>
> Jacques Derrida, *Acts of Literature*

In his "Three Dialogues" Beckett ventures a startling artistic theory. He proposes an "expressionless" art—that is, art not based on expression. According to Beckett, art is an economy of exchange; it turns into a "farce of giving and receiving" ("TD" 141) because it is based on the teleology implicit in the goal of complete and perfect expression, but perpetually fails short of its ideal because it seeks to express an ineffable idea. Expressionless art upsets this economy in the direction of a nonvolitional, nonlinear nonduality that gives itself freely and of its own accord.

Beckett sees the ideal of expressionless art realized in the paintings of Bram van Velde, but it is clear that his own art aspires to it.

Beckett is puzzled by the contradiction of having to use representational language to speak, necessarily inadequately, of things about which by definition one cannot speak. Kant was well aware of the same dilemma when he allowed for the category of the aesthetic idea: the aesthetic idea is a *Vorstellung der Einbildungskraft*, an "intuition of the imagination, which prompts much thought, but to which . . . no concept can be adequate, so that no language can express it completely and allow us to grasp it."[1]

Negative theology is thoroughly familiar with this problem at the level of the transcendent. It is concerned with the very act of *talking* about God, of our ability (or lack thereof) to represent God through language; and it is at its most eloquent when it says it can say nothing, because at that precise moment negative theology upsets conventional logic, drives it into aporia, and situates itself both inside and outside discourse. Whatever ontological claims it makes must immediately be bracketed by God's aseity. At its most rigorous it cannot make any ontological claims about the nature of God.[2] It is at a remove from its "object" insofar as it is not so much concerned with God as with the kind of language we use to speak of him. At the same time, talking about God is valuable for negative theology from a soteriological point of view and therefore it continues to talk despite the impossibility of ever capturing God in language.[3] Negative theology sees eye to eye with Beckett: the performative act of writing about the Unnamable is an end in itself, regardless of the fact that no concept can be adequate to the intuition of the imagination that gives itself when we turn our souls toward God. The speaker in *The Unnamable* summarizes the mechanism thus: "The fact would seem to be, if in my situation one may speak of facts, not only that I shall have to speak of things of which I cannot speak, but also, which is even more interesting, but also that I, which is if possible even more interesting, that I shall have to, I forget, no matter. And at the same time I am obliged to speak. I shall never be silent. Never" (*U* 294).

The problem of having to speak yet being unable to speak adequately remains Beckett's central obsession throughout his career. In

"Three Dialogues" the theme emerges in the context of his talking about three modern painters, when he suggests that art is (or should be) "[t]he expression that there is nothing to express, nothing from which to express, no power to express, no desire to express, together with the obligation to express" ("TD" 139).[4] Let us unpack the aporetic movement that is implicit here.

In the chapter on the Ineffable in his book *Logic and Existence*, Jean Hyppolite argues that the Ineffable is the absolutely singular, but instead of culminating in the absolute singularity of the Ineffable, the dialectical process of cognition cannot progress beyond the merely universal. Any proposition one may make about a singular entity (such as the individuality of a person) cannot help but slip into universals, mere abstract qualities a man or woman (universals again) possesses. "We really believe that we grasp singular, immediate being as singular, but what we say is that there is something more universal, a 'this,' a 'this one.' But everything is a 'this,' every 'I' is a 'this one.' We believe that we grasp what is richest, but what remains of this experience for us is only the consciousness of our poverty."[5] Translated into Derridean vocabulary this means that the artist is caught in a double bind. As soon as one wants to *say* the Absolute, the Unnamable, its absolute singularity withdraws as a result of inscription: the absolute character of its singularity becomes a trace. This is also Beckett's problem in *The Unnamable*. The Unnamable escapes his grasp like a slippery fish at the last moment because the moment of saying, of naming, turns it into something else, a mere trace of itself. The artist must somehow break out of this double bind. The apophatic process acknowledges it and tries to approach it through a split of its own: while the kataphatic moment aims to proclaim God's Revelation and fails at the moment of inscription when the singular turns into the trace, the apophatic moment begins with the trace and tries to recover God's singularity, his absolute transcendence, through a nonconceptual back door.

In other words, the important point is for the apophatic moment not simply to try to achieve the very thing the kataphatic moment has not (an articulation of absolute simplicity), but to remain within the moment of doubling and go not in the direction of simplicity, but triplicity: to find the "third way" in the aporia of kataphatic and apophatic. Otherwise the endeavor would, once again, turn into a futile quest for the Ineffable. The conscious language of paradox, of doubling, is ironically, then paradoxically (and then appropriately) the closest one can get to articulating utter simplicity. Expressionless art does not call for the double bind to be resolved but for it to be embraced in the language of paradox. The obligation implicit in writing derives directly from the aporetic nature of writing. For Jean-Luc Nancy the aporia of writing turns into a call, obliging the writer to answer.[6] But we need a wider angle to see how Nancy arrives at this thought.

Although often claimed to be "atheist," the term does not correctly describe Beckett's position. Conventional wisdom has it that atheism and theism are based on the same principle. And, indeed, Jean-Luc Nancy points out that to this day atheism has not managed to substitute for God, conventionally conceived as the supreme being or absolute presence, something other than another fullness or presence, another instance of supreme meaning, such as a *telos* or a good.[7] Yet any reader of *The Unnamable* or any other Beckett text can attest to the fact that Beckett is not concerned with fullness or presence. The text does not seek to fortify an ontological or epistemological position. Rather, it is self-emptying; it systematically undermines ontological positions and leaves the reader no safe place to stand, neither on the side of presence nor on the side of absence. For Beckett is not a nihilist, either. In his works, and in the most rigorous of negative theologies, a dialectical process of negation operates to negate not only affirmation, but also its presumed polar opposite, negation, and thus enters a nondual space of undecidability whose discursive manifestation is the trace. Only through the trace is it possible to keep positions from petrifying into oppositional and essentialist structures. For negative theology, what is at stake in this process is to safeguard God's transcendence: to keep him in a realm that is not of the order of beings (even if that be the order of a *supreme* being) and thus to emphasize that God will neither fit into nor answer to the patterns of human conceptuality.

Thus Beckett and negative theology both understand that there cannot be a question of the *existence* of God (or of his nonexistence, for that matter), for the term "existence" implies the order of *existents*, of beings. On the basis of this understanding Nancy points out that the question of the existence of God annuls itself because any God conceived of as a supreme being must still answer to an "authority or power"—Nancy acknowledges the inadequacy of such terms in the given context—that does not range in the order of existents.[8] Thus the attempt to keep the so-called question of God within the realm of existence amounts to saying that the world rests on the back of a giant turtle with another turtle underneath: to say that "it's turtles all the way down" does not answer the question.

Since God does not range in the order of existents, he cannot be filled with conceptual content. "God" is a word unlike any other because, properly speaking, no concept corresponds to it, while other words stand for concepts. Nancy concludes that the important thing is simply to *pronounce* the name of God and he emphasizes that this process of naming must not be understood as a process of "signification" or "designation of meaning."[9] That is, the important thing is performatively to *keep open* the iconic space that the pronunciation of God's name opens up. This is the obligation. In order for art to be expressionless, then, the compulsion that drives *The Unnamable* (to look for a way to say what by definition cannot be said) must turn into seizing the obligation of tirelessly "naming" God, in Nancy's sense, and thus to keep one's own endeavors in a space that ceaselessly destabilizes the metaphysical and the idolatrous.

Nancy's argument takes its crucial turn with some observations on the name. He points out that the name of God "de-names" the name in general, because it "names" what cannot be named, while at the same time continuing to name, to assign a name—that is, to call: "A ce compte ce nom dé-nommerait le nom en general, tout en persistent à appeler. [At this point this name would dename the name in general, while continuing to name.]"[10] The Unnamable, which the writer "creates" in the process of writing, in turn calls to the writer, obliging him to respond to that call. One can almost see an ethical obligation à la Emmanuel Lévinas here: the call of the Other results in an absolute responsibility to respond.

Let us follow this progression from de-naming to calling and finally crying one step at a time. First, Nancy's word choice evokes Marion's term *dé-nomination* with which he indicates the fully dialectical third way of negative theology. The term implies not only the process of unnaming or de-naming, but also negative theology's implication in, and potential deconstruction of, interdenominational quarrels and monetary or economic exchange. Second, a name is different from other words in that it does not stand for a generalizable concept. A name stands for a singularity, a unique being (although there may be millions of people on earth with the same name), and, as Hyppolite points out, a unique being can never be captured in language other than in generalities or concepts. Moreover, in the case of God, the name does not even stand for a being, a creature; the name of God takes this characteristic of the name to yet another level: we cannot capture the singularity of a unique being, let alone the absolute singularity of the divine, the uncreated, singular unto himself.

Further, the declamation of a name is always an appeal to an other (divine or human) that takes us beyond the bounds of our own subjectivity. God, and in Lévinas's ethical framework the other person, exceeds the boundaries of exchange. What makes one's response ethical is its unconditionality: one responds to the Other's call even though one may never have personally harmed the person, or, conversely, even though the person has never treated one especially favorably. One answers although one is not obligated by a contract formed in the present (or any present) and is thus not tied to the other person in an economy of exchange. What cannot be named and contained in a concept cannot participate in an exchange. Rather, an Other comes over us and overwhelms us, upsets the economy of exchange. So eventually, to open an empty space "without meaning" in the sense of a lack of human conceptuality, as Beckett does, also means to open a space for a different kind of meaning not defined by totality but by excess. Or, to say it in words that are closer to Nancy's, surrender *of* meaning is also surrender *to* meaning if the latter exceeds itself ("à cet abandon *du* sens qui forme aussi bien la vérité d'un abandon *au* sens en tant que ce dernier s'excède [to this surrender *of* meaning, which is just as well a surrender *to* meaning insofar as the latter exceeds itself]).[11] At this stage, for Nancy, the call turns into a cry: not into a call that calls *for* anything, but one that simply cries—in the wilderness, he remarks, or into the void of conceptual meaning.[12] It cries in the wilderness like John the Baptist, as a reminder of God and as a prophet of the return of God and to God. Beckett's absence of God signals, after all, the potential return of God. If the name of God "deconstructs" itself so uncompromisingly, then speaking of God becomes a process, an attitude, and does not necessarily require saying the word "God" (although it might), since the latter does not denote any conceptual content.

In dramatizing the case of the "humanism of the cry"—understood as a kind of negative anthropology or negative anthropotheology—Beckett deconstructs all "idolatry of the human and all anthropotheology."[13] He thus rids atheism of its conceits (of proclaiming human fullness instead of divine fullness, but still proclaiming a fullness), and implicitly theism also, since in the history of philosophy both atheism and theism find themselves on the side of fullness and presence. By deconstructing the fundamental tenet of atheism (presence) he deconstructs that of theism, too. Therefore, by presenting a post-metaphysical humanism, Beckett also opens a space for thinking about and experiencing the divine anew in terms other than those of presence and totality—namely, in terms of excess—since only a "post-humanism" can open itself sufficiently to do so. In order to allow for the saturated phenomenon to give itself in excess the subject-centered positions of humanist philosophy need to be revised and the emphasis shifted to phenomenological givenness. The subject turns into a "receiver" who submits to givenness and manifests it. As a result, the subject is still at the center insofar as no phenomenon could manifest itself in its absence, but it does not put itself there as a self-legitimizing origin, but rather it is held there by what gives itself.[14]

After "obligation" let us continue with the next word in Beckett's earlier quoted formulation concerning art's "obligation to express": expression. In the short interview excerpt at the beginning of *Shades*, a 1977 BBC documentary of Beckett's life and work, Martin Esslin ventures a predictably existentialist interpretation of Beckett's preoccupation with the obligation to express: the modern artist has to express, regardless of the fact that in the existentialist godless universe his efforts will be futile ("because you know that you die and even the greatest fame will be forgotten"). In order to be a responsible human being the artist has to express defiantly in the face of this futility, because expression, according to Esslin, is the defining characteristic of the human condition: "we experience something and because we experience it we must express it." Such an interpretation prides itself on having dismantled God as safety net, but in the process it turns the artist into a heroic figure of almost godlike proportions: the artist is able to shoulder the bleak and purposeless reality of a godless existence. He has no need for the fairy tale relied on by the majority of people throughout history in order not to have to accept responsibility for their actions.

Yet Esslin's emphasis on expression in the face of hopelessness and futility is not at all Beckett's concern in the "Three Dialogues." More to the point, Beckett questions expression *itself.* The futility is merely an aftereffect of expression; expression brings about futility. Beckett's idea is that in trying to "make it new," in trying to find ever new, more startling, revolutionary ways of expressing what fundamentally cannot be said, the avant-garde is, in fact, not making anything new at all. Beckett sees the history of art unified in the attempt to express in ever more adept and refined ways the object of its pursuits: "The more to express, the little to express, the ability to express much, the ability to express little, merge in the common anxiety to express as much as possible, or as truly as possible, or as finely as possible, to the best of one's ability" ("TD" 142–43). Yet what art, according to Beckett, fails to acknowledge is that, since its "object" is unnamable, inexpressible, ineffable, it is following a futile path in attempting to express, mediate, and hence conceptualize that which by its very nature cannot be conceptualized. Art is caught in a vicious circle of attempting in ever new ways what cannot be achieved ("There are many ways in which the thing I'm trying in vain to say may be tried in vain to be said" ["TD" 144]). It remains in the vicious circle of its efforts and within the economy of exchange Beckett diagnoses in language and conceptuality.[15] It redefines the boundaries of what is acceptable, but it does not bring about a fundamental change of perspective. All it disturbs is "a certain order on the plane of the feasible," Beckett summarizes provocatively ("TD" 139), eliciting from his real or fictitious interlocutor the objection that there is no other plane for someone who is, after all, a creator of material objects: "What other plane can there be for the maker?" ("TD" 139). Beckett answers: "[L]ogically none" ("TD" 139). But, one surmises, the demands of a logic of noncontradiction are precisely what Beckett expects artists to disregard.

Beckett proposes an art that recognizes this circle of ever new sameness and turns away from it, "weary of its puny exploits, weary of pretending to be able, of being able, of doing a little better the same old thing, of going a little further down along a dreary road" ("TD" 139). He proposes an art that is indifferent to the whole paradigm of expression and thus hypothesizes the possibility of art beyond the limits of representation. "Representation" and "expression" are related terms since both imply a dualism between what is thought to be "real" and what is a copy: the object of perception and its representation or the original thought and its expression, respectively.

In Beckett's artistic theory, the entire question of expression (and how to create an art not bound by the limits of expression) again draws on the relationship of *Darstellung*, or sensible presentation, and *Vorstellung*, usually translated as the representation of an image or an idea. Which comes first, and, as a result, which one does one privilege? For Kant, a *Vorstellung* always precedes sense perception. The referential model of expression defers to a preceding *Vorstellung* that it expresses.[16]

Is art, then, to be thought of as *Vorstellung?* The representation of an idea? Or is it, rather, *Darstellung*, or sensible presentation, without a representation to subtend it? Beckett's advocacy of expressionless art seems to indicate that his ideal is the latter. The term "expressionless" does not imply bland, or boring, but rather the opposite: a concentration of means so that the materiality of art itself, the intensity of the visual image or the texture of poetic language, can emerge with force. It is therefore doubtful that Beckett's expressionless art can be aligned with minimalism as it is framed in art history as a reaction to expressionism. Minimalism, Roland Barthes points out in his lectures on the Neutral, tries to present the object "in plain obviousness, with the clarity of an irrefutable reality," so that "a depersonalized and even mechanized facture" results. Minimalism wants "to banish all emotion, all anecdote."[17] Yet this is not what happens in Beckett, nor is it at work in Barthes's Neutral either. Emotion, or better affect (to avoid the subjectivist connotation of emotion), is not absent in Beckett. Rather, it is concentrated as sunlight is bundled with a magnifying glass and "processed" or "formatted," as Barthes has it, in the process.[18] Merely to excise emotion would be a counter-reaction that confirms the conceptual framework that situates emotion and mechanization as polar opposites. Beckett focuses on the tactile quality of art and on its sensuousness, not on its conceptual content, although it, too, plays its part since there is no *Darstellung* without a sense of *Vorstellung* in it, even in art that understands itself as *Darstellung*, or else it would cease to be art. Beckett's art is to hit the audience in its materiality, and thus to free itself from the shackles of the concept, both in the creation and the reception process.

We have seen that the iconoclastic debate also takes hold with reference to *Darstellung* and *Vorstellung*. It is impossible to venerate an icon through worship if the icon is conceived of as *Vorstellung*, as a mere representation of the "real"; this would be blasphemous and idolatrous. It is necessary to develop a theology of the icon that frees itself from the dualistic implications of a reference to *Vorstellung*. Such a theology must upset the hierarchical logic of real and copy, as St. Theodore's does. There is of necessity continuity between the divinity and its icon because, if Christ and his saints could not be depicted in the temporal realm, the divinity of Christ's incarnation would be in doubt. But an icon of Christ is not a representation of the divine, but a *Darstellung*, a presentation of his divinity. Because it is an image the icon situates itself squarely within the realm of representation, but at the same time is also outside it because it functions by a nonmimetic logic. This nonduality of inside and outside is iconic in Jean-Luc Marion's use of the term. Beckett's art of nonexpression aspires to the same state of affairs at the level of the transcendental.

His "new" art, in order to leave the "dreary road" of expression behind, must not redefine itself in a polemical gesture of newness by which the avant-garde sets itself off from its predecessors. It must not so much turn *against* the paradigm of expression as treat it with equanimity so as not to be bound by it: turning against it would immediately reinscribe the new art in the discourse of metaphysics. It would rest on the same dualism as the mode of artistic expression, based as it is on a distinction between something to express and something from which to express. And, in fact, in the advent of the new art the notion of the avant-garde itself needs to be deconstructed, since it relies on a linear model with military connotations.

Along these lines Kevin Hart points out that the aim for negative theology cannot be an exit from metaphysics because "the *denial* of metaphysics is itself a metaphysical gesture."[19] Like deconstruction, negative theology cannot exit from metaphysics, but negative theology has the superior tools to complete the deconstructive effort deconstruction itself only begins. Deconstruction, it has been argued,[20] deconstructs identity but valorizes difference, whereas negative theology at its best (that is, when it is understood that negative theology is not merely a corrective to positive theology) deconstructs both components of the binary and situates itself in a third, fully nondual space neither inside nor outside metaphysics. Crucially and aporetically, the way "out" only materializes once one no longer desires to find it.

When discussing André Masson and his pursuit of "painting the void" ("TD" 139), Beckett objects to the phraseology and prefers "obliteration of an unbearable presence" ("TD" 140) to "void." "Void," after all, is a charged term, inscribed in metaphysics as the opposite of existence or fullness. It is, as such, a positive term (although its signification is negative): presence and void, though opposites, are categorically the same. Substituting a negative term for a positive one makes no difference to the ontological nature of the statement being made. "Obliteration of presence" tries to leave open a nondescript space or nonentity not filled with positive content (not even of a negative kind). The phrase attempts to insinuate destruction without replacement. "What is the use of seeking justification always on the same plane?" Beckett objects ("TD" 140). Masson does not openly acknowledge the paradox he tries to be rid of ("this anguish of helplessness is never stated as such" ["TD" 140]) because he assumes that such an acknowledgment can only be stated explicitly (which is impossible) and so his endeavors remain locked into metaphysics. Instead of a negative ontology an art is needed that makes no ontological claims whatsoever.

It helps to remind oneself that the kinds of presence to be obliterated by Derrida and by Masson are quite different: Derrida tries to obliterate metaphysical presence, whereas Masson contends with the presence of the very thing that for Derrida is the answer: paradox. He is, Beckett says, "literally skewered on the ferocious dilemma of expression" ("TD" 140) in trying to express paradox or aporia—the very thing that defies conceptualization. Masson attempts to complete the deconstruction by trying to paint, as the art critic Duthuit's voice has it, "inner emptiness, the prime condition, according to Chinese esthetics, of the act of painting" ("TD" 139). Yet the project is undertaken with the distinct aim to establish the data of the problem to be solved ("in search of the difficulty rather than in its clutch" ["TD" 139]).[21] Masson does not even get as far as Derrida. He keeps producing merely a metaphysical shadow of painting as *Darstellung*.

The presence Masson tries to "vaporize" by obliteration is unbearable because it is "neither to be wooed nor to be stormed" ("TD" 140) and produces therefore the "anguish of helplessness" ("TD" 140) inherent in every paradox. The paradox Beckett is thinking of here is, of course, the one of being "unable to act" yet "obliged to act" ("TD" 145) that is at the root of the artist's inability to express the Ineffable. Paradox has the healing effect of stumping the mind into temporary inertia, catapulting one outside of well-trodden paths by forcing recognition of realities beside the ones our deeply engrained epistemological modes yield. Yet, according to Beckett, the avant-garde (and, one might add, Derrida) must repeat this shock of recognition over and over because it "seek[s] justification always on the same plane" ("TD" 140). It valorizes difference by "making it new," thus remains in the orbit of metaphysics and therefore needs another revolution, another deconstruction, as soon as fronts have hardened once again.

Beckett's ideal artist deconstructs both identity and difference and therefore escapes the vicious circle of endless deconstructions. This possibility of being both inside and outside (language, metaphysics, the relative), to at the same time express and not express, is what is at stake in the "third way" (Marion) or "Middle Way" (Nagarjuna) "beyond every denial, beyond every assertion,"[22] which negative theology consistently evokes. The iconic is a nondual mode in which binary questions of either/or and inside/outside lose their relevancy.

Two of the most stimulating contributors to the question whether and how such a middle way can be thought are Jacques Derrida and Jean-Luc Marion, especially in their mutually inspiring theorizations of the gift. It is fair to say that Derridean deconstruction and negative theology share their most fundamental concerns, and even the way they propose to go about addressing them, although they disagree on some fundamental points. It is precisely their disagreements that tend to bring into relief the most challenging aspects of negative theology.

It is a function of the nature of the questions at stake that Derrida and Marion remain true to the aporetic tenor of the discussion by admitting that their respective positions are at the same time "very close and extremely distant" from one another, "others might say opposed."[23] In the end, the either infinitesimally small or unbridgeable differences between them remain unresolved because, puzzlingly, despite their closeness they work from fundamentally opposed points of view. For Derrida, language is solely a system of internal differences; for Marion, it makes reference to a reality that exceeds the finitude of language—a reality without the characteristics Derrida posits to be common to all onto-theological metaphysics, because unbound by the concept. Derrida's pertinent point in his discussion with Marion is how, given our epistemological limitations, we can posit such a transcendental. How can it be what it is and still be intelligible to us? Is not every theorization of it automatically an idolatrous act limiting God to language and to the categories of what is humanly conceivable, necessitating in turn the endless trace of deconstructions? Or, if not, then how can one proceed to an "iconic" understanding of God and still be a human being ensconced in language and the relative? Marion argues that, as a saturated phenomenon, it is, precisely, not intelligible to us, but this does not mean that we cannot theorize it. What gives itself phenomenologically can be described in phenomenological terms. This does not imply conceptualizing it, but grasping why it so consistently evades our conceptualizations.

Derrida furthers his argument by considering the nature of the gift. He asserts that the gift is founded on a system of exchange, a self-perpetuating economy in which a donor gives a gift, but in so doing inspires in the recipient the obligation to reciprocate. The recipient is left with the guilt of debt. It can be argued, then, that the donor does not give at all, but hands the recipient a blank IOU to be filled at his discretion. A gift that gives itself without reserve, in excess and without the expectation of reparation, would open up the restricted economy beyond finite inscription in language. The source of such a gift, or rather the gift itself, since there could no longer be a distinction between giver and gift, between *causa agens* and *causa finalis*, can only be kenotic.

According to Derrida the true gift, which gives itself freely without expectation of compensation, is unthinkable within the economy of philosophy, but in this impossibility to think it lies its potential for liberation. Indeed, the gift carries within itself an original ambiguity; it is poisoned at the root (Derrida plays with the German word for poison, *Gift*). As soon as the gift is given, the excess sets in motion an economic circle that, in turn, annuls the excess that constitutes the gift because another gift will be given in return. For one thing, then, the gift merely "gives time" until it is to be paid back. But this also means that it is automatically inscribed in a circle that implies the temporization of writing.[24] The gift becomes synonymous with the supplement (that which is simultaneously excess and lack) and with *différance*. It is based on a constitutive ambiguity in that it annuls itself at the very moment of coming into existence.

As would be expected, Derrida embraces this impasse. The gift does not adhere to a conventional either/or logic but upsets it in challenging the Western mind to think beyond what appears to be a logical opposition to an inclusive logic of both/and. By attempting to think the impossible the mind spirals toward what within the paradigm of Western reason can no longer be called rational. Derrida develops Marcel Mauss's observations on the dynamics of potlatch as a demonstration of power in autochthonous communities: one family or clan gives a material "gift" to another. The latter must follow suit with a larger gift in return in order to save its honor, since not to give would offend the other party and imply poverty and low social status. Now it is the first party's turn again to give in excess of what it has received, until virtual capital (and debt) exceeds the material property in the community. Maybe a family is engaged in potlatch with a number of different creditors, who could not all be reimbursed at the same time. So potlatch spirals first into virtuality. This is itself a kind of madness that takes for real something that does not exist but actually brings it into existence by way of its consequences. At its climax this spiral tips over into what appears to be pure madness when large quantities of property are destroyed by their owners in what Mauss takes to be an attempt to avoid the impression of desiring repayment. At this point the logic of exchange is broken. Derrida evokes the image of Abraham on Mount Moriah prepared to slay his own son, who abandons the rational for faith and plunges into the unpredictability of madness.

The absolute status of ethical obligation and responsibility intersect with the role of obligation in Beckett's artistic theory. One has an absolute obligation toward every other person and yet one has to make a choice among several: one cannot be equally present to everyone.[25] This aporia of absolute call and necessarily inadequate relative response mirrors the writer's inadequate response to the call of the Unnamable in the process of writing.

For Derrida, the structural madness inherent in the concept of the gift provides a way of glimpsing that which is beyond language as a restricted economy without actually being able to escape from this economy: there is, he has been telling us, nothing outside the text—the only reality humanly accessible is immanent. God would not be God if he were not the wholly other. Instead, the impossible as it presents itself in the aporia of the gift is itself the moment of liberation. The gift is a limit concept and "as such," by its (non-)nature, reveals the limitations of conceptual discourse by opening out into what cannot be grasped by discourse. Like *différance*, it demands vigilance so as not to slip back into metaphysical limitations: "[T]he gift," Derrida says, "is totally foreign to the horizon of economy, ontology, knowledge, constantive [sic] statements, and theoretical determination and judgment"[26] and functions in a realm of which we know nothing because its principles are alien to those of our own experience. Therefore, "if there is a gift . . . it must be the experience of this impossibility" of the gift to appear as such,[27] that is, neither as a "regular" Husserlian "poor" phenomenon within a restricted economy nor as what Marion calls the "saturated phenomenon," because, Derrida insists, there is no "phenomenology without as such."[28]

For both Derrida and Marion, the gift *as such* is completely alien to exchange, but for Derrida the epistemological position is a necessary one. We may give ourselves in faith, as Abraham does, to the knowledge that something beyond our epistemological grasp *is*, but it remains wholly other, entirely beyond our grasp and therefore "conceivable" only in the form of aporia: of a form that opens into an ungraspable but nonetheless real beyond. Necessarily, then, it is *Abraham* who, in the sacrifice of Isaac, gives the gift to God and it is Abraham who must ensure that what he gives is indeed a genuine gift. Through his unconditional faith in a supra-conceptual reality he upsets and terminates the economy of exchange. To Marion this epistemological bias must appear as if Derrida continued to think the gift within the horizon of economy and hence of the conceptual. Marion makes quite clear that, like Abraham, we facilitate the gift in faith, opening ourselves to it, but the essential ingredient "comes to it from elsewhere," as he says in *God without Being* about iconography.[29] Marion, then, envisages a gift that gives *itself* in the same aporetic way in which Derrida's gift is given. This is what Marion calls the "paradoxical" or "saturated phenomenon"—the phenomenon without the "as such." With this idea Marion revises the fundamental tenet of phenomenology, its subject-centeredness, and appears to Derrida as if he seeks to have his cake and eat it too: to call himself a phenomenologist and at the same time break with its most fundamental assumptions. Instead of an infinite intention or ideal that no intuitive content is able to fill, there is a flood of intuitive content causing the intention or concept to overflow. It stretches our cognitive faculties and blueprints to an extent no concept can contain. The intention, not the intuition, is deficient and all our ways of grasping and conceptualizing go out the window. Marion remarks that the latter is something the saturated phenomenon shares with Kant's aesthetic idea: to the extent that Kant was able to theorize a deficient intention, the aesthetic idea foreshadows the saturated phenomenon.

Because the saturated phenomenon appears in the realm of phenomenology we can use phenomenological terminology to talk about it without reducing it to relativity. In so doing we speak not of its absolute nature but of the way it appears to us. To make this clear, Marion has preferred the term "counter-experience" to "saturated phenomenon" in *Being Given* and thereafter.

Derrida's ploy of the "nonconcept" escapes reabsorption into the conceptual less than Marion: *différance* turns into a concept signifying the nonconceptual. Neither Derrida's tireless efforts to find ever new names for it nor his vehement protestations concerning its use could prevent *différance* from becoming the central term within the terminology of deconstruction—a name that even Derrida resigned himself to. One may still object that the Heideggerian ruse of putting concepts under erasure, which Marion also uses consistently in *God without Being*, eliminates the duality of conceptual and nonconceptual only symbolically, and Marion faces a considerable challenge in attempting to circumvent the same difficulty Derrida faces with *différance*.

It is not clear why Derrida musters such loyalty to phenomenological principles in being as opposed as he is to the saturated phenomenon, which he calls "the first heresy in phenomenology."[30] He, more than anyone, has made it his vocation to question philosophical givens. There is a difference in perspective: if "the text" and therefore philosophical/ phenomenological categories are the only unsurpassable horizon, then indeed Marion's "solution" is unsatisfactory. One cannot build an argument on phenomenological categories only to deny them later. Like *dif-*

férance the saturated phenomenon is reabsorbed into metaphysics because merely to *say* that it is nonfinite and hyperabundant does not yet actually make it so. It can only become fully operative when it is part of a system that presupposes philosophical–theological continuity. This also means that in a purely textual context, which the literary or semiotic analysis of Beckett's texts and plays necessarily belongs, the two competing theories can at best be equally if differently plausible. One does not exclude the other.

At the same time we must remember that Marion does not propose a theology of the gift so much as a *phenomenology* of the gift. From his perspective the hyperabundant gift will only be acceptable as the "norm" in a post-metaphysical phenomenology that no longer accepts as dogma the Husserlian definition of the phenomenon. It is true that the saturated phenomenon may be divine (such as Christ as a gift from God the Father), but it need not be. What this means for our question, the economy of expression and how to break it, is that by enlisting Marion's help we do not wander into territory alien to Beckett's world. Marion's perspective is philosophical and immanent, not theological. In *Le visible et le révélé*, Marion speaks of the "banality of saturation" to emphasize that saturated phenomena are accessible to everyone in everyday experience. The occurrence of saturated phenomena is not confined to an exclusive group of mystics or theologians. Marion in fact shows that in many cases one can experience something either as an object (a common phenomenon) or as a saturated phenomenon. For example, one can touch for information (to find a light switch in the dark) or for sensuousness and love, as in touching a lover. Like Beckett, he tries to think post-metaphysical experience, and like Beckett's art, Marion's phenomenology of the saturated phenomenon can take us to the brink of religious experience or encounter but not beyond. Theology will have to speak of the actuality of mystical encounter; phenomenology can speak only of its possibility.

Somewhat surprisingly, Derrida does not question the Husserlian definition of the phenomenon. For him, there is no phenomenology that does not disclose the phenomenon in its essence. For Marion to claim a place for the saturated phenomenon in phenomenology is to turn phenomenology into something else, or conversely, by being part of phenomenology the saturated phenomenon has to defer to the "as such" and stop being a saturated phenomenon as Marion conceives of it. The saturated phenomenon cannot really be post-metaphysical if it claims to be in continuity with a discipline that has traditionally affirmed presence.

To Derrida, negative theology is another such discourse that cannot escape its metaphysical assumptions. He does not question a particular corrective version of negative theology that has come to dominate the West through St. Thomas Aquinas. To Derrida negative theology's verbal acrobatics serve no other purpose than to affirm God's ineffable presence in a realm that claims immunity from deconstruction. Although he has modified his position in later texts toward affirming an aporia in negative theology, his early position as articulated in *"Différance"* still basically holds:

> [T]he . . . the detours, locutions, and syntax in which I will often have to take recourse will resemble those of negative theology, occasionally even to the point of being indistinguishable from negative theology. . . . And yet those aspects of *Différance* which are thereby delineated are not theological, not even in the order of the most negative of negative theologies, which are always concerned with disengaging a superessentiality beyond the finite categories of essence and existence, that is, of presence, and always hastening to recall that God is refused the predicate of existence, only in order to acknowledge his superior, inconceivable, and ineffable mode of being.[31]

Along similar lines, he insists in *Sauf le Nom* that although negative theology questions each ontological or theological proposition by "suspend[ing] every thesis, all belief, all *doxa*," it fundamentally affirms the ontological foundation because "in the most apophatic moment, when one says: 'God is not,' God is neither this nor that, neither that nor its contrary' or 'being is not,' etc., even then it is still a matter of saying the entity [*étant*] such as it is, in its truth, even were it meta-metaphysical, meta-ontological."[32]

It is questionable whether negative theology really gathers itself back into such hyperessential presence. Some less rigorous versions of negative theology do, and these Derrida takes to be representative. The renowned Plotinus scholar A. H. Armstrong makes a distinction between two rival construals of negative theology, one of which he calls

"Middle-Platonist apophasis" and the other "Neoplatonist apophasis."[33] In the first, apophatic theology functions as a corrective to its kataphatic counterpart and is fundamentally analogous to Aquinas's dialectical movement of *via affirmativa*, *via negativa*, and *via emanentiae*. Whatever can be said about God can never be adequate to the fullness of the divine itself because language is a means of signification that is adequate only to creatures, not to the uncreated. Nonetheless, the qualities attributed to God do apply to him, but in an infinitely more outstanding, divine way: "[A]s we have seen, calling God good or wise doesn't simply mean that he causes wisdom or goodness in creatures, but that he himself possesses these perfections in a more excellent way. As expressing these perfections the words apply first to God and then to creatures (since the perfections derive from God); but because we know creatures first, our words were first devised to describe creatures and so have a manner of expression appropriate only to creatures."[34] The *via negativa* in this case signals the inherent inadequacy of the *via affirmativa*, but it does so in a merely corrective way. As Kevin Hart points out, the negations pertain only to the mode of signification—language—and not to the actual qualities that are signified: God *is* what we say he is, just in a way that surpasses what language is able to convey. Derrida is right—this version of the positive/negative dialectic gathers God into a positive presence. On the highest, transcendent level God is again affirmed as the highest value, and his aseity is compromised because reduced to the level of value (a category that pertains to the realm of beings).[35]

Neoplatonist apophasis, in Armstrong's opinion the pure and genuine version of negative theology, is not satisfied with a correction of the positive by the negative, but moves instead to what Denys Turner calls a second-order level discourse of "negations of the negations."[36] This version is fully dialectical, ascending by way of ever-increasing uncertainty to Dionysius's "darkness of unknowing." This implies also that apophatic discourse does not necessarily make its points by way of explicitly *negative* language (although well-known exponents of the apophatic tradition have chosen to do so) if this use of negative language results in a valorization of negativity. It has to negate this leg of the dualist binary as well, so as to produce a self-subverting statement that questions the distinctions between positive and negative, interior and exterior, and so forth, distinctions that the first-order level has maintained.

In a certain respect kataphatic theology taken to its extreme automatically turns into apophatic theology, similar to the way an extremely metonymic text can only flip to the metaphoric mode, and not by chance are the apophatic and the kataphatic intertwined, with a positive statement followed by a negative one. In *The Divine Names*, Dionysius finds such an abundance of names for the divine that there can be no doubt that none of them describes the divine adequately. Instead of a process of naming, Dionysius's text is a process of de-naming, or non-naming—of *denomination*.[37] The confessional and monetary allusions of the term are significant: boundaries of confessional denominations are human inventions that a God without Being crosses as much as those of mercantile give and take. In its final stages, *The Divine Names* spirals into *The Mystical Theology*, not as a corrective, but as a necessary conclusion. In the nondual darkness of unknowing both affirmation and negation are deconstructed.

On this basis, Kevin Hart can summarize that "we do not need a third theology, one neither positive nor negative—a theology of paradox—for negative theology, properly understood, *is* that theology: a discourse which works at once inside and outside onto-theology, submitting its images of God to deconstruction."[38] Hart makes an important terminological observation: the word *hyperousious*, which Dionysius uses to denote God's state of being or nonbeing, is misleadingly translated in some English renderings as "superessential" (cf. the 1920 translation by C. E. Rolt). Yet while the English word suggests that God is the highest being, higher than created beings, "[t]he Greek word . . . makes no such claim; indeed, the prefix *'hyper'* has a negative rather than a positive force. To say that God is *'hyperousious'* is to deny that God is a being of any kind, even the highest or original being."[39] Jean-Luc Marion agrees with Hart's reading.[40] In other words, *hyperousious* signals a deconstruction beyond Aquinas's version of negative theology, one that deflates Derrida's objection almost to the point of disappearance.

The word *ousious* makes unmistakably clear that Dionysius puts forward an ontological argument, not mainly or only an epistemological one. It is not merely due to our creaturely limitations that we cannot fathom the mode of God's being. Rather, God has intrinsically, as it were, no being, because *ousia* is a characteristic of creatures. For although negative theology is in one way a kind of second-order discourse that is concerned with theological *language,* making sure, as Hart puts it a little confusingly, "that human speech about God is in fact about *God* and not a *concept* of God,"[41] it nonetheless makes ontological claims about God, if only to deny this ontology since all that falls under the rubric of ontology is of a philosophical kind, applicable only to finite creatures. In fact, Hart's statement makes clear that it must be possible for the divine to be manifest in language. The fact that God transcends the conceptual does not mean that he is nowhere present in language, but everywhere present in experience (of language and otherwise). Negative theology must not establish an opposition between language and experience. One misunderstands the Dionysian ascent if it is assumed to culminate in the rarefied and reified transcendent silence of "mystical experience." The distinctly modern overtones of individualism inherent in this view are quite opposed to the apophatic spirit. "Individualistic" experience is complicit with the emphasis on (self-)expression with which Beckett reveals himself to be so impatient in the "Three Dialogues."

Rigorously practiced apophaticism takes a rather different position on the question of experience. It situates itself securely in the everyday because apophatics can only be a way of life, a fusion of the intellectually cognitive with the experiential. Enlightenment, the Soto Zen Buddhist tradition emphasizes, is "just sitting." The mystical experience (rather than the nonduality of the negation of negation, which is a second-order discourse on that experience), though not experientially empty as Denys Turner claims, does not give itself to experience but rather to counter-experience: to that which will not be reduced to any of our experiential categories. In this sense, Turner is right to say that its power is instead its capacity to shape and transform human experience, so that, although nothing is changed, everything is changed: through a nondual approach the "phenomena" of the world cease to be self-existing and are thus no longer phenomena in the Husserlian sense.[42] The rift between our own fragile selves and the outside world disappears.

■   Beckett's text abounds with economic terms and metaphors: "insuperable indigence" ("TD" 141), "esteemed commodities," "ultimate penury," "destitute" ("TD" 143), "possession-poverty" ("TD" 144), "expense" ("TD" 145). He sees "conventional," that is "expressive" art, which includes all art other than van Velde's, caught in an economy of exchange. Even if one does not share Beckett's idiosyncratic concerns and obsessions with the pursuit of the Unnamable and even if one disregards for a moment the problematic of *Darstellung* and *Vorstellung*, it is easy to see why he frames his artistic theory in this way: the artist "gives" his audience a conceptually translated version of his artistic genius (fetishized as it is in Western culture), which he has received by way of intuition, a muse, or divine inspiration. Such are the metaphors traditionally at hand in Western society to describe the artistic process. The audience acquires a material token (and hence proof) of the artist's genius of expression, his ability most fully to express what no one previously had been able to express. In fact, partly because art is so thoroughly inscribed in an economy of "spiritual" exchange, the work of art, most notoriously painting, enters the realm of monetary economy and becomes a significant economic asset. Millions of dollars change hands so that paintings by artists who, society agrees, are most fully masters of their expressive powers can switch ownership.

We habitually approach the world through antitheses and we apply the same categories to art, but, Beckett claims, this need not be so. At considerable risk ("let us for once be foolish enough not to turn tail" ["TD" 143]) it is possible radically to abandon the accustomed thought structures of exchange and duality and to venture into unfamiliar territory. The irreducibility of literary language is an adventure, a journey into the peril of *Erfahrung*. It is an experiential journey into perilous territory because all our established categories with which we make sense of our experience will fail to grip there. But such a move would make a qualitative difference, not just a quantitative one. It would not just rearrange boundaries "on the plane of the feasible" ("TD" 139): "There is more than a difference of degree between being short, short of the world, short of self, and being without these esteemed commodities. The one is a predicament, the other not" ("TD" 143).

Importantly, Beckett singles out world and self as our most valuable possessions: the world (as opposed to privileged reserves such as monasteries) is that which imposes the ubiquitous quantitative measurements that surround us; and the world is what we perceive in opposition to self. The self is indeed the most prized possession in modernity and at the same time the one on which we have but a tenuous grip, given its built-in evanescence in the face of the passage of time and eventually death. David Loy sees "the basic anxiety of our lives" as a contradiction between permanence and impermanence: "Despite the efforts we make to deny our temporality, we are all too aware of aging and death; yet on the other hand 'we nevertheless feel and experience that we are eternal' (Spinoza)."[43] Or, as Beckett puts it in *Proust:* "The mortal microcosm cannot forgive the relative immortality of the macrocosm. The whisky bears a grudge against its decanter" (*P* 10). Because we habitually experience the world as a duality of apparently permanent objects separate from ourselves, our solution to the pressing awareness of our own transience is to deny it by hanging on to the illusion of an equally self-existing self. To this end it is essential to construct a narrative of our lives to create the illusion of cumulative achievement toward a permanent record. Given the nature of narrative, it focuses primarily on past and future and thus paradoxically confirms our transience by reducing the present to an isolated moment in, as Loy appropriately terms it, a "'time-stream' understood to exist 'out there'—a container, as it were, like space, within which things exist and events occur."[44] The first thing to exist in it is the self: a nontemporal entity trapped irreversibly in the flux of time, as we believe to our detriment. This is not least the dilemma Beckett's short text addresses. For if Beckett's thoughts were to be taken seriously, more would change than merely artistic theory or practice, but even the very way we relate to the world generally would be altered. As Heidegger says at the beginning of "The End of Philosophy and the Task of Thinking," "if the answer could be given it would consist in a transformation of thinking, not in a propositional statement about the matter at stake."[45]

What keeps us floating in the stream of time and functioning in the economy of exchange is the obligation to "express." The term appears in the first part of the text in which Beckett analyzes the status quo of artistic practice. The artist is at the mercy of his need to express but lacks the means to do so. His means perpetually fall short of his aim, a fact that does not make the need disappear: "Like a child in mud but no mud. And no child. Only need."[46] The artist is bound by this inescapable aporia: "unable to act, obliged to act, he makes, an expressive act, even if only of itself, of its impossibility, of its obligation" ("TD" 145). Beckett thus concedes that unless the premise of conventional art (the insurmountable need to express) is let go of, expressionless art is impossible and therefore has to be attempted repeatedly. One could say that the avant-gardist practice Beckett describes here is an incomplete deconstruction, the Derridean one. Because it is incomplete the Derridean model must resort to the force of aporia over and over to break up petrified thought structures in repeated deconstructive efforts. A "permanent" obliteration of presence here is as impossible as the expressive act itself—the artist is stuck in a dilemma. But always, for Derrida, aporia is the place to begin, not to give up. Having considered the challenges art faces at the limit of representation, we can now ask to what extent there is room in the artistic theory of the "Three Dialogues" for a third way that is not only Derridean, but fully nondual.

In order to "complete" it the artist has to let go of the very paradigm of expression. This is the nondual, fully dialectical deconstruction. The question is what precisely is changed by this complete deconstruction, since it is obviously not the artistic product itself: to the onlooker a van Velde canvas appears to be situated as much within the canons of Western art as any other; it seems to express just as much or as little. The painting, "the expression that there is nothing to express" ("TD" 139), riddled as it is with irresolvable contradiction, becomes a limit concept, like the gift. It is bound by the laws of the conceptual, but becomes an icon of the nonconceptual. Heideggerian *Gelassenheit* will show how.

The very structure of Beckett's text in "Three Dialogues" allows for a third way. Beckett proceeds by way of dialectical progression, introducing in its third movement what he hails as the solution to the dilemma of expression, namely, in principle, no solution at all, but simple acceptance of the dilemma. The idiosyncratic dialogic form ensures that the text can come to a satisfactory end, providing even some closure, without running the risk of appearing to dodge the rigorous demonstration of feasible results other genres would demand. It circumvents the linear structure the conventional academic text calls for and sides with other discursive forms, such as Platonic dialogue and, crucially, literature. "Three Dialogues" is a multivoiced text and achieves further distantiation by putting words in the mouths of (semi-)fictional characters. Because the "Three Dialogues" present themselves as semifictional we cannot even say for certain that Beckett really held the beliefs they set forth. Plato's dialogues, for instance, are conventionally treated as if Plato held the views he develops, but there is no conclusive evidence against the proposition that they are in fact discursive exercises set up to refute hypothetical points. Platonic dialogue is concerned less with the development and proof of a new thesis than with showing conclusively the invalidity of a given premise. Likewise, Beckett does not so much want to outline a completely new artistic theory (let alone an unassailable or noncontradictory one) as show the dead end of art as we know it. And then he ventures into thoughts that could indicate a new direction, but does not claim to have found a panacea.

Of course, Plato does proceed by unassailable logic and reason and in this sense constructs linear arguments. Beckett, on the other hand, presents three notoriously elusive texts that draw extensively on allusion and the writerly filling-in of blanks on the part of the reader. He situates his text securely in the literary realm, not the philosophically discursive one. Apart from a few early and rather self-conscious works of criticism, he never emerged from behind the mask of the artist. Further framing is produced by the tactical move of writing about painting rather than about his own area of expertise, literature. The measure serves as an ironic guard against the text's being taken too seriously as a scholarly work: Beckett is—so he would like to signal to critics eager to pin him down—only dabbling in the subject matter he tackles: "the critic as amateur," as Lawrence Miller puts it, both in the original and the colloquial denotation of that word.[47]

He presents this short text, which has repeatedly been treated as his artistic credo, as a series of linguistically adorned and playful (semi-)-fictional dialogues rather than as a linear theoretical text. No matter to what extent Duthuit the art critic in fact held the views ascribed to him here, his voice has nonetheless passed through Beckett's aesthetizing and fictionalizing process. The same goes, of course, for Duthuit's interlocutor. Beckett himself prefers to present his theoretical views through the inherently ambiguous structures of literary genre. The text fully attests to the lack of confidence Beckett has in the theoretical text to challenge, let alone exceed, the confines of expression and representation. Any primacy granted to the theoretical-philosophical bias, as is inherent in Derrida's position, is to Beckett an illegitimate foreshortening and reduction.

This important difference also has consequences for the way in which the problem of the limit of representation presents itself to Beckett, working as he does within a discourse that is by definition multivoiced and multivalent. Much of the ground for which Derrida fights in philosophy is a given in literary discourse, as Derrida himself acknowledges: "If there is no essence of literature—i.e., self-identity of the literary thing—if what is announced or promised as literature never gives itself as such, that means, among other things, that a literature that talked only about literature or a work that was completely self-referential would immediately be annulled."[48] The reason why literature does not as yet annul itself is that it is made to be expressive of conditions in the world, that is, is representational. Nonexpressive art, then, aspires to the ideal of self-annihilation. And yet, in what way can Beckett's artist claim to transcend representation and to have found the solution to the expressive dilemma if he produces "*[t]he expression* that there is nothing to express" ("TD" 139; emphasis mine)? Surely expressionless art is going nowhere if it is merely the *expression* of a lack of expression. How does one keep from making of "this fidelity to failure, a new occasion" ("TD" 145) and hence a new expressive act? The artist makes an expression, but at the same time his "hands have not been tied by the certitude that expression is an impossible act" ("TD" 143). That is, on the one hand he does not "transcend" the conceptual, on the other hand he is not limited by it. How is one to integrate these conflicting positions?

Lawrence Miller rightly points out that "Beckett is concerned . . . to preserve the integrity of the artist's 'predicament,' and to deny its conversion into a problem that may be solved,"[49] which seems puzzling because what Beckett thereby seemingly advocates is the continuing, obsessively circular pursuit of the dilemma. Not so: what he asks is the abandonment of the *will* to transcend the dilemma of having to express yet being unable to express and an acknowledgment of it as the fundamental aporetic given of artistic creation. Acceptance of the problem is the only way to be free from it. Unlike in Derrida, here the force of aporia alone is not liberating, but liberation ensues once the aporetic structure is accepted and built upon.

Criticism predominantly considers Beckett's work to be internally unified and essentially preoccupied with the same questions throughout.

The plays are treated as commentary on the novels and vice versa. But is Beckett's work really static throughout? In particular, it is doubtful that he remains concerned with the pursuit of the dilemma of expression, which he articulates to perfection in *The Unnamable* ("I can't go on, I'll go on" [*U* 418]). *The Unnamable* can be seen as Beckett's ultimate statement concerning the limits of representation in a deconstructionist linguistic mode. With its completion Beckett had painted himself into a corner. He had so thoroughly dealt with the issues at hand as to render further writing by himself in the same mode impossible, and in fact he experienced a creative drought afterward. It does not seem farfetched to suggest that his late work for the theater pursues not so much the same questions by different means, but in fact uses the means specific to the theater to investigate a problematic that is an extrapolation of his previous concerns: the potential harbored by the pursuit of the dilemma is exhausted, but fruitful perspectives open up once the dilemma is taken for granted—accepted in repose instead of uneasy consternation or celebrated in revolutionary glee, as deconstruction does.

Beckett makes clear that the limit that the artist cannot pass is *itself* conceptual. It is not primarily and immediately the limit of the conceptual, that is, the transcendent. The dilemma itself is only the *product* of the volitional linearity of expression. So, what needs to be overcome is will. The idea of willing nothing, of nonwilling, appears in different incarnations throughout the diverse canons of apophatic literature: Buddhist *sunyata*, Plotinian *henosis*, Eckhart's detachment or *Gelassenheit*, Marion's "gaze of boredom" all aim to illustrate this idea.

For the most part (Plotinus, Eckhart, to an extent Marion) these straight apophatic approaches presuppose an unproblematically theological universe: as soon as humans show themselves to be receptive to it, that is, as soon as they commit themselves to the spiritual path, the divine dimension will enter their lives as a matter of course. For instance, Eckhart's spark of the soul, the *Fünkelein* to which Beckett refers in entry 690 of the *Dream Notebook* as "the organ by which the personality communicates with God and knows him,"[50] presupposes an anthropological–theological continuity that the Beckettian worldview does not have. The spark of the soul is proportionate to the divine itself. It contains in essence that which is beyond it, and as soon as the spark has been recovered from the infilling of attachments not only has communication been established between human and divine, but the two have become one by way of a merger of the divine element in human nature and the divine itself. As Denys Turner puts it, "Eckhart's detachment, we might say, is archeological rather than architectural."[51]

Beckett's world, on the other hand, is distinctly (post-)modern and arises from a predominantly secular context. It lacks the easy continuity of the theological worldview. As Linda Ben-Zvi points out, Beckett's world is gray rather than black;[52] he does not deny the Absolute, but the Absolute is no automatic given. His work is pervaded by longing for it, a call for it, and even a response to its call, but at the same time a skepticism as to whether it will, in fact, "occur." It prepares a space for what it does not *expect* to occur because expectation would reinscribe it in an economy of exchange. Beckett's nonwill is more evocative of Heidegger's, who is influenced by the so-called mystical tradition, but situates *Gelassenheit* within a phenomenological framework. Being is not God (and neither is *différance*), although it cannot completely shake off the proportions of the metaphysical God. Rather, Heideggerian *Gelassenheit* attempts to establish a nonduality between subject and object, human and world, disregarding God. Yet because of the nondual ground of Being, *Gelassenheit*, although not theologically motivated, makes a space for God. Thinking in the Heideggerian sense—the thinking of *Gelassenheit*—is "a gift or a grace, an event that overtakes us."[53] By way of Heideggerian *Gelassenheit* we will encounter a different relation to language and the text than the conventionally significational one, a relation that indicates the way "out" of Beckett's expressive dilemma and that allows for a theologically coherent apophatic gift to give itself in language.

The "project" of going beyond will is beleaguered by an aporia. The realization that will keeps thought structures locked in the dualistic patterns of representation, and finally the desire to abandon will as a result of this realization, is immediately followed by defeat: the will not to will is still a sort of will. But, Heidegger reasons, it is a different kind of will than the one that drives our quotidian desires because it indicates that willing itself has become questionable. By willing nonwill one prepares oneself for, shows oneself to be receptive to, the "real" nonwill. In apophatic terms, the will not to will is the first-order level of negation, which is still conceptual. Afterward the effort has to transcend this antithetical moment to a third one that implies neither to will nor not to will but neither and both. This is the second-order level of the negation of the negation, an "essential" and "originary" self-negating negation, at which the artist finally confronts the nonconceptual. Yet because *Gelassenheit* is not bound by will, and is in fact impossible within the patterns of will, this third moment is, of course, beyond one's volitional control. There is no "awakening of *Gelassenheit*" but only "staying awake for *Gelassenheit*" because "we do not of our own accord awaken *Gelassenheit* in ourselves."[54] *Gelassenheit* is a fundamental repose: a letting-go and letting-be (all of these valences are implicit in the German). *Gelassenheit*, Heidegger emphasizes, is not quietism or passivity because it is outside the distinction between activity and passivity. It is a moment of nonduality. Therefore, the thinking, painting, or writing it enables is not *outside* the thinking of representation. It is not the "real," authentic, uncontaminated way of being in the world, outside of our present corrupted, fallen nature, but the realization that we will only find the "real" once we stop looking for it.

Beckett sees such an act of nonwill in the "inexpressive" ("TD" 143) art of Bram van Velde. Although van Velde uses the conventional array of artistic means his tradition offers him (ones that operate within the economy of expression), he does so with a different starting point. He accepts the impossibility of expression and can hence move freely within the spectrum at his disposal, without using it to the same compulsively expressive end. What emerges from this for Beckett's artist is the freedom to fail, as of necessity, by any conventional standard of efficiency, productivity, output, causality—expression: "van Velde is the first to desist from this estheticized automatism, the first to admit that to be an artist is to fail, as no other dare fail," whereas art usually "attempts to escape from this sense of failure" ("TD" 145). According to the conventional view the artist will in ever more refined ways ("by means of more authentic, more ample, less exclusive relations between representer and representee" ["TD" 145]) represent the truth "in a kind of tropism towards a light as to the nature of which the best opinions continue to vary" ("TD" 145), depending, as Beckett insinuates, on which version of truth is most prevalent at the time, or which means are deemed to reveal the truth most successfully: the most romantic, realistic, surrealist, theistic, humanist depending on which the artist subscribes to. Beckett finds, in other words, even in the most radically subversive of artistic movements a positivistic tendency for which "the irrationality of pi [is] an offense against the deity, not to mention his creature" ("TD" 145).

In his final statement Beckett resists the suggestion that van Velde's art harbors such a positivistic tendency:

> I know that all that is required now, in order to bring even this hor-rible matter to an acceptable conclusion, is to make of its submis-sion, this admission, this fidelity to failure, a new occasion, a new term of relation, and of the act which, unable to act, obliged to act, he makes, an expressive act, even if only of itself, of its impossibility, of its obligation. I know that my inability to do so places myself, and perhaps an innocent, in what I think is still called an unenviable situation, familiar to psychiatrists. For what is this coloured plane, that was not there before. I don't know what it is, having never seen one before. ("TD" 145)

Beckett declares himself unable to find "a new occasion" in van Velde's art that would turn his artistic endeavor into another expressive act. We are faced, then, with art that both is expression and is not, and while this is unacceptable by the standards of the logic of noncontradiction, here it is the necessary conclusion. The paradox will not be resolved one way or the other. This is the crux of Beckett's theory: the paradox of the im-possibility of expression ("I can't go on, I'll go on") and any paradoxical multivalence is not to be resolved but to be accepted. The artist contin-ues to use the means her tradition puts at her disposal (those of expres-sion). But she does so from a position of *Gelassenheit*, which does not change the phenomena that surround us: a tree is still a tree and what was an expressionistic canvas still looks like one. ("The ontic range of *nirvana* is the ontic range of the everyday world. There is not the sub-tlest difference between the two.")[55] And yet they are changed insofar as we look at them differently from within a Heideggerian *Gegnet*, which Heidegger defines as the open as a place of gathering. Between *Gegnet*, which derives from the usual German word "Gegend" (for "area" in the sense of "countryside"), and *Gelassenheit* there is neither a cause and effect connection nor a transcendental–horizontal relation. The *Gegnet* lets the thing be; it allows it to give itself. *Gegnet* is a surrounding openness that does not define itself in opposition to a constituting subject, as the horizon does. A subject casts phenomena within a horizon that exists only in relation to it. Thinking as *Gelassenheit*, however, is not the will and *Vorstellung* of a constituting subject. The horizon as the confines of the constituted world dissolves into *Gegnet*. So the horizon is really part of the more encompassing *Gegnet*. As a result, we are never *outside* *Gelassenheit* and *Gegnet*, but sometimes we see only the horizon that we construct from our subject-centered vantage point. In other words, the *Gegnet* is never elsewhere, even when we are not in it.

The paradox itself loses its fascination and instead of mulling it over the artist can devote his energies to what can be done once one tacitly presupposes it as the inevitable precondition of any artistic endeavor. Everything is the same and yet all is changed. There is no immanent realm with a transcendent one in opposition to it. The transcendent is in the immanent and vice versa; there is merely "a difference of perspective, or rather a difference in the way they are 'taken.'"[56]

Hence Nagarjuna's distinction of cognitive and guiding notions is in fact only apparently a dualism. The distinction is necessary at the relative level in order to remind oneself that our conceptual horizon is not the only one. Because of the teaching of impermanence there are no self-existing things in Buddhism; words and concepts have no stable reference. In everyday contexts ("your lunch is in the refrigerator," to use Loy's example) using concepts as if they had "true" referents is not too problematic, as long as one keeps in mind that the cognitive notions one uses in the process are merely human constructs. This same only apparently referential way is used to speak about the Absolute, which means that whatever concept is used to describe it can only be a so-called guiding notion "to suggest appropriate ways of coping with the putative realities on which it rests for its meaning and to which it lends meaning" and "serving to lead men toward freedom, but not claiming to describe any reality or convey any ultimate truth."[57] A guiding notion is a way of speaking of the Absolute in relative terms that not only acknowledges its own inadequacy, as Western theistic apophaticism does also, but rather not even *attempts* to achieve adequacy to a reality imagined to be existing independently of it. This is because there is, in Buddhist understanding, no unchanging transcendent reality. Buddhism here is more "pragmatic" than Christian apophaticism. It does not want to offer an ontology but an epistemology that allows the end of suffering. It is concerned more with liberation in this life than in the world to come. A guiding notion has no truth value, but use value; it is eminently practical insofar as it has achieved its purpose when it has aided students on their paths to liberation, to *nirvana*. In this endeavor any putative absolute essence of the divine is irrelevant. The apparently dualist distinction between guiding and cognitive notions is, then, a function of human limitations and from the perspective of the Absolute it does not exist. Therefore it is essential to remind oneself, necessarily conceptually, that there is no difference between *samsara* and *nirvana* because this realization is the volitional precondition, the first-order negation, that will keep us from trying to "achieve *nirvana*," to *will* our own salvation by, as Loy puts it, trying to become real.

What does Heidegger's "thinking of *Gelassenheit*" mean for language and for Beckett as an artist working with language and situating himself firmly in the multivocity of literary discourse? It means that the word will be able to present, rather than represent. Heidegger is in the footsteps of the Jena Romantics, who saw Kant's aesthetic idea embodied in the language of poetry. Only poetry can create the vitality of life through language because the figurativeness of poetic language transcends conceptuality. Figurative language is autonomous of the mimetic. At the beginning of his essay "Das Wesen der Sprache (The Nature of Language)" Heidegger makes an important distinction between treating language in a conventionally conceptual way, based as it is on the distinction between word and referent, and a radically different way of approaching language, namely through *Gelassenheit*.[58] This way is experiential: "Mit etwas, sei es ein Ding, ein Mensch, ein Gott, eine Erfahrung machen heißt, daß es uns wiederfährt, daß es uns trifft, über uns kommt, uns umwift und verwandelt."[59] ("To undergo an experience with something—be it a thing, a person, or a god—means that this something befalls us, strikes us, comes over us, overwhelms and transforms us.")[60] It involves the recognition that language is not separate from us but that we *are* language, or that language is at least inseparably part of us: "So sind wir denn allem zuvor in der Sprache und bei der Sprache. Ein Weg zu ihr ist unnötig."[61] ("[W]e are within language, at home in language, prior to everything else.")[62] This abolishes the split between ourselves and what we think, and between our thoughts, imagined somehow to exist separately before they are put into words, and the expression of those thoughts in language. Based on this realization Heidegger advocates undergoing an experience with language, "the house of Being [das Haus des Seins]," in which poetry becomes the voice of Being.[63] Poetic discourse, for Heidegger, exemplifies a kind of nondual, nonrepresentational thinking through *Gelassenheit*, "without science, without philosophy."[64] Now, in rigorous apophaticism or, if you will, deconstruction, the reification of poetic discourse as privileged, which this view suggests, is as suspect as a dangerously "kataphatic" conception of Being based on ontological difference. But the basic conception of a radically different, nondual way of inhabiting language is very useful. The Unnamable can emerge from the interstices of language if language is inhabited and experienced because the nondual will not be absent from language (or it would not be nondual). Such a conception of language does away with the distinction between word and referent and with the supposition that there is or can be adequacy between word and referent and that this adequacy finds expression in the word.

The idiosyncratic audacity of Madhyamika Buddhist philosophy opens up a way of speaking of ultimate realities that is likewise not based on an implied, and therefore at least attempted, adequacy between expression and the reality it "describes." A guiding notion is not expected adequately to describe the Absolute because there is no Absolute in the form of a stable referent. Instead, it has served its purpose if it has brought the student face-to-face with the Absolute. A dilemma of the "I can't go on, I'll go on" kind as Beckett poses it in *The Unnamable* does not arise in the Madhyamika model. Madhyamika does not hold on to the idea of a divine whose nature is proclaimed to be ungraspable in language but still posited as somehow hypothetically verifiable separately from the initiate's own transformation.

The crucial distinction between guiding and cognitive notions is what frees the Beckettian artist from the expressive dilemma: the artist still produces what looks like an "expression" but now it does not matter whether it is inadequate to the Unnamable; in fact, the question does not even arise. It does not matter whether—lapsing for a moment into representational logic—the expression has anything at all in common with the Absolute, its referent (supposing that one could find out). What matters is that the work opens up a space in which we, the audience or reader, may be helped to come face-to-face with it. Crucially, the work of art still looks like expression, bound by the conventions of the representational, but it is produced and received with the tacit understanding that it is a guiding notion.

But, one might object, does not the fact that Beckett's work never does end the torturous cycle of "I can't go on, I'll go on" contradict all of the above? Where is the liberation in the excruciating, almost physical pain of witnessing *Not I*, for instance? In Nancy's words one could say that even if there is no expression, there remains the obligation to "name." It is this process of "naming" that keeps the text in a process of self-subversion of its metaphysical assumptions, or rather, that keeps proclaiming the meta-metaphysical as if this proclamation were a request from elsewhere, not an expression of a tortured I, since this I needs to be decentered, post-subjectivist, kenotic to make the proclamation possible.

Chapter 4

Metaphor and Metonymy in *Not I*

Beckett's theoretical explorations of an expressionless art in the "Three Dialogues" do not remain without aesthetic and artistic consequences. A steady "neutralization" progresses throughout Beckett's work, especially his late plays and prose writings. Colors, still used to startling effect in *Happy Days*, for instance, disappear in favor of shades of gray, and likewise acting and delivery are reduced to an increasingly neutral style from which all exuberance and emotion are excised while the prose itself tends toward increasingly pared down sentences. "Too much colour, no no, too much colour," Beckett kept repeating to Billie Whitelaw when rehearsing with her for *Not I*. "By which he meant: 'For God's sake don't act.'"[1] And yet this radically minimalist, "expressionless" theater is intensely evocative.

For Roland Barthes the neutral is "that which outplays . . . the paradigm, or rather I call Neutral everything that baffles the paradigm," which he understands to be the binary framework of the sort that generates meaning in the West.[2] Surveying vast intertextual fields Barthes quotes Lao-tzu, from Jean Grenier's *L'Esprit du Tao*, which allows him explicitly to link the neutral to the colorless, the emotionless, and the will not to will: "I am as if colorless . . . neutral as the newborn who has not yet felt his first emotion, as if without project or will."[3] Barthes approaches the neutral in art through what it undoes—namely, the colorful—based as it is on the contrast of primary colors such as blue and red: "[I]t's the opposition par excellence, the very motor of meaning (phonology)," he says, alluding, of course, to the voiced/voiceless binary. "[T]he monochrome (the Neutral)," on the other hand, "substitutes for the idea of opposition that of the slight difference, of the onset of the effort towards difference, in other words of nuance: nuance becomes the principle of allover organization . . . that in a way skips the paradigm: this integrally and almost exhaustively nuanced space is the shimmer . . . the neutral is the shimmer: that whose aspect, perhaps whose meaning is subtly modified according to the angle of the subject's gaze."[4] The monochrome style of Beckett's visual images itself—not just their material minimalism or "emotionless" acting style—undoes conceptual binarisms. The disorienting effect this has on the spectator contributes to the plays' evocativeness as part of a multilayered network of nondual undecidabilities.

This chapter approaches *Not I* through the visual image and narrative technique in order to determine how the ideal of "expressionless art" finds its way into Beckett's own work and what it means for him artistically. I investigate how the horizontally metonymic and the vertically metaphoric dimensions in Beckett's art interlock, relying for this purpose in part on David Lodge's useful distinction, adapted from Roman Jakobson, between the metaphoric and metonymic poles of modern literature. Metonymy progresses along a horizontal axis of notional association or combination, metaphor along a vertical axis of substitution. The question is whether Beckett's reduction is horizontal, secular, atheological, and moves primarily along the metonymic pole, or whether it tends more toward the metaphoric pole and toward a full-fledged vertical religiosity, or whether—and this I would like to suggest—the peculiar tension in Beckett's work derives from pulling equally strongly in both directions. According to Beckett and Maurice Blanchot writing is a movement along a horizontal axis toward a point whose transcendental (vertical, metaphorical) implications come into existence and into focus only in the process of writing, that is, in the horizontal pursuit of that point. Writing turns out to be an aporia of the metonymic and the metaphoric poles. We will see that the metonymic and the metaphoric form such an aporia in Beckett's art.

Lodge categorizes modern literature along the metaphoric/metonymic divide. Metonymy and its cousin synecdoche are not both subforms of metaphor, that is, simply figurative transformations of a given statement. Rather, metaphor and metonymy are diametrically opposed because they are generated by opposing principles. Metaphor belongs to the selection axis of language and works by way of substitution. Lodge's analogy here is dress: one selects just one item from a set (or paradigm) that is constituted by a range of tops. If one has already selected a t-shirt, one does not need a blouse and hence substitutes a t-shirt for a blouse. The items are substituted on the basis of similarity. In Lodge's master sentence "Keels ploughed the deep," "plough" can be used instead of the literal "cross" because the movement of a plough through soil is reminiscent of the movement of a ship through sea. Metonymy, on the other hand, belongs to the combination axis of language and works by way of contiguity or natural association. Metonymy is to put an attribute or an adjunct in the place of the thing meant: keels are parts of ships and depth is a property of the ocean. Hence "keels" finds its way into the sentence not so much by substitution as by a process of expansion and deletion: the long, nonfigurative version of Lodge's exemplary sentence would be "The keels of the ships crossed the deep sea."[5]

In other words,

[p]*loughed* has been selected in preference to, or substituted for, other verbs of movement and penetration . . . which are conjoined in the code of English (by belonging to a class of verbs with approximately similar meanings) . . . . *Keels*, on the other hand, is conjoined with ships both in the code (as nouns, as items of nautical vocabulary) and in the notional message . . . . The contiguity of keels and ships in many possible messages as well as in the code reflects their actual existential contiguity in the world, in what linguistics calls "context," whereas there is no such contiguity between ploughs and ships.[6]

Metonymy, then, consists in a purely horizontal movement. It proceeds by way of notional association. Metaphor, on the other hand, works by way of a paradigmatic shift from *parole* to *langue* that is vertical, because there is no "natural," "existential" (as Lodge calls it) connection between a metaphor's tenor and its vehicle. In order to establish the connection a jump to the systemic (or paradigmatic) axis of language (*langue*) is required.

Although both the verbs "to cross" and "to plough" belong to the same paradigm (because of the similarity of the movement of a plough through soil and of a ship through water) "it is an essential feature of a metaphor that there must be a certain distance between tenor and vehicle. Their similarity must be accompanied by a feeling of disparity; they must belong to different spheres of thought."[7] There is, then, a certain similarity between tenor and vehicle on the basis of which a group similarity can be established so that other people, for example readers of a literary work, will be able to make the same connection between tenor and vehicle. Only in this way can the metaphor be intelligible. But making the connection involves a leap from one notional context to another, in this case from that of a nautical context to that of agricultural machinery. The two items cannot be conjoined in the message because only one of them is required, but they are conjoined in the system that underlies the specificity of the message, which in turn makes possible the vertical leap that is the peculiarly startling joy of reading metaphors: the tension of similarity and difference that opens up between tenor and vehicle is responsible for the specifically metaphoric semantic field that, in the best metaphors, always involves an element of surprise. (If there is no surprise, the metaphor is dead.)

Here is already an indication of why Lodge's distinction between the metonymic and the metaphoric modes proves useful with respect to determining the relationship between apophaticism and Beckett's art: metaphor's verticality acknowledges (semantic) dimensions not immediately present in the horizontality of the syntagmatic message, just as religion is based on an acknowledgment of transcendent dimensions beyond the horizontality of worldly existence. Thus, for Lodge there is no question that the metaphoric strand of literature is the more "religious."[8] Metaphoricity manifests itself in Beckett's late work for the stage primarily in the visual dimension. There Beckett's work is inspired by non-representational, nondual aesthetic forms and nonduality is the core of apophatic theology.

Not I is a play of extreme reduction: action and movement are led back to a static stage image that consists solely of an isolated, disembodied mouth and a faceless, unidentifiable, therefore strangely selfless hooded figure whom the audience sees only from behind. There is no color except for the small but prominent red dot in a sea of blackness that is Mouth. Furthermore, as Billie Whitelaw's recollection of Beckett's exhortations indicates and a viewing of her performance confirms, Mouth delivers its breathless tale in a monotonous voice at breakneck speed. *Not I* moves toward the colorlessness of extreme reduction on a number of planes simultaneously by removing, first of all, the context of embodiment and, as a result, the cohesion of self and narrative continuity, and arguably dramatic alterity. The case can be made that by denying his character, Mouth, the continuity of selfhood, Beckett elides the necessarily dualistic relationship of alterity between one character and another and finally between character and audience. In order to have full-fledged apophatic nonduality, however, one needs first a fully formed dualism between self and other, and between self and the absolute Other, the transcendent God. Instead, this interpretation would hold, Beckett slides along a horizontal, metonymic axis of fragmentation: a fragmented text is complemented on the visual level by a body part, Mouth, which takes the place of coherent character. Moreover, Mouth denies her own subjectivity and by extension the subjectivity of the other. In the television version of *Not I*, though not at all in the stage version, this elision of subjectivity in Mouth is complemented by complete disappearance of the dramatic other. Auditor is excised from the play. In this interpretation Beckett turns away from a metaphysic of presence but then does not allow its alternative, nonduality, to ripen to fruition because he reduces its prerequisite, duality, to a kind of pre-dual stage that has neither self nor other. The result is a nonoppositional space that remains pre-dual rather than nondual, because it has fewer of the ingredients necessary for a full duality, let alone nonduality.

But is the play really that fragmentary and is Mouth really the sole (paradoxically decentered) focus of the play? Or do critics tend to emphasize what they see as fragmentation because they approach the play with the deeply engrained reference points of fullness and whole-ness in mind? Because Beckett's (and many other avant-gardist play-wrights') theater is in part a reaction to the naturalistic stage, the latter lingers as an unconscious if unsatisfactory standard. If one compares *Not I* with the "fullness" of the naturalist stage, Beckett's stage will in-variably appear as lack; it seems bare and pared down. Likewise, Mouth's identity will seem fragmented before the backdrop of concepts of whole-ness and centered subjectivity. What happens if one takes emptiness as a standard and starting point, if one sees Beckett's stage not as poten-tially full and therefore in fact half-empty (or half-full), but, as Les Essif puts it, "as potentially and therefore essentially empty"?[9] One has to see Mouth's verbal torrent not as a scattering of self but as a kind of pro-grammatic self-emptying. In such a view the state of being emptied of self is seen as a positive ideal. It becomes a kenotic movement in which the human self-emptying of ego is complemented by divine kenosis to-ward the "end" of being face-to-face with God in nondual unity. Maybe Beckett's dramatic development as a whole, and *Not I* in particular, would no longer slide along a metonymic axis of fragmentation toward complete (and fairly predictable) destruction or deconstruction of the subject, but work steadily toward an increasingly clearer articulation of his artistic vision: a metaphoric depiction of emptiness—physical, but more importantly, metaphysical.

The text of *Not I* is certainly metonymic, but the text is only one dimension of the play, and arguably not the most important one. Too much Beckett criticism neglects theatricality, and especially Beckett's carefully crafted stage images, in favor of a textual approach, forgetting that Beckett was intensely interested in the visual arts, frequenting art galleries all over Europe, often planning entire trips around the indi-vidual pictures he wished to see. The stage image of *Not I* yields valuable perspectives in connection with strategies of reduction on the textual level. I trace the major strategies of reduction in the play, beginning with Beckett's removal of the context of embodiment, continuing with the removal of narrative continuity and concluding with the removal of the continuity of selfhood or identity. Throughout, we will keep in view both the metaphoric and the metonymic trajectories to find out how they interlace and what this means in terms of an apophatic vocabulary.

■   Let us begin with the most far-reaching and most obvious strategy of reduction in the play, Beckett's removal of the context of embodiment. Doubtless the isolated, tiny, brightly lit, chattering mouth lost in the enormous darkness of the stage space is the play's most captivating and most radically original artistic move and its effect on the audience is remarkable. The immediate effect of *Not I* is visceral, experiential—not intellectual. And since the audience's aural memory is relatively short given the circumstances, the spectator enters the play primarily through the *image* of Mouth, which is constant, rather than the *character* of Mouth (if it still makes sense to talk about Mouth in such terms). Primary access is not through the naturalist route of character, constellation of characters, or even plot, and not primarily through the text, which remains inaccessible because of the enormous strain it puts on the audience. In fact, by isolating a single body part to represent his character, Beckett does not allow the audience to build a relationship with a complete fictional person. A fully physically present body stands for a continuous identity complete with past and future. Instead, Beckett presents just a mouth, without even so much as a name. The concept of character is stretched to the breaking point. Mouth is nobody (too metonymically fragmented to be anybody), but also everybody (metaphorically representing the human condition) by being nobody specific.

Fragmenting the body and isolating specific body parts, is, of course, a metonymic procedure: to have a part stand in for the whole is synecdochic, and synecdoche is a subform of metonymy. Les Essif, however, pertinently points out that a reduction of a naturalist character to a shape strategically situated in a visual field is also a reduction to form.[10] Essif argues that "the reduction of the character to form implies a serious argument against claims of corporeal fragmentation. There is a tremendous difference between the literal value of a body part illustrated in a medical dictionary and the metaphorical value of one featured on a theatrical stage."[11] An object or character is stripped of the context or utilitarian value it usually inhabits on the naturalistic stage and orients itself differently as a component in a primarily aesthetic visual composition in which it fulfills a part that is quite different from its usual context based on natural metonymic contiguity. The contiguous context is overridden by compositional demands.

Furthermore, the critical emphasis on the fragmentation and visual as well as narrative metonymy of Mouth is concerned only with one-half of the stage image, but the stage image forms a metaphoric totality of which Mouth is only a part. Auditor's presence is a considerable counterweight. A perspective that problematizes the loss of dramatic alterity in the play focuses on Mouth as a solitary presence, and *Not I* is, in fact, the closest Beckett ever came to writing a mono-drama. *Not I* occupies an extreme position within the Beckett canon: in all of Beckett's other plays the theatrical other, even if not physically present on stage, is of a more verbally articulate kind and therefore comes slightly closer to being a conventional character (cf. the off-stage voices in *Footfalls*, *What Where*, and even *Rockaby*), although no "character" in Beckett's late drama is developed along the lines of an identity modeled naturalistically. Auditor, on the other hand, is merely a silent, towering presence. A mono-drama would do away with dramatic alterity completely and thus dismantle a basic premise of theater, but Beckett stopped just short of going the whole way. Auditor interacts with Mouth, although the audience does not hear his interlocutions. Presumably he is the source of the interpolations that cause Mouth to backtrack and correct herself.

Auditor's presence establishes a curious balance on stage: what Mouth has in activity he compensates through size. The tiny, frantically hyperactive Mouth is counterbalanced by Auditor's silent hugeness. The play strategically generates tension within the stage image itself—a kind of motionless dynamism—and between the audience and the image as a whole. *Not I* does not consist solely of Mouth's breathless flight from itself (to whose fleeting presence an audience would indeed find it difficult to relate), but of the dramatic totality of the (thwarted) interaction between Mouth and Auditor as watched by the audience. Auditor, Mouth, and the spectator form a totality of perception consisting of ear, mouth, and eye.

The image thus created for the audience not only forms a formal and aesthetic unity, although this emphasis on form is an important precondition. Because of this formal emphasis, the stage image has to *mean* something. It is not merely imitative of the world in a kind of drawing room aesthetic, but it is rather in an allegorical relationship to it. Most of Beckett's work, and especially his late work for the stage, remains utterly unintelligible unless read metaphorically to signify a fundamental problematic of the human condition. According to Lodge all drama tends toward the metaphoric pole, but

> many modern playwrights have put an extreme stress on the metaphoric dimension in drama. In Beckett's plays, for instance, there is no progress through time, no logic of cause and effect, and the chintz and upholstery of drawing-rooms has given way to bare, stark acting spaces, with perhaps a chair, a row of dustbins and a high window from which nothing is visible (*End Game*). These plays offer themselves overtly as metaphors for the human condition, for on the literal level they are scarcely intelligible.[12]

Hence Lance Butler, for instance, insists on characterizing Beckett's work as "ontological parables": metaphorizations of existential philosophical problems.[13]

Auditor is often neglected because he is far less dramatic in effect than Mouth and, in fact, the television production of *Not I* with Billie Whitelaw, over which Beckett had editorial control, had no choice but to omit him in the process of adapting the play to the new medium. Yet his importance for the play in general and for the visual composition of the stage image in particular emerges with great force, especially when one takes into account Beckett's sources of inspiration for *Not I*. Surprisingly his main interest seems to have been Auditor's unobtrusive presence.

The standard accounts of Beckett's life and work generally point toward two sources of inspiration for the play: Caravaggio's painting of the *Decollation of St. John the Baptist,* which Beckett had seen in Malta, and an Arab woman clad in a djellaba "crouched in an attitude of intense waiting" whom Beckett observed from a street cafe in Morocco and who turned out to be waiting for her child to return home from school: "Every so often, she would straighten and peer intently into the distance. Then she would flap her arms aimlessly against her sides and hunker down once again."[14]

The Arab woman is clearly an inspiration for the figure of Auditor, while the title of Caravaggio's painting would seem to suggest the image of a head separated from its body, a mere step of further metonymic fragmentation away from the image of an isolated mouth. In fact, Beckett's reflections prompted by the painting progressed along rather different lines. Like Beckett's stage image, Caravaggio's painting consists of two parts. The painting leans heavily toward the left, where in the brightly lit foreground the gruesome scene of the beheading is taking place. Far off to the right (the painting is more than five meters wide), shrouded in darkness and hidden behind a barred window, the viewer finally notices a witness to the scene other than herself. Beckett told Gordon Armstrong: "Some years ago I visited the Valetta Cathedral in Rome [sic; SW] to view Caravaggio's *The Beheading of St. John the Baptist.* I stood there a long time in front of the painting. Gradually I noticed that I was not alone, that behind the screen at the side of the church [in the painting] was the face of a man watching me observe the scene of the beheading."[15] What primarily sparked Beckett's interest, in other words, was not Mouth, not the scene and center of the "action," but the silent observer in the margins, unnoticed at first and apparently unimportant, who turns out to be indispensable to an understanding of the work, painting and play alike. Suddenly, Mouth appears almost as an afterthought or a kind of dramatic externalization of the condition that brings about Auditor's resigned helplessness. "[Beckett] told Hume Cronyn and Jessica Tandy . . . that Auditor was the real inspiration for the play."[16] In this light the title of the play, usually read to refer to Mouth's refusal to accept the first person pronoun as referring to her own biography, acquires a different valence: "[N]ot I but he, watching me watch a visceral assault on another individual."[17]

In almost Derridean fashion Beckett takes a seemingly unimportant detail in the margins of the work and points out how the work hinges on this detail, how it changes not only the dynamics of the work internally but, more importantly, how the author, in this case the painter Caravaggio, uses it to turn the reception process of the painting into a self-conscious experience that allows the viewer no unambiguous place to stand. It is unclear whether the silent witness behind the window reprimands the spectator for her voyeuristic activity or whether he conspires with the viewer and will go out into the world together with the viewer to bear witness to an unspeakably brutal crime. In both cases the marginal turns out to be the center of the interpretation and cannot be dismissed. Auditor and Mouth are inextricably joined, to the point of appearing to represent two strata of the same personality or two faces of the same human condition. Mouth can be seen as an externalization of what is occurring in Auditor's head, or the *whole* stage image can be read as an externalization of a state the play induces in the audience. The relentless onslaught of Mouth's monologue fills the audience's heads, works on its nerves, and there produces a version of the state of mind in which Mouth finds herself, and the audience's reaction to it is likely to resemble Auditor's.

Antonin Artaud, like Beckett, knew of the inadequacy of "expression" and opted for a process of "dissimulation," which includes the deliberate exploitation of the extralinguistic arenas of theater. Les Essif takes Artaud as a starting point for his explorations of the "Concentrated (Empty) Image behind the Fragmented Story in Beckett's Late Plays," and quotes as follows from *The Theatre and its Double:*

> All true feeling is in reality untranslatable. To express it is to betray it. But to translate it is *to dissimulate it* [Artaud's emphasis]. True expression hides what it makes manifest. . . . All powerful feeling produces in us the idea of the void. And the lucid language which obstructs the appearance of this void also obstructs the appearance of poetry in thought. That is why an image, an allegory, a figure that masks what it would reveal have more significance for the spirit than the lucidities of speech and its analytics."[18]

It should not concern us here whether Artaud's void, Beckett's void, and that of negative theology are identical or whether Artaud's strategy of "true expression" can successfully render the void. Essif, for one, is convinced that "a truly Artaudian metaphysical approach to Beckett's theatre—one which reveals rather than obstructs our awareness of the void—would *fundamentally* prioritize visual over narrative story and concentration over fragmentation, as well as emptiness over fullness."[19] What is important is rather that the process of dissimulation that is at work here is a metaphorical one of translation into an alien paradigm, so that the emerging image does not describe and capture (a process that is necessarily derivative) as much as create from scratch an image that will produce an "experience," for lack of a better term, similar to the original—that is, of the same existential substance but not necessarily of the same phenotypic material. The reception process, then, involves the same retranslation process that thrives on the associative field between tenor and vehicle. What Beckett tries to produce is, in other words, not adequacy to the original, but similarity of experience.

Another inference from Caravaggio's painting that so impressed Beckett emphasizes the inseparability of Mouth and Auditor in the dramatic totality of the play. If *Not I* was Beckett's attempt to depict a disembodied voice, an existential condition, a "voice crying in the wilderness"[20] (rather than a conventional character), then one figure in the painting finds its way to equal parts into Auditor and Mouth: an old woman—the only one in the painting unmistakably to express her horror—who, oddly, covers her ears rather than her eyes, as if in a futile attempt to block her ears to an inner scream of pain, necessarily silent. Her hands covering her ears are meant, it seems, rather to keep her head from exploding from the impact of the scream inside it. The figure triggers connotations of Edvard Munch's *The Scream*. There, too, the scream is palpable and yet it is uttered in a painting: mute, silent, and unheard. Billie Whitelaw describes her difficulties in performing in *Not I* thus: "What happened to me was a terrible inner scream, like falling backwards into hell."[21] Despite appearances, in *Not I* it is Auditor who utters the silent scream in his gestures of "helpless compassion" (*SP* 215) and by the end of the play the audience does the same, its nerves worn thin by the torrent of sound coming from Mouth. In fact, when Beckett redirected *Pas Moi* in Paris in 1978 he increased the emphasis on Auditor especially at the end of the play: "Auditor now covered his head with his hands 'in a gesture of increased helplessness and despair, as if unable to bear any longer the torrent of sound.'"[22] His gesture here is even more reminiscent of the old woman in Caravaggio's painting. Mouth, then, is literally a voice crying in the wilderness, unheard and unhearing, but Beckett's emphasis is on the silent scream her pain (which might be Auditor's pain) produces in Auditor and the audience. The externalization of Auditor's state, which might be Mouth's, is a way of dramatizing the kind of existential experience of anguish with which the play is concerned. Like Munch's painting, *Not I* is a representation of anguish and pain as an existential human condition, untied to specific circumstances or analytic ideas. "I am not unduly concerned with intelligibility. I hope the piece may work on the nerves of the audience, not its intellect," Beckett told Tandy or Cronyn.[23]

If Auditor is removed, as happened for technical reasons in the original production of *Pas Moi* in Paris in 1975, the dramatic conflict between Auditor and Mouth disappears. Beckett agreed to the change only reluctantly and then reinstated and reinforced Auditor's presence in the 1978 production. *Not I* is not a monologic play. It relies on the alterity of Auditor. The communication between Mouth and Auditor, minimal and warped though it may be, is essential to the dynamics of the play.

■ If Mouth and Auditor are formal abstractions dramatizing the human condition, we need to look at the stage image from a formalist point of view. As in his near-elimination of dramatic alterity in order to emphasize it, Beckett explores the very limits of the theatrical medium, stretching theater to its breaking point. If, as Paul Lawley (quoting Ezra Pound) pertinently points out, the medium of drama consists not only in words but "persons moving about on a stage using words," then most of Beckett's late stage images (including that of *Not I*) verge on the anti-theatrical.[24] Movement is virtually eliminated and even the visual stimulus of the static image is reduced to a minimum: a tiny mouth and a shadowy monk-like figure seen only from the back.

Enoch Brater sees that the analogues and precedents for the stage image seem to be found in other visual media much more readily than in earlier drama, and he draws an explicit parallel with painting: "Beckett's stage space in *Not I* looks very much like a surrealist painting come to life."[25] It is reminiscent of surrealism, which in Lodge's typology is metaphoric because it presents objects in close proximity or juxtaposition that are in no relationship of natural contiguity to each other. There is no continuity between monks and isolated spluttering mouths suspended in midspace, except that the former in all probability possess some form of the latter, though most likely not the spluttering variety. Any relationship of contiguity that could be established between Mouth and Auditor is at such a level of generality that it becomes meaningless. The image of the mouth onstage is certainly a fragment, which suggests metonymy, but on the visual level it does not appear in contiguity with, say, other fragmented body parts, as it does on the aural level.

Stanton Garner also notes the pictorial nature of Beckett's late stage images. Beckett "subordinates movement to position," limiting movement to a kind of movement within stillness.[26] Mouth moves rapidly but remains in its place and Auditor's minimal movements, too, remain confined to one location. Paradoxically, proxemics as a theatrical force is emphasized because of its near elimination. A burst of movement, expected on the theatrical stage, would provide relief and release—both of which Beckett does not grant his audience. In addition to this lack of motion, depth is indeterminate in Beckett's late stage images, Garner observes.[27] The depth element of his visual compositions does not seem to interest Beckett; he treats them much rather as two-dimensional pictures. This is a logical derivation from the lack of movement, since depth becomes interesting only when one has characters moving through space changing their spatial relationship to one another. Because the images are to be observed from a frontal position only (the audience's perspective of the proscenium arch), depth becomes doubly unimportant since the audience for its part cannot change position and move around the characters.[28] Frontal orientation is further emphasized by the characters' frontal posture (cf. *Krapp's Last Tape, Not I, Rockaby, Ohio Impromptu, Catastrophe*) and frontal illumination.

And yet, despite these "antitheatrical" tendencies, the image is stunning in its theatrical effect and in the tension it generates. "To the objection visual component too small, out of proportion with aural, answer: make it smaller on the principle that less is more," Beckett defends his theatrical strategy.[29] Brater concedes that "Beckett's 'drama stripped for inaction' . . . implies, ironically, an extraordinary amount of tension radiating from the stage, simultaneously visual, verbal and aural."[30] Three times during the play the spectator shifts her focus from Mouth to Auditor, a process that emphasizes what Brater calls a "stark antagonism" between them.[31] There is contrast and tension, but precisely for this reason there is also balance. The images of Mouth and Auditor are peculiarly complementary: the small but intensely active and brightly lit Mouth audience right is balanced by the towering but silent and "*fully faintly lit*" (*SP* 216) figure of Auditor audience left. Both are perched on the edge of the stillness of an electric hum between repulsion and attraction. Big and silent balances small and active—and this holds true as

much for the internal dynamics of the stage image as for the balance between the hyperactivity of the (short) metonymic text, or aural component, and the vast blackness of the metaphoric stage image, or visual
component. Brater notes that it is "difficult to tell if *Not I* is primarily
spectacle or literature—'ill seen,' or 'ill said.'"[32] Far too often in Beckett
criticism, the theatrical and visual aspect of his work recedes behind an
analysis of the text.

Beckett's "less is more" is not a mere flippant remark. It should be
taken literally and seriously. It is possible to approach emptiness posi-
tively if one detaches oneself from an uncritical acceptance of wholeness
and centered subjectivity as paradigms to aspire to. The strategies of
reduction Beckett employs both visually and textually then appear no
longer as driven by the negative goal to eliminate visual stimulus and
destroy the coherence of the text, but by the goal to concentrate and
transcend. To be sure, Beckett moves toward increasing emptiness of
the stage space, but if one detaches oneself from the conventional valorization of fullness and the concomitant negativity of emptiness, this can
be seen as a kind of full emptiness, an affirmative negativity, concentration rather than lack.

Stanton Garner recognizes the importance of the stage images in
Beckett's art, noting the unusual control Beckett assumed over it, and
despite his "phenomenological" approach, wont as it is to notice presence before nonpresence and fullness before emptiness, he acknowledges
the importance of the darkened, empty space as a constructive force:
Beckett's use of light as an "active, even aggressive determinant of the
theatrical image . . . throws into relief the darkness around it. . . . Through
its sheer predominance in plays such as *Not I* and *Rockaby* [darkness]
acquires pressing visual weight."[33]

What makes the dark empty space stand out especially is Beckett's
off-center positioning of his concentrated images. In chapter 2 I referred
to Junko Matoba's article on Japanese ink-splash paintings and the empty
space and off-center position in Beckett's stage images, as well as to
Norman Bryson's essay "The Gaze in the Expanded Field." With *Not I*
we can add to what we earlier observed regarding the visual manifestation of nonduality in Beckett's art. The off-center position introduces a "pull" into the stage image. The "figure" is not merely surrounded

evenly on all sides and therefore framed by the darkness. Rather, the figure pulls to one side, or sometimes a kind of balance not unlike the "golden section" ensues, in which the tension between the pull of the object and the counterweight of the dark stage space remain in precarious equilibrium. Both Matoba and Bryson find a more positive role for the empty space than Garner, for whom Beckett's stage images are "a celebration of subversion and imbalance."[34]

Bryson emphasizes the importance of the "dark or unmarked remainder" in Ch'an ink-splash paintings, which, by virtue of the Buddhist underpinnings that govern their "production," operates at the limits of representation.[35] It is this dark space that opens the "object" up to all the places where the viewer and the object are not, to all the other views that are excluded.[36] The flight lines of the converging perspective that govern the conventional representational image lock the viewer into a specific position in relation to the image. This position is supported and held in place by the frame. In Ch'an painting the image emerges from the nonduality of the painter's subjectivity with the objective world and gestures toward this "universal surround" by opening itself up beyond the frame, by freeing painting and viewer from a relationship of enframing and allowing *sunyata* (emptiness) to enter the image through *Gelassenheit.*

Recall Beckett's recollections of viewing Caravaggio's painting in Valetta. His experience of gradually becoming aware of being watched by the sneaky witness behind the barred window at the far right margin of the painting parallels precisely Sartre's description of the person in the park who is thrown back on himself by the rustling bush or the voyeur peeking through a keyhole who suddenly hears steps behind him (see chapter 2). Where previously there was a clear hierarchical power relationship of predatory watcher and objectified watched in place, the converging flight lines of this relationship are now destabilized by a competing third party around which some of that energy now groups itself. The scene moves from a straight duality to greater heterogeneity, as the subject competes with another subject (the other watcher behind the bush) for the unchallenged centrality of his position. This frees the "object" from its lack of agency, so that this party, too, can compete with the other two. At any one point, two subjectivities are engaged in a kind of staring duel, and it is from this that the destabilization results. This also implies, however, that the fundamental pattern of a subject–object duality based on a stable subject position remains intact. Two dueling parties attempt to force the opponent into submission and acceptance of the object position. This model is now permanently destabilized merely because each party has to divide its attention between two opponents competing with it and each other for this stable position. There is, in other words, now a constellation in place that inevitably destabilizes itself in the perpetual effort to establish stability and hierarchy. The Sartrean model remains confined to destabilization in the pursuit of the old stability based on a subject–object divide.

This model can only be dislodged if it is replaced by one that does not allow for conventional subject–object divisions. Such a new model would not have to be destabilized because it would not be in pursuit of stability, and at the same time it cannot be defined as unstable because it does not define itself in opposition to stability. Bryson convincingly argues that this can be done by allowing *sunyata* as the darkened or unmarked area to enter the picture. *Sunyata* opens the picture beyond the frame to the surrounding universe, which has in fact entered the picture during its production: it was created in nonduality of subject and object, artist and world.

As a result, the off-center position of the "figure" in Ch'an painting arguably does not introduce elements of subversion and imbalance into the image, as Garner, mistakenly, I think, diagnoses in Beckett's stage images. There is nothing the figure can be in imbalance with because there is nothing the figure can be in opposition to. I suggest that a careful distinction ought to be made between imbalance and a kind of nonfixity as a result of nonattachment. "Imbalance" is a negative descriptor whose positive reference point is balance, whereas nonattachment in the Buddhist understanding avoids such polarizations (despite the lingering linguistic markers of duality) and is fully nondual and dialectical. It follows from this that "stasis" is no accurate term to describe Beckett's stage images either, as it has a negative valence whose positive reference point is "motion," or "progress." I prefer "stillness" to stasis. The term is sufficiently neutral not to be immediately associated with an opposite and Beckett himself suggests it to describe the peculiarly ambiguous nature of his late work: stirrings still.

■   The stage image of *Not I* is metaphoric, nondual, and motionless, and the text appears to be completely at odds with it. It is metonymic and engaged in linear pursuit. Or is it? The impression of stillness or balance radiated by the visual stage image has a dramatic counterpoint in the play's aural dimension. There is, it appears, no stillness in Mouth's (near) monologue. She pours out her reflections and recollections in a continuous verbal flow, a torrent of sound that moves along a horizontal axis of free association: "gradually realized . . . she was not suffering . . . imagine! . . . not suffering! . . . indeed could not remember . . . off-hand . . . when she had suffered less . . . unless of course she was . . . *meant* to be suffering . . . ha! . . . *thought* to be suffering" (*SP* 216). The individual thoughts and images that pop into Mouth's head are connected, yet not by a universally acknowledged principle of deduction, but through the associative patterns of Mouth's mind. Association functions by way of a pattern of close proximity in space and time: a (metonymic) relationship of contiguity. The instantaneous, momentary workings of this mind are further emphasized by the lack of complete sentences. Mouth's thought fragments find their expression in sentence fragments, all of approximately equal length. There is no hypotaxis, but a dominantly paratactic relationship among the fragments. The interrelationships of the fragments are primarily of a temporal or causal kind ("till . . . then . . . till . . . when" [*SP* 219]), which again suggests horizontal progression.

If one figures into this paratactic, fragmented, associative picture the enormous speed with which a performance of *Not I* takes place, it comes as no surprise that reference relationships often remain unclear. On first exposure no audience member will grasp precisely the content and meaning of Mouth's ramblings and, as Beckett's directions to Tandy and Cronyn indicate, the play is not intended to appeal primarily to the intellect. Instead, isolated intelligible fragments will leap out of the jumble, but what they refer to may not be so clear. "[T]ill it was back in her hand," Mouth says, and then backtracks and clarifies: "the bag back in her hand" (*SP* 219). For a reader of *Not I* it is clear from the context that the "it" refers to "bag" three lines or six fragments before, but the immediately preceding fragment suggests "mouth" as a subject: "mouth half open as usual . . . till it was back in her hand" (*SP* 219). Once removed from context (a process facilitated by the fragmented structure and fast delivery), the fragments enter into different relationships with one another: a mouth held in someone's palm, a hand disconnected from its body in someone's lap ("sitting staring at her hand . . . where was it? . . . sitting staring at her hand . . . there in her lap" [*SP* 220]), or noted for its position at the end of an arm, as if it were not always there but rather sometimes took off on its own ("glad of the hand on her arm" [*SP* 221]). Beckett evokes these images of physical dismemberment consistently throughout the play and obviously delights in their ambivalence: each fulfills a coherent function on the level of narrative (it is clear from the context that the hand on Mouth's arm is someone else's comforting touch) but, seen in fragmented isolation, each also underscores the metonymic elements of the stage image (apart from adding a touch of the bizarre).

So far it appears as if *Not I*, at the level of language and narrative, is straightforwardly metonymic. And yet Lodge shows that this metonymic mode can slide over into the metaphoric when explored to its limits—the other pole manifested in *Not I* (and many other plays) most readily in the visual component of Beckett's art, the stage image.[37] It can hence be argued that the metonymic, when explored exhaustively, turns into the nondual flipside of the metaphoric, since in the metonymic mode no further development is possible.

There is more. Before we look in detail at how an essentially metonymic text can be made to support the purposes of metaphoric writing by assuming characteristics that are metaphoric in their aims and assumptions, it has to be said that there are instances in the text of *Not I* that are in fact indicative of the metaphoric pole. The series of *Not I* manuscripts held by the Beckett archives at the University of Reading reveals a loss of narrative continuity brought about by a movement away from naturalist narrative detail:

> birth . . . into this world . . . this world . . . [of a] tiny little thing . . . [five pounds] . . . in a godfor— . . . what? girl? . . . [yes] . . . tiny little girl . . . birth into this . . . in a godforsaken hole . . . in the bog . . . named - . . . what? . . . what? . . . [the downs? . . . godforsaken hole in the downs?] . . . no . . . no! . . . the bog . . . godforsaken hole

in the bog . . . named . . . named . . . [forgotten] . . . [to] parents unknown . . . unheard of . . . he having vanished [into] . . . thin air . . .
no sooner [done] . . . [his devilish work] buttoned up his trousers . . . and she similarly . . . .[38]

What is being *omitted* here is naturalist detail that makes one association flow more logically into the next. The more naturalist a narrative is, the more it tends toward the metonymic pole. But Beckett breaks
up the continuous storyline of naturalism, pushing his obviously metonymic text further toward metaphor. Take the specification of the ambivalent "godforsaken hole," the place where Mouth lives and the vagina
whence she came into the world, as being located in the downs or the
bog. Also excised from the text are grammatical function words that establish the relationships between the fragments of speech. The reader
now has to infer the relationship between the juxtaposed fragments
more than was previously the case. This can be done fairly easily because the text is still metonymic and it still preserves at least the rudimentary structures of narrative. What makes mainstream film the metonymic genre par excellence for Lodge is the fact that it moves lineally
through space and time, following the conventional conception of time
as "a series of discrete [that is, metonymic] moments," and that in so
doing it creates the illusion of life.[39] Mouth, on the other hand, prefers
to relate her story in a fragmented, though associative manner.

Her philosophical reflections are interspersed with biographical an-
ecdotes of her gathering cowslips in the fields, of her going to the super-
market, and of her being stared at in the public lavatory. These would
lend themselves to being related in a conventionally naturalist style. But
she does not relate these incidents in linear progression. Instead she
adds to each theme throughout, each one identifiable by a recurring
phrase, and returns to them at regular intervals. First she relates the incident in the field when "the buzzing" first occurred (*SP* 216), then gets
sidetracked into reflections on what the purpose and origin of the buzzing might be, and finally returns to her encounter with the buzzing
"back in the field" twice more (*SP* 221, 222) before the curtain falls. Likewise, she returns to her "sudden urge to . . . tell" (*SP* 222), which always
occurs in the wintertime (*SP* 222), a second time after having first al-
luded to it about five minutes previously ("always winter some strange

reason" [*SP* 219]). Her more abstract reflections on "the buzzing" (*SP* 217–19, 221), the "sudden flash" (*SP* 217–19), the "mouth on fire" (*SP* 220), and "the brain . . . raving away on its own" (*SP* 220) are not of a linear kind either. They recur throughout in a similarly thematic way identified by variations on a theme: "whole body like gone . . . just the mouth" (*SP* 220, 221); "something she had to . . . had to . . . tell . . . could that be it" (*SP* 221); "but the brain" (*SP* 217) "something begging in the brain" (*SP* 220), "and the brain . . . raving away on its own" (*SP* 220), and so on. Mouth obsessively returns to these themes as one does to dilemmas, never finding a solution yet always having another stab at them. The text becomes repetitive and circular, rather than linear.

Beckett's text shows the symptoms of a metonymic text that uses the structures of metonymy to support and further the metaphoric mode. It is a metonymic text on the verge of metaphor. This does not mean that metonymy is really "like" metaphor. The two are opposites, but metonymy is the nondual opposite of metaphor, like the flipside of a coin. Together they generate the transcendental conditions of the aporetic movement of writing Blanchot so vividly describes.

Lodge shows how Gertrude Stein, one of the most uncompromisingly methodical experimental writers, had radically to switch modes once she had explored the metonymic mode exhaustively, "with an unflinching resolve," and reached the point of crossing over from one mode to the other. This path led her conclusively from the extreme metonymy of *The Making of Americans* to the metaphoric mode in *Tender Buttons*. She goes from extreme length and verbal constructions to extreme brevity and nominal constructions.[40] As a dramatist, Beckett has at his disposal a wider array of expressive means than the prose writer. Apart from the prose dimension there is the visual and proxemic dimension. Instead of switching to a new artistic phase, as Stein did, Beckett pulls towards the metonymic pole *and* the metaphoric pole with equal intensity within the same work—two modes which, although they require a radical switch from one to the other, are in a relationship of peculiar logical inevitability to each other.

The dominant textual trait out of which the prose of the play is woven is strategic repetition with a difference: themes recur with slight variations or identical lines recur in slightly altered contexts. Beckett does not go to quite the same lengths of diligence with his pattern of repetition as Stein does in "Picasso," for instance ("One whom some were certainly following was one who was completely charming. One whom some were certainly following was one who was charming. One whom some were following was one who was completely charming," and so forth), but all the major ideas of the text recur with variation more than once, perpetuating the impression that the text does not really go anywhere, but rather returns obsessively to the same preoccupations. The text has movement, but the movement is circular rather than linear. Mouth is going round in circles obsessively and manically. The stage directions require the actor to ad-lib from the text while the curtain is rising and to continue behind the curtain for ten seconds until the house lights are up. The play is merely a snippet from an ongoing torrent of speech. When the curtain goes down and the audience's eye on the scene closes, Mouth goes through the same or a very similar cycle all over again. Seen from a distance, the narrative dimension, apparently so full of motion, is static.

Stein shows in "Picasso" and elsewhere in her repetition-with-minimal-variation texts that it is possible to reduce motion in the metonymic mode to such an extent that the texts no longer recreate a dynamic movement through time and space (which would be proper to the metonymic mode), but rather insinuate continuous sameness—an impression of never-ending now. This technique of minimal variation is still metonymic because based on iterative difference no matter how miniscule, but it is at the extreme end of what the metonymic mode can do before the artist has stretched it to such an extent that it flips over into the metaphoric mode. Employed also by Beckett in *Not I* and elsewhere, to a somewhat lesser extent than Stein, this technique has the effect of "converting the dynamic into the static, the temporal into the spatial; this is entirely consistent with the aim of metaphor-oriented Symbolist and Imagist verse, or Pound's definition of the 'image' itself, which presents an intellectual and emotional complex in an instant of time."[41] Not incidentally, imagism itself is iconic. The Imagist poem is to *present* the thing by bypassing the referentiality of language. After this Stein switched to the metaphoric mode of the short prose poems in *Tender Buttons*, which she thought of as portraits or still lifes. (Note the analogy to the stillness of Beckett's stage images.) In language the desire to have an intellectual and emotional complex present itself in an instant of time is necessarily an approximation not only because of the inherently temporal nature of language. Language, having to use the detour of words, appears mediated, whereas painting appears to address the senses directly. Beckett's stage images approximate painting in their extreme reduction of movement. Although drama, as much as poetry, is a "time art," Beckett's stage images remain largely unchanged for the duration of the plays.

The isolated mouth, equally present in the aural and the visual dimensions, is therefore the connecting link between the metonymic aural dimension, with its intimations of physical and other fragmentation, and the metaphoric visual dimension. *Not I* aporetically pulls toward both the metaphoric and the metonymic poles and creates the iconic quality of Beckettian writing.

Another way of looking at the same mechanism is to say that horizontal linearity (of humanist reason, for instance) has to be exhausted before there can be a space for the self-giving of the transcendent. Mouth goes through the motions of her iterative mind, caught in the confines of "the brain . . . raving away on its own" (*SP* 220), unable to exit from the vicious circle of trying to make sense, returning obsessively to existential conundrums that have her stumped: the meaning of human existence ("tiny little thing . . . before its time . . . godforsaken hole . . . no love of any kind" [*SP* 216]), the role of suffering in it and ways to defy it ("unless of course she was . . . *meant* to be suffering . . . ha! . . . *thought* to be suffering" [*SP* 217]), and the possibility of impossibility of mercy ("brought up as she had been to believe . . . with the other waifs . . . in a merciful . . . [*Brief laugh*] . . . God" [*SP* 217]). It is doubtful that Mouth ever finds the way out of the obsessions of her mind, but the audience is able to take refuge in the quiet balance of the stage image.

Beckett's work is full of episodes that show human reasoning run wild. He illustrates the human inability to calm existential anxiety by covering all eventualities, by trying to order the world conceptually by means of reason so that nothing is left to chance. The sucking stones episode in *Molloy* is a prominent example (*Mo* 69–74), as are Watt's methodical musings about the mysterious availability of hungry dogs to eat the leftovers of Mr. Knott's dinner (*W* 88–97). Trying to have every possibility covered is, Lodge points out, one way of avoiding the selection process of metaphor: "A more radical way of denying the obligation to select is to exhaust all the possible combinations in a given field."[42] Lodge is alluding here to Molloy's attempt to devise a system that will ensure that all of his stones will be sucked equally.

While Lodge is right and I would not attempt to argue that the episodes of obsessive ordering in Beckett's texts are not metonymic, it should be pointed out that there is a difference between the attempt to exhaust the possibilities by finding a rule to which they will all adhere and the attempt to "use everything," which Lodge isolates as a defining characteristic of Stein's *The Making of Americans:* "'Using everything,' the megalomaniac desire to cover, eventually, the whole field of human contiguities with language, defies the practical necessity to select, and insists on the essential uniqueness or 'difference' of each human being underlying their superficial similarity or 'resemblance' to each other."[43] Beckett's people, on the other hand, are frightened by this proliferation of difference, which they perceive as chaos. In their own way they make an attempt at selection in the sense that they abstract from the chaos and try to formulate a system governed by rule, even (or especially) if that rule will eventually cover everything.

Even in Beckett's prose works the metonymy of such exhaustively systematic reasoning is transcended into some form of metaphoric presence, such as the mysterious Mr. Knott (Mr. Not?). Among Beckett's works for theatrical and televisual performance, *Quad* contains—in fact *is*—the most prominent example of such metonymic rational systematization, while on another level it epitomizes the metaphoric pole. The systematic scurrying of the five hooded figures is contained by a "set" and a stage image of utmost reduction and simplicity: it consists merely of the peculiar monks—more Cartesian than Carthusian—within a faintly lit quadrangle. The set does not change throughout the performance, and neither does the camera angle. The camera maintains its position in front of and diagonally above the stage. As a result, the figures' frantic scurrying is contained by an entirely static image and again the tension or balance between the metonymic and metaphoric poles is operative—this time in a much starker fashion than in *Not I* because of even more radical reduction. Here both dimensions confront the spectator on the visual plane since all verbal language has been eliminated.

Finally *Quad* and *Not I*, as much as any other Beckett play, raise the question of meaning. What does *Quad mean*, since at the level of "plot" it is not intelligible? At this point Beckett's work becomes ultimately metaphorical and charged with transcendental meaning. Garner remarks that Beckett's would almost be an "'art of indeterminacy' were it not for the precision with which Beckett specifies the conditions of instability."[44] Nothing is left to chance; everything is meaningful. The precision of Beckett's stage directions, the minuteness with which his figures move about the stage and the reduction to bare essentials inspire a search for meaning that is by necessity beyond the conventional plot of the contained fictional world. Along with plot, the other cognates of linear continuity and contiguity disappear: there is no progression through time, no cause and effect logic, and no stage set imitating the natural world. Naturalist fourth-wall theater and film try to make their audience believe that what they see *is* the world, whereas Beckett's stylized sets and dialogues leave no doubt that they are meant to *stand for* something else. To an extent, Lodge points out, this is the case in all theater, regardless of how naturalist it is, because theater depends on being recognized as performance, not the natural world: "[O]ur pleasure in the play depends on our continuous and conscious awareness that we are spectators not of reality but of a conventionalized model of reality, constructed before us by actors who speak words not of their own but provided by an invisible dramatist. The curtain call at which the actor who died in the last act takes his smiling bow is the conventional sign of this separation between the actors and their roles, between life and art."[45]

For this reason Lodge argues that naturalism in theater is really an aberration of theater's metaphoric nature. "Arising out of religious ritual (in which a symbolic sacrifice was *substituted* for a real one) drama is correctly interpreted by its audience as being analogous to rather than directly imitative of reality."[46] As a reaction to the naturalist trend that has dominated especially commercial theater throughout the twentieth century, many avant-gardist playwrights have made a point of emphasizing the metaphoric dimension of drama—Beckett among them, according to Lodge.[47] *Not I* is read by critics in the most fundamentally metaphorical terms: as mystical encounter (Acheson, "Madness"), conversely, as a metaphor for the impossibility of salvation (Zeifman,"Being and Non-Being"), or as a Jungian-inspired model of identity (cf. Howard, "Not Mercies"), although many of these interpretations become quite "unmetaphoric" in their specificity. The play of metaphor is lost and the text pigeonholed. Brater, by contrast, asks himself whether the play does not go "so far toward simplification and abstraction as to raise the question of whether it refers to anything outside itself."[48] *Not I* would then have fulfilled the Derridean dream of a self-annihilating piece of literature, freed from any referentiality and hence self-erasing.[49] But this is not how *Not I* has been read, and to read it in such a way would indeed make it an anomaly in the theater, which even more than the other literary genres is based on communication and hence arguably more immediately connected with human existential concerns.

■   The question of what *Not I* is *about* leads to the strategy of displacement that is most centrally the concern of most interpretations of *Not I:* the elision of selfhood in Mouth and, hence, in the speaking voice. If *Not I* is about anything very obvious, it is Mouth's persistent refusal to acknowledge as her own the experiences she describes. Defiant of Auditor's admonitions or corrections (his part of the dialogue the audience can only speculate on), Mouth continues to tell her story in the third person. Her refusal of the first person singular pronoun is so viciously insistent and its suggestion so obviously painful (Whitelaw in performance clenched her teeth as if waiting for the pain to pass) that *Not I* has been seen in connection with mental illness. Mouth, it has been suggested, is schizophrenic (Acheson, "Madness") or at least deeply disturbed. Like a survivor of some unspeakably traumatic experience, it could be argued, she tries to externalize that experience and distance herself from it by pretending that it happened to someone else. And now Auditor assumes the role of the psychiatrist who tries to reconcile the two autonomous halves. Then the question becomes whether Mouth's psychological split is thoroughgoing and we are indeed listening to Mouth's conscious self raving away, or whether parts of her unconscious trickle in, as in a dream. Carl Jung's theory of the shadow is often cited in interpretations of *Not I*. James Acheson surmises (with Brater) that "Mouth *has* been taken over by her shadow—the sum of her 'uncontrolled emotional manifestations.'"[50] But if that is so, it remains unclear how Mouth is able to be very consciously in control when she has to be in order to rebuke Auditor. "For God's sake! This craze for explicitation!" one hears *Catastrophe*'s Director groan in the background (*SP* 299).

One problem with such interpretations is that the text does not provide sufficient information to support them. One cannot decide on the basis of a text that is barely seven pages long whether the character depicted in it is schizophrenic in any clinical or even merely meaningful sense without lapsing into speculation. Much like *The Unnamable, Not I* operates at such a level of abstraction that it will support any number of "literal" interpretations: yes, one can speculate that Mouth was raped, as Jessica Tandy suggested much to Beckett's dismay, and even find indications in the text that can be read in this way.[51] Invariably, one will drag the text down to a level of specificity it had already transcended, and as a result the interpretation, even if applicable, will always explicate only a fraction of what the text itself comprises. To an extent, this is the fate of any interpretive effort, but it becomes more pronounced the steeper the drop from abstract text to specific interpretation. Indeed, Beckett's texts are self-referential insofar as they are about language itself. They problematize and question the very process and paradigms of the production of meaning and the nature of meaning itself. Traditional interpretive efforts that attempt to impose narratives on the work to explicate it are anachronistic because they try to reinscribe the work into a representational paradigm that it consciously puts into question. They quickly meet their limitations because it is not possible to procure "meaning" unproblematically in Beckett's texts.

For these reasons I do not attempt a traditional narrative interpretation of *Not I* but limit the discussion here to an analysis of the dissolution of Mouth's subjectivity in the light of Lodge's typology. The majority of interpretations of *Not I* see it as a kind of failed autobiography and offer the diagnosis that in order for Mouth to "get better" she will have to acknowledge her own biography as her own and thus stop the mad run away from herself that assumes the rhetorical shape of metonymic horizontality. The metonymic form with its implications of fragmentation is seen as something counterproductive that must be remedied by stepping back into the safe haven of the master narrative of a centered subjectivity. "Audiences beholding the versions of *Not I* which include Auditor may come to recognize that the entire set is an image of Mouth's complete self," Patricia Howard asserts in accordance with such humanist interpretations, and continues, "[t]he 'I' is the union of the conscious and the unconscious, of body and of spirit: the human

being as unique and integral."[52] Auditor once again appears as the benevolent giant whose admonitions Mouth had better heed if she wants
to achieve an integration of her whole personality and thus be freed
from her pain.

Yet such nostalgia for traditional "metaphysical" centeredness is
not at all in keeping with the perspective Beckett expounds elsewhere in
his work. Especially in *The Unnamable* he systematically undoes all certainty, dismantling at the level of the novel a conventional construct
plot, narrative, and character, and at the level of epistemology all ontological certainty based on the centrality of the subject. Beckett disman-
tles the subjectivity of the speaking voice. The speaker of *The Unnamable*
knows that he thinks. What he remains unsure of is what mode and level
of existence or being, if any at all, can be ascribed to him on this basis.
The "subject" ventures beyond subjectivity.

At the same time, Beckett is not someone to revel in the bleak uncertainty and hopelessness of the meaningless void, despite persistent
claims to this end from Beckett's so-called existentialist critics. Hersh
Zeifman's position on *Not I* is consonant with the tenor of those voices:
"The Mouth . . . refuses to listen. Thus salvation is shown to be unattainable in Beckett's plays, not simply because it doesn't exist, but because the characters won't admit that it doesn't exist, and are therefore
denied the only kind of 'salvation' possible to them: the 'peace' that comes
from finally accepting that there can be no real peace.[53] While it is true
that Mouth does not listen and that Didi and Gogo refuse to acknowledge that their hope of Godot's arrival is futile, this does not imply that
all hope would fail if they did. It is the (pseudo-)existentialist critics'
choice to identify Godot with (false) hope and an abandonment of the
idea of Godot with staring the existentialist void in the face. The result
is that these critics understand Beckett's people to be caught between
the horns of a dilemma: either they continue to exist in the hamster
wheel of the inauthenticity of *mauvaise foi* or they confront the "truth"
that there is no meaning. Both forms of existence are versions of mean-
inglessness. There is no room left for authentic existence, which still
figures so prominently, if untheologically, in Sartre's philosophy. To a
critic who does not accept the postulation of a void beyond *mauvaise foi*,
the cyclical nature of Didi and Gogo's hell might merely imply that their
conceptual attachments forbid them to risk an existence beyond *mau-*

vaise foi, where they would encounter genuine hope. What genuine existentialism and negative theology share is a common concern with cutting through human delusions and constructs in order to enable authentic existence, but the latter they configure very differently, of course.

By no means do Beckett's texts endorse the characters' situation (beyond compassion for their self-created hell) or present their mode of existence as inevitable and inescapable. The obviously stylized nature of Beckett's dramatic dialogues and sets, however, draws attention to the constructedness of the dramatic situation and hence to the presence of the dramatist beyond the stage who has arranged the text in terms of metaphoric meaning. The implicit presence of the dramatist as the purveyor of meaning can well be read as a logocentric limitation in Derrida's scheme; what it also achieves, however, is a distantiation from the text: the audience reads the play as an artistic construct, not an inescapable force of nature. The artist implicitly points toward the way out.

Beckett's pervasive humor and the irony with which the characters' frequently dismal existences are infused are further means by which he achieves distance from the dramatic situations and allows audiences to envisage other, better, modes of existence. The most basic form of irony, where the intended meaning is opposite or near opposite to what is actually said, where meaning is that which is *not* said, by definition opens up a dimension beyond the text. Most of Beckett's characters, notably the speaker of *The Unnamable,* have a remarkable degree of ironic distance from their own situations. A problem manifests itself only when this irony is then read as a stable representational paradigm on the basis of which it is possible to *translate* Beckett's "cryptic" texts into interpretations that produce representational discourse on particular topics.

As soon as one does not look for a paradigm of representation but reads Beckett's irony and humor rather as self-subversive mechanisms meant to undermine the very assumptions of a representational logic, then the text of *Not I* stops appearing as an instance of failure (failed autobiography and failure to produce representational discourse) because the paradigm of stable subjectivity cannot be applied to it. The majority of critics approach Beckett's work with ideas of fullness and wholeness (the complete body and the centered self) as reference points, even when these reference points are criticized, and then they see *Not I* as a case of unachieved integration or, at best, as participating in the fragmentation of the subject as a postmodern commonplace. Enoch Brater, for instance, calls the "disintegration" of *Not I* an "ontological disaster."[54] But is it really such a disaster if one shifts one's perspective from a bias toward fullness to emptiness? Emptiness here should be understood in all shades of its three implied meanings: literal emptiness of the stage space; emptiness in the sense of nondual *sunyata;* and emptiness in the sense of a process of self-emptying implicit in *kenosis.* The kenosis of the text is what shall concern us now.

In a cursory article on the parallels between negative theology and Beckett's art, which regrettably overlooks a few crucial distinctions (such as the fact that Christian negative theology is still a theism), Marius Buning sees clearly that *"Not I* may be interpreted not only as dramatising *Mouth's* [sic] confrontation with her own Jungian shadow (as Enoch Brater has shown), or as a flight from self-perception and self-acceptance, but also as a struggle to give up the Self in order to become aware of a wholly 'other' reality, although it cannot be put in words."[55]

The premise of Jina Politi's article on *Not I* also offers an interestingly divergent starting point and an argument in favor of Mouth's refusal to accept the first person singular pronoun. In bold opposition to the vast majority of criticism on *Not I,* Politi questions the benevolence of Auditor. As she understands it, Auditor tries to impose on Mouth a discourse written for her by others as her autobiography: "Like *The Unnamable,* the play appears to centre round the pressure exercised by the discourse of Authority upon the subject to accept as axiomatic the truth of their description," and she concludes, forcefully, that "[t]o try, then, together with the Auditor, as with most Beckett critics, to read *Not I* as a miscarried 'autobiography,' is to assume the terroristic position of an inquisitor who by hook or by crook tries to subjugate Mouth's narrative to the authoritative law of a subjectivist genre; secure the authenticity of the subject's discourse; pass judgment; close the case and dismiss the audience court."[56] I would not go so far as to read into the play such a strong antagonism between Mouth and Auditor, for it neglects the balance as well as a semantic complementarity between them. Furthermore, Politi's emphasis on Mouth's "right *to author*"[57] remains noticeably within the discourse of subjectivity by maintaining that there is indeed a self to choose and to construct autonomously. Politi is able to see a positive force behind Mouth's refusal to accept the "I" but she does not go far enough in her critique of subjectivism.

Maybe we can look at the metonymic flow of words as a kind of emptying out of language, a kenosis that has as its end the emergence of the transcendent, "wholly 'other' reality" Buning mentions. The subject empties itself in a torrential outpouring of that which constitutes its ego-centered subjectivity and in this process the divine likeness can emerge. Here the allusion to St. Paul in the title of *Not I* comes into play: "I have been crucified with Christ; it is no longer I who live, but Christ who lives in me" (Gal. 2:20), and also "But by the grace of God I am what I am, and his grace toward me was not in vain. On the contrary, I worked harder than any of them, though it was not I, but the grace of God which is with me" (1 Cor. 15:10).

Yet *Not I* is not simply the representation of an "I" divesting itself of its subjectivity in order to allow the nondual divine beyond ego-attachments to emerge. If its self-deconstruction stopped here, the play would still move at the level of representation. On a further level of abstraction the text itself divests itself of its subjectivity. What takes place in the play is a kenosis of discourse. The text goes through a process of strategic self-emptying that frees it from all objectified externality: all authorial authority, all narrative—in short, all dogma of the concept.

As Derrida emphasizes, no text belongs to the *via negativa* "pure and simple." If this were the case, negative theology would have turned its own discourse into a monument. The subversive power of the *via negativa* would have been forfeited because it would turn into just another positivism. "Negative theology" cannot and must not be a unified discourse. Therefore, secular texts, too, are "in some way contaminated with negative theology."[58] The text is split just like the apophatic process is split into a kataphatic and an apophatic moment, and the kenosis of the text is a process of perpetual undercutting of every positive statement. For example, Mouth relates that "she" found herself "in the dark," rather than the light, though "not exactly . . . insentient" (*SP* 217), a statement that undercuts and modifies the absolute postulation of darkness and the state of "nonbeing" it approaches. Nonetheless, she is uncertain of spatial position, "whether standing . . . or sitting" (*SP* 217). And just as the reader has convinced herself that this is a fairly miserable situation to be in, the "speaker" insists on her lack of suffering (*SP* 217). At this point all theories about what might have happened to Mouth go overboard again. The text makes it consistently impossible to build a coherent theory of who Mouth is, what might have happened to her, and what the nature of her predicament is.

The apophatic undercuts the everydayness of a postulation (for example, "God is good") in order to preserve the absolute transcendence of God and at the same time that transcendence emerges precisely in the interstices of language because the content of the paradoxical statement that emerges in the process of negation overflows the usual semantic boundaries of a logic of noncontradiction: how can something be one thing and its opposite? The mind boggles. So the apophatic simultaneously *undercuts* in a horizontal process of subversion or deconstruction and it *preserves* transcendence, while linguistically transcendence must be understood as an aporetic moment of undecidability. These tendencies of simultaneous subversion and preservation can be found in the metonymic and metaphoric poles of the play: the metonymic undercuts, the metaphoric preserves. One could say that, although metaphor and metonymy are irreconcilable poles, in *Not I* they work together toward a nondual transcendent.

The notion of kenosis of discourse in *Not I* is fortified by Blanchot's short text—"Where Now? Who Now?"—concerning the narrative voice in Beckett. Blanchot, like Beckett, pinpoints the loss of narrative authority by focusing on "having lost the ability to say I."[59] Both writers know that the subject needs to be challenged for full-fledged kenosis of discourse. The "I" disappears in Beckett's text. What remains are "empty images revolving mechanically around an empty center that the nameless 'I' occupies," Blanchot says.[60] His focus is the earlier *Unnamable;* by the time Beckett's reduction process reaches *Not I* the speaker has most literally lost the ability to say "I." The voice in *Unnamable* could still be argued to try to work out, futilely, what kind of subjectivity might be ascribed to it, while the voice in *Not I* no longer even attempts such unification. Beckett's text becomes a vehicle for a central preoccupation in Blanchot's own thought: the advance in writing and in literature of a *neutral* space that "expresses nothing"[61] because a neutral space cannot be a vehicle for a subjectivity that would seek expression for its innermost ideas. *The Unnamable* "is precisely experience lived under the threat of the impersonal, the approach of a neutral speech that speaks itself alone."[62] In this neutral space the text *itself,* emptied of all interiority such as authorial intention, plot, character, or readerly intention (in the phenomenological sense of the term) performs its own fundamental emptiness.

This idea of the neutral space of writing, detached from the individuality and the temporal existence of author and reader, is connected with Blanchot's divergence from Heidegger in his interpretation of the notion of death as a guarantor of personal singularity. For Blanchot death is not only the moment that defines a person's life in its singularity (since no one else can die my death), as it is for Heidegger. It is also the opposite: in death one is deprived of the world of action, or of possibility, that defines one's own existence as singular in the sense that what is possible is what one can achieve through one's actions and action is a vehicle for one's individuality. Hence Blanchot calls death the "impossibility of possibility," in divergence from Heidegger's "possibility of impossibility," the generator of all other possibility in life. In Blanchot's model of a contested subjectivity these two "versions" of death as possibility and impossibility vie with one another, simultaneously affirming and negating subjectivity.[63]

Blanchot, like Beckett, wants to open us to an end of possibility, externality, and action—which in turn opens us beyond the world of subject-centered action in which language appears merely as a utilitarian carrier of information. He confronts us with an Other in what Blanchot calls the "Outside" of language. Language as writing is an experience of loss and dispersal where language is not the mode with which *inner* thought is expressed, but rather is confronted with an *outside*, an unpredictable, completely irreducible space. Given the way the neutral space is "structured," the path to this outside is a path toward a nonorigin: the origin is always already split. The neutral is neutral in that "it cannot be central, does not create a center, does not speak from out of a center."[64] In Nagarjuna's understanding, it does not posit a thesis and therefore cannot be faulted. It grasps language in a space "outside" the binary distinctions that conventionally govern comprehension, a space "where speaking would neither affirm being nor need negation in order to suspend the work of being that is ordinarily accomplished in every act of expression."[65] To confront the neutral is not just another possibility, but the very point where possibility, will, and power are exhausted. To underline his point Blanchot distinguishes between the work and the book. The work (of writing)—as opposed to the book as cultural object, operative in the power structures of the world—is a never-ending task of slippage during which the "nature" of literature— the trace—necessarily remains ineffable, emerges only in what litera- ture manages to say without saying it, because any conceptualization of its nature would place the work immediately on the side of the book.

It becomes clear that despite its name the Outside is not outside lan- guage at all. It does not function by way of a logic of exclusion that would situate it either inside or outside. Rather, it is inside *and* outside at the same time, sacrificially (if you will) offering up its own concepts to deconstruction immediately. Strictly speaking, it is neither inside nor outside because it does not advance any concepts in the first place. The Outside is an aporetic space in which the rules of conceptualization do not take hold. A figure that is both inside and outside is iconic (function- ing within the realm of representation but not bound by its rules), and in the context of Beckett's work it certainly retains its visual overtones.

It is important that Blanchot calls the Outside the "Outside" for yet another reason. With this name he hangs on to an impossible structure of transcendence, but transcendence nonetheless. The notion of an out- side of language is not unlike Derrida's impossible appeal to the end of metaphysics, which cannot be reached because there is no way of leaving metaphysics behind without committing a metaphysical gesture. In its iconicity and its structural transcendence the Outside assumes the posi- tion of the sacred. It is a kind of displaced sacred in the horizontal, tran- scendental realm—like the holy in an absolutely irreducible space.

I have no doubt that Blanchot is right to propose such a neutral space in Beckett's work, but he needs to be careful before claiming Beck- ett unreservedly as his spokesperson. There are important, if minute, differences between the two. The Blanchotian Outside is a space of end- less dispersal devoid of the gathering or concentration that emerges from Beckett's process of reduction. In Beckett's work this dispersal also takes place, to be sure, most notably in *The Unnamable*, and still in later minimalist works such as *Worstward Ho*, where every assertion is sys- tematically put under erasure in the moment of slippage between affir- mation and negation. At the same time, however, the short sentence fragments of *Worstward Ho* imitate the concentration we have already observed in the stage images. Beckett "chops up" complex sentences to halt forward motion, making it possible to contemplate a thing in itself: a place and a body and how it feels to be a body in space, rather than "a place . . . for the body to be in," as Beckett's sentence would read were it ordinarily punctuated: "A place. Where none. For the body. To be in" (*WW* 89). Ordinarily punctuated, the "place" would automatically enter into a causal relationship with the body.

Beckett's space goes into a phase of concentration after an indispensable process of dispersal that ascertains that what is being concentrated is not merely our own partial conceptuality. Or maybe it would be more accurate to say that the simultaneous result of Beckett's process of dispersal is an uncanny concentration. Such a formulation would foreground the aporetic impulse in which Beckett's artistic endeavors are "grounded." For the same reason, Blanchot's neutral space also lacks Beckett's fascination with the immediate, momentous self-giving of painting that increasingly found its way into his own art. Blanchot's neutral has nothing new or fresh that gives itself. It is eternal only in the sense that it endlessly repeats and regurgitates. Beckett does this too, but the repetitions "culminate" in concentrated images of momentarily eternal stillness and repose. In both phases of dispersal and concentration the text appeals to, creates, and performs an iconic space at the limit of discourse.[66]

Chapter 5

The Empty Space of *Quad*

By the time we reach *Quad* the main divergence between Beckett's perspective and apophatic discourse becomes apparent: Beckett comes to realize explicitly the very thing apophatic discourse takes for granted—namely, that what cannot be said in language emerges in the interstices of language, in the moment of slippage. By comparison Beckett first embraces the moment of slippage in pursuit of the impossible, and then tries to halt its movement once he realizes that pursuit is futile and misguided. For apophatic theologizing, every proposition one makes about the divine reveals itself to be in need of correction, and often it is corrected by a directly contradictory proposition. The apophatic statement emerges from the tension between the two irreconcilable propositions. The proposition "God is beyond (language or reason)," for instance, is immediately caught up in a performative contradiction by setting up two conceptual spaces, one immanent and one transcendent. It generates a conceptual dualism in need of correction. The structures of apophatic discourse then demand the contradictory statement to be made: "God is immanent." The tension between these two statements generates, Michael Sells thinks, the textual or semantic equivalent of an experience of the divine. Sells prefers to call this an "event" rather than experience, and avoids the connotations of individuality and quiddity that sometimes accompanies the concept of experience. In apophatic discourse such questions as "Do mystics of different traditions experience the same thing?" and hence "Can we treat the mystical experiences of various traditions as equivalent?" are pointless since what is experienced does not fit such substantialist categories. The word "event" helps to shift the focus from subjectivity to givenness, but it can be just as laden with "metaphysical" implications as the term "experience." Jean-Luc Marion prefers to speak of "counter-experience," and in his phenomenology of liturgy Jean-Yves Lacoste prefers "nonexperience" and "nonevent," which might give the mistaken impression of being consonant with the position of Denys Turner, who categorically denies apophatic experience. But Marion actually means something quite different: "counter-experience offers the experience of what irreducibly contradicts the conditions for the experience of objects," that is, it overflows and exceeds all our conceptual blueprints for making sense of what gives itself to experience.[1]

Since *every* statement is in need of correction, however, the regression is endless and every glimpse of the nondual "beyond" is only fleeting. Apophasis does not have an issue with the forward movement inherent in the fleetingness. God cannot be pinned down and the forward movement is not teleological. Apophasis recognizes itself as discourse (that is, as different from the actual "event") and accepts the limitations of its discourse.

For Beckett the problem presents itself differently. First, up to and including *The Unnamable*, he engages in a questlike pursuit of the unnamable—a pursuit apophatic language cannot attempt because it does not assume that it can achieve adequacy to the divine in language. Once he recognizes this pursuit as futile and questions the ideal of adequacy, he tries to abandon all questlike, linear, sequential structures and therefore, finally, language as such.[2] The aporia of writing concerns Beckett throughout, but its acceptance leads to artistic manifestations quite different from the gleeful pursuit of the aporia in *The Unnamable*. The motionless stage images of his late work are, then, not only indicative of a tendency toward metaphoricity, but also of a fundamental mistrust of language. This means that if Beckett's art indeed progressively works toward reduction of the narrative/temporal element because, as he proclaimed in his early German letter to Axel Kaun, the inadequacies of language became increasingly painful to him, then his late play for television, *Quad*, must be seen (and has for different reasons been seen) as the artistic crest of this reduction.[3] It abandons language entirely in favor of the undivided intensity of the metaphoric visual image. What makes *Quad* quintessentially theatrical, despite the fact that it abandons traditional notions of plot and character, is that it reduces, crystallizes, and foregrounds elements of artistic expression that are specific to the theater. Beckett turns toward another medium, the visual dimension of the theater, to further an artistic vision that defied further development in prose. Clearly this trajectory is idiosyncratic to Beckett's predilections rather than written into the media themselves: apophatic writers are at home in iterative language, while paintings can be viewed dualistically from the position of a transcendental ego.

Two foci emerge: first is Beckett's attempt to stop motion in order to avoid any semblance of teleology. Here Gilles Deleuze's argument in "L'épuisé" is a useful foil because it advances some similar ideas while drawing radically different conclusions. Whereas Deleuze finds the idea of exhaustion with its nihilist implications essential to understanding *Quad*, I argue that there is exhaustion in *Quad* only to the extent that the domain of the rational is exhausted so as to make room for a more contemplative intelligence that reflects the nondual principles in *Quad*. As with *Not I*, I illustrate the iconic as a formal force rather than attempt to find hidden allegorical meaning. There is a counterproductive danger to allegory about which Beckett was well aware. One elucidates an abstract text with a specific interpretation and thus narrows rather than broadens one's understanding of the text. The dominantly mimetic, metonymic *Film* is easier to read allegorically; in fact, the narrative structure seems to call for a parallel narrative on the allegorical level. A metaphorical text, by contrast, hints at depth impossible to match in allegory.

Second, this formal concern leads directly to the aesthetic of nonduality in *Quad*, both in the composition of the visual image and in the acting. For the apophatic theologian the structures of discursive reason reflect an alienated consciousness split into subject and object, whereas

the nondual mind is engaged in an integrative form of contemplation—
theoria, in Plotinus—contemplation not directed at an objectified *something*. This emerges with particular force as soon as one traces the acting
style Beckett favors throughout his late work (and which in the absence
of dialogue carries the play) to the twentieth-century aestheticians of
the theater who have left their marks on *Quad:* Edward Gordon Craig
and Oskar Schlemmer. A major influence on Craig (and to an extent
Schlemmer) is Heinrich von Kleist's essay on the marionette theater, for
which Beckett, in turn, has expressed great admiration. In this essay
Kleist passionately argues for a consciousness unalienated from itself.
To be sure, Beckett is not a Romantic and would have difficulty proclaiming the *unity* of consciousness, but both Kleist and Beckett redefine
consciousness in counterdistinction from the dualistic implications of
the transcendental "I," and both perform a horizontally displaced version of the mystical encounter with God. For the Romantics this is to be
found in the union of human consciousness with nature; for Beckett it is
to be found in an expressionless dramatic style and an acting style to
suit it, one not based on the projection of a *Vorstellung*, but on *Darstellung*
and givenness.

In his early letter to Axel Kaun, who tried unsuccessfully to win
Beckett's enthusiasm and expertise as a translator for a proposed Ringelnatz translation into English, Beckett speaks of his inability to produce
official English because it appeared to him pointless, like a veil waiting
to be torn that is draped over the things, or the nothing, behind it.[4] He
considers it his calling—any contemporary writer's calling—to poke one
hole after another into the "terribly arbitrary materiality of the word-
surface" (*D* 53) in order to dissolve it, or, to say it with Maurice Blanchot, indefatigably to turn the book into the work of writing.[5] He is
aware of the ambitious nature of this undertaking and emphasizes the
importance of modesty: "For the time being one has to make do with
small steps. First of all, it can only be about somehow devising a method
that will present [*darzustellen*] this contemptuous attitude to the word
literally [or: by means of words; Beckett is punning]" (emphasis mine).[6]
He then draws a parallel between what he has in mind and the "logo-
graphs" (*D* 53) of Gertrude Stein where "the linguistic tissue has at least
become porous."[7] Yet he qualifies the parallel straight away. Unfortunately Stein has come close to his ideal only by accident. As far as Beck-

ett is concerned, Stein still shows too much respect for language. She is in love with it ("The unhappy woman (is she still alive?) is without doubt still in love with her vehicle"),[8] she teases it, plays with it, and this playing becomes an end in itself. She is so taken with the things language can do that the "solution" of the problem itself recedes into the background, is of secondary interest to the effects she creates. What was intended as deconstruction ends up as reification; what was intended to break up the surface in fact turns into just another surface.

This criticism of the Steinian method is neither synonymous with a rejection of the capacity of language to produce the semantic equivalent of an "experience" of truth, of language's capacity to present, nor is it a rejection of a meaningful universe outside the constructions of language. Language as such (apart from its petrified forms maintained through "grammar and style" [D 52]) retains the capacity to tear the veil, but it is important to see it for what it is: a vehicle, a means (not to an end but to *no* end), not an end in itself. No valorization of language is taking place here, but that does not mean that language is meaningless. It simply does not occupy a privileged position in a hierarchy of means. Beckett will use any means to uncover the something or nothing (nothing) behind the surface conceptualizations of language. Structurally, it is important to recognize the clearly articulated dualism in Beckett's statement about the something or nothing behind the surface of language. It is a dualism that is essential to any theological enquiry. There is the relative and there is the absolute. Whether this truth is something or nothing is for Beckett another question and remains to be seen, but the premise he works with is a fully articulated dualism of immanence and transcendence.

Two details in the passage from his letter to Kaun quoted above are striking. One is that Beckett should stress the preliminary nature of the strategy he proposes, implying that once one has some practice, has exhausted the potential of the "method," and has altered people's linguistic sensibility, there will be other, more far-reaching means. Second, he wastes no time and provides an analogy from the world of the visual arts: he mentions Feininger, presumably Lyonel Feininger, the Expressionist/Cubist painter and Bauhaus instructor.

Beckett is an extremely, maybe quintessentially visual artist—an oddity in someone who worked primarily as a writer, but an intriguing fact considering that he worked in the theater and other visual media and had ample opportunity to express his visual temperament there. His predilection for the visual emerges even in his prose writings, especially his late novels, whose structure is pictorial, not narrative. Especially *Ill Seen, Ill Said* tends to read like a screenplay. Each paragraph presents a particular scene as if describing a stage set, illuminating one detail after another in the spotlight of its gaze, thus making it visible for the reader: "The cabin. . . . Chalkstones of striking effect in the light of the moon. . . . Rigid with face and hands against the pane she stands" (*ISIS* 50–51). Its emotionless sentence fragments at times resemble directions for camera angles in screenplays ("Close-up then" [*ISIS* 57]; "the hands seen from above" [*ISIS* 66]; "Close-up of a dial" [*ISIS* 76]). Thematically, as the title suggests, the novel is concerned with seeing phenomena for what they are, or with one's inability to see them for what they are "nor by the eye of the flesh nor by the other" (*ISIS* 56) and with one's inability to represent the real. "Such the confusion now between real and—how say its contrary? . . . And such the farrago from eye to mind" (*ISIS* 72). Indeed, how to say its contrary? Is there a contrary? It isn't "copy" or "fake." The artistic presentation is just as real as the real; iconicity is not based on a logic of copy and original. St. Theodore sincerely countersigns Derrida's and Beckett's texts.

Beckett's closest friends were not fellow writers, but almost all visual artists: Jack Yeats, the van Velde brothers, Henri Hayden, and Avigdor Arikha are the most important ones. But, as Stanton Garner points out, "Beckett's temperament was more deeply visual than a study of allusions and influences might suggest."[9] Few writers for the stage have retained the same amount of control over their theatrical images as Beckett, who specifies their composition in minute detail and who often worked as a director of his own plays, thus assuming ultimate control over the work as a *Gesamtkunstwerk*.

In his essay "L'épuisé," Deleuze also ascribes particular importance to the visual in Beckett's art. The essay is about the television plays in general (for Deleuze the culmination of Beckett's art) and especially about *Quad*. Deleuze starts by distinguishing between fatigue and exhaustion, assuming exhaustion to be the "goal" of all Beckett plays: "The fatigued person cannot realize anything anymore, whereas the exhausted one can no longer create any possibilities."[10] Maybe there is an echo here of Blanchot's idea of death as impossibility? The former, due to his fatigue, cannot choose from an array of possibilities, whereas for the latter the very possibilities have disappeared. Deleuze proposes a kind of hierarchical progression of "languages" Beckett invents in order to exhaust the possible. This progression is useful in illustrating the means by which Beckett will attempt to poke holes in the surface of language in order to get at the "something or nothing" behind it. Thus far Deleuze is a fellow traveler, but we part ways when he draws his conclusions.

The first such language, according to Deleuze, is a "disjointed, cut-up, chopped up" language of enumerations, a language of nouns Deleuze finds especially in the novels up to and including *Watt*. It is characterized by the same combinatory logic that is responsible for the sucking-stones episode in *Molloy*. The second language is a language of "voices" that works no longer with combinatory atoms but with "streams to be blended and mixed." It is to "exhaust the words themselves," as Deleuze puts it, by exhausting the streams from which they are made.[11] Those streams are the other possible worlds. The third language is that of "the visual or acoustic . . . image, provided one frees it from the shackles with which the other two languages hold it back." In the first case the shackles would be those of a combinatory, rationalistic imagination, in the second an imagination held down by memories that root the image in the past.[12]

Deleuze then offers a remarkable sentence, which appears in rather unmotivated a fashion in his text and appears atypical of its nihilist tenor. Unless I misread, I agree with the implied purpose of Beckett's forays into the language of visuality: "It is very difficult to tear away everything that is connected with the image . . . . It is very difficult to create a pure, immaculate image that is nothing but image, to arrive where it appears in all its singularity, without being burdened down with anything personal or rational, and to penetrate to the indefinable as if to a celestial state."[13] The image Deleuze talks about frees itself from its metaphysical shackles and does not need to renew its deconstructive efforts. It is iconic. One wonders given Deleuze's agenda to what purpose, unless for irony, he employs the religious allusions in this sentence, for the religious, insofar as it is built on a relationship of immanence and transcendence, or more generally of self and Other, depends on a fully formed dualism in order to overcome it. This means that in order to have a fully formed Other a certain gathering has to take place. One will have to affirm something, whether it is indeed a something or a no-thing. The movement that takes place in Deleuze's vision of Beckett's art, however, is purely one of dispersal: to exhaust the potential of space and to disperse the power of the image. The end of this dispersing process is, in other words, a nihilistic one.

What attracts Deleuze to the image is its ephemeral quality. It can, Deleuze says, itself become process. It can detach itself from its object and become an event that does not need to realize itself in a body or object, "similar to the grin without cat in Lewis Carroll."[14] Deleuze does not spend much time demonstrating where in Beckett's work he finds instances of purely potential images. His most convincing example is the Stuttgart television version of *Eh Joe*, which *suggests* a smile by showing merely the possibility of one in the eyes as well as a few upward-curving wrinkles around the mouth but does not show the mouth itself.[15] It is not clear why Deleuze insists on treating this example as a potential image rather than a full-fledged but synecdochical image. Moreover, what he describes could just as well take place (through inflection of voice, for instance) in what he calls "acoustic" images—images created by means of language and mediated by language, but also images created by way of sound, presumably both musical and purely sonic, although Deleuze refers explicitly only to musical ones. There is nothing specific to visual images in the theater in the phenomenon of potential images Deleuze describes, though there seems to be a distinct difference between visual and musical or sonic images.[16]

It seems to me, first of all, that theatrical images especially have a much *closer* relationship to their "signifiers" (for example, actors) than ones mediated by language, and hence cannot as easily be separated from the physicality of their object, and second that Beckett's stage images do not disperse their power or potential. Because theatrical images tend to "show" rather than "tell," they have, this time in Charles Sanders Peirce's terminology, an "iconic" quality to them. They convey their story by a set of signifiers that bears a certain resemblance to the signifieds. The actor playing Hamm, for instance, should exhibit some of the defining characteristics specified for the character of Hamm in order to cut a convincing figure. And neither of the two, Hamm nor the actor, could disappear without sacrificing the inherent nature of theater (or, to a large extent, television), whereas a word can comfortably stand in for what it signifies. Of course, this does not mean that the two are inseparable. Any number of actors with given characteristics are suitable for a given role. But it does mean that there is a close connection between the image in its potentiality, which is also the one physically realized on stage, and the immediate physicality of the actors that anchors the play in the real world.

Further, Beckett's theatrical images are ephemeral only insofar as they remain part of an art form that unfolds in time. They will disappear as soon as the play has come to an end, and this ephemerality is important, but within this definition they become as pictorial and unchanging as possible. Within the limits of this unchanging and static composition they have hardly any means of dispersing their power or potential. They remain physically static but dynamically charged within their physical stasis. I agree with Deleuze only insofar as the image is the most encompassing and effective means by which Beckett breaks up the surface structures of language, yet not for dispersal but for a gathering of potential and concentration in reduction.

In the plays of the 1970s and 1980s, Beckett embarks on an exploration of the play as image that gains in definition and momentum as he experiments with increasing levels of reduction. In most of these works language continues to have a role, but it is increasingly subordinated to the visual realm as the narrative dimensions of the plays shrink. Dominated by patterns of repetition and meant to visualize internal states rather than external action, the language dimensions of the plays do not have much of a story to tell. The near disappearance of narrative and the disciplined exploration of the visual is a confluence in which Beckett stretches the limits of the theatrical, but most importantly in which he confronts the limits of the horizontal metonymic narrative. It approximates and converges with almost entirely still stage images that resemble paintings more than the moving and shifting world of theater. Although Beckett only approximates stillness in both the domains of narrative and of the visual image, a development toward the stillness of the aesthetics of painting is traceable here. This changes the perception of time in Beckett's art. The audience is urged to let go of its conceptualization of time as linear progression.

Except for his attempts at poetry, Beckett's works fall within the two narrative literary genres, the novel and drama. I here rely on Seymour Chatman's proposition to subsume both novels and drama under the heading of "narrative." Under the traditional narrow definition the term "narrative" applies only to primarily diegetic forms of literature, excluding primarily "mimetic" forms such as drama. Chatman points out, however, that "there is no great difference between the structures of the 'what,' the *story component* told by epics and enacted by dramas. Both rely on sequences of events, and both present a chronology of events different from the chronology of the discourse."[17] What the subsumption of novel and drama under the heading of "narrative" emphasizes is that they are both time arts (that is, arts in which the passage of time is significant) in a way in which painting is not. They depend on time in different ways, obviously, since one can go back and reread a few pages in a novel but one cannot turn back time in a play and watch the first act again) and that they are both defined by horizontal, linear (narrative) unfolding in time. Prose, as categorized by David Lodge, has a natural tendency toward the metonymic pole of literature, which is horizontal in movement and hence accompanied by a strong sense of the passage of time or the movement through time. Drama, on the other hand, is dominantly metaphorical, but its narrative dimension is equally defined by the passage of time. The fact that both drama and prose are "time arts" in this sense does not of course mean that the *stories* they tell have to be related in a linear fashion. The stories unfold according to a given sequence of events, but that sequence may be jumbled up in the narrative, which may start with the end or the middle. This does not, however, change the actual sequence of events. Both novel and play can use flashbacks and other methods to disrupt the chronology of the story on the level of discourse. The impression of linearity nevertheless remains because in their reception these art forms depend on the passage of time. This means, Chatman points out, that they prescribe an order in which the audience will take in the information. In a play or a novel one has no choice but to start on the first page or to follow the play from the moment the curtain rises to curtain call. And if one skips thirty pages, or if one leaves the auditorium, there is no guarantee that the rest will still make sense.[18] In such a case one may have successfully rebelled against the inherent structures of the genre. One has, however, not exposed oneself to the work in the way deemed meaningful by the artist.

Paintings, on the other hand, are a nontemporal art form because they do not prescribe a particular sequence in their reception. They offer themselves all at once, in a single blink, to viewers who can then proceed to process and digest them at their leisure. The viewer can start wherever she chooses, go from general to particular or vice versa, return to a particular detail repeatedly, and so on. The viewing of a picture also takes (place in) time, but it is only the viewer's work that is temporal here, not the work itself. "Paintings *present* themselves as if they were holistic; verbal narratives as if they were linear," argues Chatman. "They do so regardless of how any given spectator or reader goes about perceiving any given work."[19]

This external passage of time during the reception process is characteristic of drama and Beckett can do nothing about it. What he can do something about is the internal passage of time at the level of story. The texts (both drama and prose) written after the trilogy *The Unnamable*, *Molloy*, and *Malone Dies* are increasingly dominated by patterns of repetition or circularity, or variations on themes that, despite their miniscule forward motion, suggest stillness or at least a standing still rather than motion. At the level of narrative this means that the text is not driven forward by action. The texts do not tell anything that could be classified as genuine stories. Nothing happens; there is no action. "In the mid-1960s," S. E. Gontarski remarks, "Samuel Beckett's fiction took a dramatic turn, away from stories featuring the compulsion to (and so solace in) motion, toward stories featuring stillness or some barely perceptible movement, at times just the breathing of a body or the trembling of a hand."[20] Of those so-called closed-space novels, *Worstward Ho* best epitomizes the terminal point of this stage of Beckett's artistic development. Here we have what could be called "descriptions" or "images" of internal (psychological) states. They describe the "core" of the sentiment by increasingly finely tuned approximation: "Dim light source unknown. Know minimum. Know nothing no. Too much to hope. At most mere minimum. Mere-most minimum" (*WW* 91). Process and action, indicated by verbs, have disappeared alongside the parts of speech that express them.

Even the paragraphs, as larger units of "narrative," are barely in causal, chronological, or otherwise logical connection. They are set apart from one another in the typescript, intensifying the impression of a virtual spotlight that comes on to illuminate one particular state before switching off to illuminate another, and to return to the first within the space of a few pages with another approximation. The paragraphs are like short photographic exposures. Gontarski summarizes Beckett's achievement in the closed-space novels in a similar vein: "Beckett did something new not only with his own fiction but with fiction in general—a reduction of narrative to points of space."[21]

Where his earlier work, especially *The Unnamable*, still evokes the impression of being in pursuit of something despite its own better judgment, Beckett's late work embraces the fundamental emptiness at the root of literature, that which Blanchot calls the "neuter" or the "Outside"—the result of its drive to cancel itself out. The origin recedes as one approaches it; literature will never be one with itself and coincide with itself so as to be reducible to an origin.

The trilogy had exhausted the linear motif of the quest, the narrative par excellence, at all levels: literally at the level of plot, technically at the level of narrative technique (it is no accident that the sucking-stones episode that so epitomizes Beckett's "combinatory" style is in the trilogy), and philosophically with respect to Beckett's project of (un)-naming the unnamable. After the trilogy Beckett's preoccupation with what is behind language shifts from trying (futilely) to capture it in language to finding poignant images that will be *Darstellungen* of it without trying to be equal to it. He abandons the model of adequacy.

Porter Abbott thinks that "narrative was where Beckett dealt with the inevitability of time. So instead of abandoning narrative, he sought to change it from within, setting himself the impossible task of reforming its temporal logic."[22] But when he was struggling with the "impossible prose" of the closed-space novels, Beckett had not steered himself into a dead end. The stage images allow a closer approximation to the complete stillness of painting than the temporality of prose. Abbott summarizes: "From then [after *Godot*] on, most of Beckett's plays are quasi-paintings—of a Mouth in *Not I*, a head in *That Time*, a face in *Eh Joe*, a single figure standing by a bed in *A Piece of Monologue*, two identical figures seated at a table in *Ohio Impromptu*. . . . [B]y and large these are staged pictures, curiously disturbed by the action of speaking or by discrete, repeatable movements."[23] It is important to let the priorities sink in: while it is arguably as "unnatural" to the theatrical genre to have stage images that do not move as it is unnatural in the novelistic genre to have prose that aspires to complete stasis, the difference is that a still stage image *can* present itself holistically, whereas a linguistic image in a prose text will always unfold in time, no matter how much the author excises movement and action from it.

With *Quad* a turn away from language and narrative is completed. Beckett embraces the image that fails to tell a story of any kind. The hooded figures' pacing takes place within time, but it lacks the teleological aspect of narrative. No matter how decentered and devoid of closure even the most postmodern of postmodern narratives might be, the smallest unit of narrative composition, the sentence, moves irreversibly toward its own completion as a sense unit (in time). By contrast, the figures in the square do not move toward anything. They exhaust all the possibilities of how and in which constellations four figures can traverse the sides and diagonals of a square, but this does not happen with a view to mastering a given field. *Quad* does not give the impression that there is an end to the "characters'" pursuits. When one round of combinatory pacing is completed another one begins. The figures go through the motions over and over ad infinitum, so in all their movement there is really no movement at all. Rather, there is an evocation of eternity in the sense of an everlasting now, which is the only intimation of eternity temporal beings can have. As Michael Glasmeier in his perceptive article on *Quad* observes, on the one hand this type of going on and on makes one nervous (not least because as twentieth-first-century Westerners in the claws of capitalism we are used to being fruitfully employed in some kind of teleological endeavor and cannot well tolerate the impression of doing something merely for the sake of doing it); on the other hand, it is soothing because it gives rise to the feeling of continuity that cannot be disrupted.[24]

The pacing, then, takes place without a goal, for its own sake, without any sense or purpose being ascribed to it. This said, it is of course possible to see it as being very much part of a (pointless) teleological endeavor. This would put it in line with all the other instances in Beckett's work of a combinatory logic running wild. These instances are invariably futile attempts to control an unpredictable world by rational means, but mastery is never achieved, simply because the world does not function exclusively according to rational principles. Overcome by anxiety the characters apply their combinatory logic to the most basic and mundane problems, such as the distribution of a number of sucking stones to four pockets in such a way that the stones will all be used to an equal degree. They find themselves in endless pursuit of an ever-elusive goal. Irony turns these instances into critiques both of the problems to which the characters apply their inexhaustible ratio (our propensity to lose ourselves in problems we have manufactured ourselves) and of the means applied to them (our tendency to pretend that we can be in control of the world and our lives).

The combinatory logic prevalent in *Quad* and elsewhere is a peculiarly self-sufficient form of the Cartesian cogito. In its Beckettian incarnation it pursues the "I think" as an end in itself. The Cartesian revolution is based on the very dualism that Heinrich von Kleist, Edward Craig, and Beckett set out to overcome—namely, the one between subject and object. In some of his funniest writing Beckett reveals himself to be critical of the aspiration of human reason to be self-sufficient unto itself. Beckett's people consistently attempt to apply reason to the perplexing problems of everyday existence in an effort to reduce these problems to human categories—categories they can understand—but this effort is futile. They try to cope with the anxieties and uncertainties of existence by forcing their own rational categories on the world and the world stubbornly refuses to cooperate. The sucking stones episode is a brave and futile attempt to account for all eventualities so as not to allow the vagaries of human existence to catch one by surprise. Hugh Kenner writes of it that "[n]o more desperate assault on the randomness of things has ever been chronicled."[25]

Beckett mocks reason as an exclusive and self-sufficient path to knowledge by making the discrepancy between the "problem" and the means applied to solving it as great as he possibly can. No one in their right mind would care sufficiently to attack the problem of the sucking stones (a quotidian banality, not to mention a pointless personal perversion) with quite the same amount of method and diligence as Molloy. Molloy is killing a butterfly on a wheel, and much of the humor of the scene derives from this lack of proportion. Beckett insists on the utmost precision and detail in the most mundane of circumstances. At the same time such descriptions are never merely funny, because it is clear that such rampant rationality is a helpless compensation in the face of far deeper anxiety.

Watt, too, is an individual utterly obsessed with method and hence a well of examples. His theories about the never-ending supply of hungry dogs to eat the leftovers of Mr. Knott's dinner have already been mentioned, but Watt does not stop short of applying the same logic to his own immediate existence, as his systematization of the process of walking illustrates.[26] Life is an ongoing improvisation and walking is an appropriate image for it: one is really off balance at each single point in the process and yet one advances and does not fall over. But one has to be prepared to make a leap of faith and trust that walking is indeed possible, although it is an activity executed, as Kenner says, "in a manner too hopelessly immersed in the *ad hoc* for analytic reconstruction."[27] If, on the other hand, one arrests the flow of motion arbitrarily in order to take the time to analyze its parts, one will in fact simply fall over; reason turns into a self-fulfilling prophesy. The "dogged systematizer" (Kenner) Watt is unable to make this leap of faith. He refuses to trust, prefers rather to trust only himself and proceeds to systematize even the simple procedure of walking, with obvious disastrous effects. He is awkward, indeed more awkward than his clueless unbalanced contemporaries who simply *walk*. Watt is continually beside himself: split and analyzing himself as if he were another, like the protagonist in *Film*.

At the same time the mirth created by all of this for the reader is accompanied by the almost tragic awareness that Beckett's people are, for the most part, unaware of the disproportion. (The obvious exception might be the narrator of *The Unnamable* with his (its?) boundless self-irony.) The "randomness of things" Kenner mentions is itself a matter of perspective. The characters are unable to admit that the surface problems to which they apply their excessively active capacity to reason are merely symptomatic of a deeper compulsion to bestow human order on a world that appears random because they lack the faith to see its fundamentally benevolent order. This is to say that Beckett is not simply compassionate with the hopeless and endless nature of their plight, although he is that, too. Beckett's works are no tacit confirmations of the way the characters have constructed the world, as inescapable hamster wheels. Instead, Beckett's humor criticizes both the characters' method and the assumptions underlying their choice of method and points to another way. I see in it an attempt to promote awareness that the characters' problems are fabricated ones, ones that would disappear together with the assumptions on which they are based once we changed our fundamentally dualist way of thinking.

This critique of rationality (we will return to it later) no doubt underlies some of the significance of the pacing in *Quad*, but it does not capture its full range. The nonteleological pacing-for-its-own-sake emerges more fully in the second shooting of *Quad*, which is shorter and slower paced. It lacks the percussion accompaniment and it is shot in black-and-white. It is difficult not to laugh on first encountering the frantic scurrying of the hooded figures in the first version, intensified as it is by the equally hectic percussion "music."[28] One cannot help but think of caged rats, albeit strangely methodical ones. The second, slower version much rather evokes connotations of a walking meditation: the figures properly *walk*, rather than scurry, with great attention devoted to the execution of every step. The alien percussion is gone and the faint shuffling sound of feet on floor (a sound properly part of walking) now constitutes the play's sole acoustic range. The aspects that made Glasmeier nervous in the first version have disappeared and what is left is merely the exercise of attentive walking for no other purpose, it seems, than that of being attentive. One no longer wonders what all that exertion of energy is actually *for*. The walking is slow and therefore less automatically directed toward an external purpose. (Even in everyday experience we are, after all, quite at ease with slow walking for its own sake, whereas we immediately assume a destination when people walk quickly.)

In the second (black-and-white) version the figures are less sharply distinguished from one another. In fact, they could be multiples of the first: in the stage directions Beckett specifies "identical white gowns" (*SP* 294) as costumes. The figures, neutral in gender ("sex indifferent" [*SP* 293]) and appearance ("[a]s alike in build as possible" [*SP* 293]), become indistinguishable. Hence the method behind the walking patterns becomes blurred. Now we have just some figures joining others in a kind of labyrinthine endeavor (labyrinths are, of course, traditionally used for walking meditations) while some others drop out to rejoin later.

The focus is on the walking, not on the method. Upon viewing the second version, Beckett is reported to have said, "Marvellous, it's 100,000 years later."[29]

It is a hundred thousand years later, one surmises, because the figures have tired of their rational pursuits. Their steps come more slowly; they are dragging their feet more than they did before. According to Deleuze, a kind of exhaustion has indeed set in: there is no purpose, goal, or preference. "Only the exhausted person is so uninterested, so scrupulous." Exhaustion, according to Deleuze, is characterized by what he calls "inclusive disjunctions."[30] No longer is only one of two given statements necessarily true; they are both true. Yet what Deleuze is driving at is not a straightforward Derridean, or even apophatic, aporia in which the two poles of an opposition fuse momentarily into a kind of nondual inseparability. Rather, the dualities between the terms remain, even are more clearly defined, but they are meaningless because they have no purpose except that of endless permutations, whose defining characteristic is an exclusively combinatory logic that is by definition without preference. For Deleuze exhaustion is in other words still part of a combinatory logic; it is inseparable from it through another "inclusive disjunction": "Does one need to be exhausted in order to be concerned with combinatorics, or is it rather combinatorics that exhausts us, that brings about our exhaustion, or both at once, combinatorics and exhaustion?"[31]

It seems to me that there are two distinct phases to combinatorics as it appears in Beckett, illustrated by the two parts of *Quad* (and by the general tension between metonymy/metaphor and horizontality/verticality in Beckett's work). The question hinges on whether one sees combinatorics in Beckett as inherently without aim or goal. It seems clear to me that, although combinatorics tries to "use everything" and refuses to make distinctions, Beckett's people try to achieve mastery over what seems to them a hostile and chaotic world, that is, they use it with a distinct purpose in mind. The desired mastery fails and the permutations continue endlessly and at this point exhaustion sets in. The rational mind exhausts itself while caught in the hamster wheel it has created by the inadequacy of the method it has chosen to attack its problem. The problem is of an existential kind and hence, like a koan, unsolvable by rational means. Taking the koan analogy further one can say that the exhaustion is not a nihilistic end in itself. From it something new begins to appear, as in *Quad II*, or more generally in the image as a formal construct that frames these pursuits.

Another way of illustrating this twofold structure is by way of the image. All the frantic action (essentially static because circular) is gathered in a single image, captured by a fixed camera position located somewhat diagonally above and in front of the playing area. There is a place, then, from which we can regard the play as well as our pursuits holistically, and from which their metaphorical significance will unfold. It is important to remind oneself that the fixed camera position in *Quad* is a conscious choice on Beckett's part. It is not the product of some supposed dilettantism of someone new to television and used to the perspectival confinements of the proscenium stage. Beckett has always shown himself to be very conscious of the possibilities and limitations of the respective media in which he works and to use different media for purposes that are specific and idiosyncratic to them. In *Film* he proves himself to be perfectly capable of working with a moving camera, and with an extremely active one at that, when he turns the supposedly "objective," disengaged narrative eye of the camera into a subjective entity, a full-fledged character in active pursuit of another.

The camera position in *Quad* is partly explained by practical necessity. In order for the viewer to follow the figures' precise trajectories the camera must be in an elevated position. Yet the position is not of necessity fixed. In fact, left to their own devices, well-meaning inept adapters to the televisual medium would probably have incorporated at least a few cuts from one camera position to another in order to make the presentation more "interesting." This happened with devastating results in the BBC version of *Not I*, which appears as part of the 2001 *Beckett on Film* project. Not only does that version excise Auditor (which would be forgivable), it then fails to zoom in on the mouth, showing the actor full length, out of costume, and in a chair rather too obviously like an electric chair, alluding to Billie Whitelaw's torturous experiences in that chair. To ruin the play entirely, the camera then proceeds to cut from one position to another, showing the actor sometimes frontally, sometimes in profile, as she delivers a monologue slowed to a pointless ramble. The contrast between the rapidity of the text and the stillness of the stage image is lost.

Quad, like *Not I*, depends on the apparent tension between the fast horizontality of the "action" and the stasis of the framed image. Glasmeier observes that in *Quad* Beckett leaves behind the last remnants of the literary: "He has become . . . an inventor of images on the basis of the experience of images. His ekphrasis does not describe, it creates."[32] It abandons the mimesis of *Vorstellung* in preference to *Darstellung*. Beckett refuses to use space to tell a story, to lay out a narrative three dimensionally in time. What he offers instead are images that fuse into a single picture, gathered and framed by the camera. Because *Quad* does not "develop" in the same way traditional drama does (along the lines of plot development, however rudimentary), in principle any individual shot from *Quad* could be singled out to represent the play as a whole. Any development takes place not in the work but in the viewer, as her reactions to the unchanging sameness of the pacing figures range from baffled amusement, to annoyance, to boredom . . . and probably back to head-shaking amusement at the minimalist audacity of Beckett's project. What remains are "images without before or after, images in naked presence"—saturated phenomena.[33]

Glasmeier reminds his readers of Beckett's fascination with the Dutch painters of the seventeenth century, especially Johannes Vermeer. Their paintings celebrate what he calls "the theatre of stasis, of frozen gestures." Scenes were not taken from nature, but they were built in the studio, "staged reality in diffuse spaces, painted stage, total artificiality."[34] The parallel between the seventeenth-century Dutch masters and Beckett's own approach is useful insofar as it draws attention to the extreme formalism they share. Vermeer, for all his realism, did not attempt naturalist "slices of life." Therefore, there are no scenes capturing life in full-blooded motion, such as running children, wildly gesticulating people, and the like. Figures appear in staged poses and are hence largely still, as they are in Beckett.

However, the fact that these paintings do not represent motion or speed does not mean that their compositions are static. In fact, as Rudolf Arnheim points out in *Art and Visual Perception*, images that arrest physical motion, such as snapshots, tend to look static—like objects frozen and displaced in space—although they capture moments of extreme action, whereas minutely balanced compositions (such as Vermeer's) are always intensely dynamic affairs.[35] Glasmeier does not distinguish sufficiently between physical stasis and compositional stasis. Beckett's theatrical images are not "frozen," although they are still. A brief look at the visual composition of Beckett's theatrical images will counter two contrary but complementary assumptions—namely, on the one hand Glasmeier's to the effect that Beckett's images are static, and on the other Stanton Garner's proposition that they are imbalanced.[36] In fact, the majority of Beckett's images are neither. This excursion into visual composition will complement the parallels between Zen painting and Beckett's images because an imbalanced composition obviously cannot adhere to principles of nonduality, and a static composition is likely to be imbalanced.

"Equilibrium," Arnheim defines succinctly, "is attained when the forces constituting a system compensate each other," but in order to be balanced a composition does not need to be symmetrical.[37] Symmetry is merely the simplest form of balance; most artists, however, work with some kind of inequality. Inequality of the two sides of a pictorial composition does not imply that the image automatically pulls in one direction: items carry different weight depending on where they are positioned in the picture, so that, for instance, a small object can balance out a larger one provided it is located in the right spot. And at the same time the stillness of balance does not mean the absence of pulling forces. In other words, Beckett's images do not need to be "a celebration of . . . imbalance" in order to be "charged with visual pull."[38] Arnheim points out that "[t]o the sensitive eye, . . . balance . . . is alive with tension. Think of a rope that is motionless while two men of equal strength are pulling at it in opposite directions. It is still, but loaded with energy."[39] Such tension is frequently more interesting than the kind Garner finds in Beckett's images because it is both more subtle and more lasting: it has no outlet for discharge and so continues to sizzle behind the apparent restfulness.

Before we look at some images to which this analysis applies, it needs to be said that indeed not all of Beckett's late stage images are like this; those that aren't are frequently images that consist of just one unit, without a second entity to establish a counterweight. In *Rockaby,* for instance, the rocking chair is positioned slightly off center; the same goes for the face in *That Time.* In both cases dead-center position would be too heavy and boring; the image would be entirely devoid of tension and motion. It would radiate a complacency inappropriate to the disturbing tenor of the plays. Significantly, though, even the off-center position chosen in these cases is not one of balanced tension. A slight off-center position will always fidget, pulling either toward dead center or toward the restfulness of the golden section. The latter implies too much restfulness for Beckett's taste in these cases. He opts for outright imbalance.

Not I, for one, is a different matter. The image is structured centrally, with Auditor on the left and Mouth on the right. Mouth can balance Auditor because she is active, bright, and small, while Auditor needs to be larger because of his relative inactivity, though faintly lit in order not to overpower Mouth. Because images are read from left to right, objects on the left carry more weight than objects on the right.[40] A large, brightly lit Auditor on the left would hence be so extraordinarily heavy he would plunge right through the floorboards. Mouth, on the other hand, is heavier than her size indicates because she is positioned eight feet above stage level—rather high when seen from the position of a seated audience member. According to Arnheim, other factors being equal, objects positioned closer to the top of a given visual field will carry more weight than objects at the bottom because our existence as gravitationally determined beings makes us accord more importance to the top: "To rise upward means to overcome resistance—it is always a victory."[41]

Similar balance can be observed in the stage image for *Ohio Impromptu*. The table at which Reader and Listener sit is positioned stage center, anchoring the image centrally. However, both figures are seated at the right end of the table, Reader at the short side, so that the audience sees him in profile, and Listener toward the right end of the long side of the table and facing the audience. In terms of pure distribution of matter it seems as if the image should lean to the right, but in fact it does not. The weight of the two figures centers around the restfulness of the golden section while the empty left half of the table reaches into the empty side of the image connecting matter with nonmatter. Furthermore, the empty half of the image is on the left, the side to which a viewer generally ascribes more weight. In a curious way it is the center of attention, framed on one side by the proscenium arch, on the other by the two figures at the table. Were the two figures seated at the other end of the table, the empty stage space would be in some danger of becoming a negligible afterthought. It would trail behind the action, as it were, rather than establish a philosophically significant counterweight. One is reminded of the numerous Zen paintings in which the bough of a tree or a bamboo cane reaches into an otherwise empty image. Consider Niten's *Crow on a Pine Branch*, where the crow itself is at the far right of the picture, its tail barely in view, while a single branch extends about three-quarters of the way across the picture, leaving the rest of the canvas blank.[42] The detail (the branch) merges with the whole that is suggested in the blankness of the canvas. The empty space offers the eye a place to rest while opening up the image to the contemplative concentration in which the image was produced, reminding the viewer that a human artifact such as the picture, if produced in the right state of mindfulness, is never merely what is represented in the picture. The "whole" including its necessarily unrepresentable dimensions are never all in the picture; and yet it is, because the empty space opens the image up to the rest. An asymmetric style opens the composition up whereas a symmetrical composition is closed and self-contained.

Quad is, of course, an entirely centered and symmetrical composition, the playing area being square and traversed by the figures along the four sides and the diagonals. The visual composition is framed twice, first by the distinct outline of the playing area surrounded by a dark undefined space into which the figures disappear upon leaving the square (a technique that makes the otherwise rigid frame of the composition somewhat permeable), and second by the dimensions of the television screen itself. The figures never diverge from the parameter of the square, except when they approach its center. There they come to a short, startled stop only to then circumnavigate the center by way of a short deviation to the right and to resume their course along the diagonal on the other side. In *Quad* the center (ominously called "O" in the early *Quad* manuscripts)[43] is where the image opens itself up beyond representation. The center is literally and figuratively the crux of the matter. It is the axis of a cross, and Beckett has, it is well known, an obsession with cross-shaped structures. It is what Deleuze calls "the potentiality of the square."[44] Here everything comes together; it is the locus of meaning, as it were. And it is precisely at this point that the movements of reason, the smooth unceasing flow of endless combinatorics, is disrupted. The methods of reason fail to grip. Reason has to admit defeat and bow before the power of something that cannot be grasped and traversed by its means.

Maybe this central point hints at a God beyond representation, possibly even the Christian God; it is, after all, situated at the intersection of a cross that prescribes the paths of the figures and in which the figures' trajectories are inscribed. Christianity deeply informs Beckett's work; in an effort to discourage literalist interpretations that try to confine him to standard popular Christian readings, Beckett called it "a mythology with which I am perfectly familiar, and so naturally I use it."[45] By and large Beckett criticism tends to tie discussions of religion and theology either to the characters or to the author himself, or to both, as in Hélène Baldwin's *Samuel Beckett's Real Silence*, which regularly commits the standard interpretive *faux pas* of ascribing to Beckett beliefs professed by his characters. But even a substantial and groundbreaking study such as Mary Bryden's *Samuel Beckett and the Idea of God* not always differentiates sufficiently between the characters' limited perspectives and what the work as a formal construct might signal. For instance, the assertion that Didi and Gogo, as victims of human violence, find it easiest to identify with the victimized, human Christ because they find themselves in a similar position[46] does not warrant the conclusion that Christ appears in Beckett's work only in a form entirely divested of his divine attributes, "as a human exemplar" of suffering, in what she calls the "kenotic mode: emptied, made destitute, and available for suffering of the worst kind."[47] "[T]his Christ has no divinity," she concludes.[48] Bryden is right to say that the kenotic is an important concept in Beckett's art, but she uses the word in a misleadingly secular way. "Kenosis" does not mean a shedding of divine attributes. Christ always has two natures, one fully human and one fully divine. What he chooses to forgo in becoming human is to use his divine nature to his advantage and in this sense he becomes a slave or a servant. Therefore, as Graham Ward points out, kenosis is rather a doctrine of divine representation: "With the doctrine of kenosis . . . we investigate exactly what it is to be incarnate. Put systematically, Christology grounds a theological anthropology, and a theological account of what we know of God and how we know it."[49] Kenosis works both ways: God chooses the self-emptying of the incarnation and at the same time humankind, through the example of Mary, is redeemed and given the chance to divest itself of ego in a kenosis and to become fully deified.

Bryden's cruelly persecuted and slaughtered Christ puts rather too much emphasis on suffering because, as undeniably aware of human suffering as Beckett shows himself to be, his work is not full of unrelieved pain and squalor. It is also very funny—*Waiting for Godot*, Bryden's example, being a case in point. Beckett has a keen eye for presenting human folly with a gentle humor that emphasizes that his people's self-created hell is not the only way. There is a kind of redemption in Beckett, but it tends to appear after the play is read or watched and the work is done. No Beckett character experiences redemption (with the semi-ironic exception of Murphy, who blows himself up in his chair during one of his meditations). In the meantime we need help understanding the nature of our self-created hells, because only when we understand our dilemmas to be of our own creation can we be open for redemption, and it is this concern that is prevalent in Beckett's work. Fundamentally, redemption in Beckett is possible only as an act of self-recognition: it is up to the reader to garner enough momentum from Voice's "fuck life" (*SP* 282) in *Rockaby* to act on the desire for a different type of existence. Whether this means entrusting oneself to the saving grace of a transcendent power is up to each audience member, but it is a decision based on the entirely secular delivery granted by the realization that we are the makers of our own prisons. Christian redemption, dependent as it is on Christ's saving grace, is present in Beckett's work only insofar as none of the characters, not even a self-reflective one such as Voice in *Rockaby*, is able to liberate herself from her circular existence solely by the power of her own human will, though the will not to will is a necessary condition for divine grace to occur.

The two natures of Christ provide a structural hint of a far deeper fascination on Beckett's part with the cross. At the beginning of *Waiting for Godot* Vladimir evokes the cross and the crucifixion scene, and thus the two thieves crucified with Christ: "One is supposed to have been saved and the other . . . damned" (*WG* 6). Vladimir is preoccupied with the fact that the accounts of the four Gospels do not agree and wants to know why he should believe the one in which the thief is saved, so that it looks as if what attracts the tramps' attention is indeed "an eschatological queue in which a salvation quota system is of direct relevance."[50] But Beckett's fascination with it went deeper. What interested him was the essential undecidability of the question whether one will be saved or not. The cross gives reason for hope, but like any genuine hope, love, or forgiveness it is not based on a bargain: we cannot expect to be saved, and thus hubris is kept at bay. Beckett loved a particular formulation of this undecidability, which he, correctly or incorrectly, ascribes to St. Augustine. Its parallelism reflects the undecidability rhetorically and the parallelism's strict formalism satisfies Beckett's strong formalist vein. He remarked to Harold Hobson: "I take no sides. I am interested in the shape of ideas. There is a wonderful sentence in Augustine: 'Do not despair, one of the thieves was saved. Do not presume, one of the thieves was damned.' That sentence has a wonderful shape. It is the shape that matters."[51] According to Chris Ackerley's *Annotated Murphy*, Beckett took the sentence from Robert Greene, who ascribes it to St. Augustine.[52]

Like the two natures of Christ, the cross becomes a sign of ambivalence under whose sway the categories of dualist logic fail. The question how someone can be both fully human and fully divine boggles the mind, and indeed, there is no "logical" solution. There is no other way than to accept it in its rankling ambivalence by which it generates meaning. To attempt to make sense of it solely by rational means is to sooner or later exhaust the rational mind and to accept semantic overflow. As a strategy, as we saw earlier, it is akin to the well-known Zen Buddhist practice using koans.

Gilles Deleuze, however, sees in the squiggle the figures perform to circumvent the center the very mechanism by which *Quad* achieves the exhaustion of space—an assumption that is in complete agreement with his nihilist interpretation: "To exhaust space is to withdraw from it its potentiality by making any form of coming-together impossible."[53] In other words, because the figures do not collide, they are able to continue their combinatory pursuits indefinitely, exhausting the potentiality of the space in the process. Granted, coming together is not synonymous with collision, but what other possibility is there short of radically rewriting Beckett's play, which regularly has more than one figure arrive at the center at the same time? Surely a collision would not equal the potential of the space's coming into its own but would be merely an abortion of the play, a kind of misfiring and starting again. Were one, on the other hand, to rewrite the play in such a way that the figures traverse the center in sequence (by, for instance, making them start from their respective corners in minutely calculated intervals), the exhaustion of the potentiality of space could indeed continue ad infinitum or until physical exhaustion puts an end to the exercise, but it would be a pointless exercise because if one does not acknowledge the existence of the center in a way there is no potentiality to exhaust. The space is exhausted to begin with. My point is that every time one of the figures acknowledges the existence of the intraversable center, the potentiality of the space and the image is reconfirmed so that it cannot be exhausted. While Deleuze would like *Quad* to peter out into apathetic nihilism, Beckett in fact *affirms* something beyond representation, metaphorically epitomized by the empty spot in the middle of the set, and for the experience of this, the exhaustion of rational conceptuality (but not exhaustion per se) is a precondition.

Philosophically, metonymy is subordinated to metaphor in Beckett's late art and a purely rational (horizontal) intelligence to a more contemplative (vertical) intelligence epitomized by the stage image, and there is a corresponding principle at work at the level of visual composition. For, while there is metonymic motion in all of Beckett's late plays, this motion is not in a relationship of tension with the general metaphoric stillness of the images. "Beckett subordinates movement to position," Stanton Garner writes, "circumscribing motion within the bounds of invariant location. The effect, far from transforming the performance image, is to confirm the fixity of position in that image"; and a page later he summarizes that "movement . . . highlights the solidity of location . . . endowing objects and figures with a sculptural quality."[54]

By approximating his stage images as far as possible to the stillness of pictorial compositions, Beckett not only furthers an abstract artistic project. In the reception process these late plays also concretely and experientially alter the way we relate to time. If movement is reduced to the absolute minimum necessary not to overthrow genre definitions (of theater as a time art), this also displaces our conventional perception of time as movement and change. This conventional perception is based on the dualistic idea that unchanging objects exist in time as if in a container.[55]

Genuine nondual perception of time, on the other hand, does of course not depend on actually stopping time in the sense of ceasing all activity. Rather, one "becomes" time, so that there can be neither stasis nor flux because one has, in effect, deconstructed the contrast between them: there can only be a concept of flux if there is an idea of stasis and vice versa. The Buddhist law of impermanence hence does not imply renunciation of permanence and unconditional embrace of change, but rather an attitude of nonattachment. Letting go of our attachments to permanence means not embracing the other extreme, which would be another attachment. The result is that time becomes eternal. It is the closest human beings can come to being immortal in this world.

This moment is represented in *Quad* through stillness in change, or change in stillness. The figures' pacing, although "still" in the sense of not contributing to any development, plot or otherwise, is nonetheless a reminder of the image's fleetingness. No single "frame" can be caught and kept. Each one is slightly different and falls away, but then none needs to be "kept" because each represents the play as well as any other. Likewise, in *Not I*, although the composition remains unchanged throughout, the opening and closing of the mouth is a reminder that one is looking at a fleeting composition in a theater that will disappear as soon as the play is over. Any displacement of the dualism is, in other words, necessarily fleeting, just as the moment of nondual union with the divine cannot last because, through having a body, or through our obligation to tell others about our experience, we always still have one foot in the temporal camp, although the experience is eternal while it lasts.[56] Displacement is a necessary condition of the project. Even in the still-life prose of *Worstward Ho* there is the distinct awareness that displacement is necessary:

A place. Whence none. A time when try see. Try say. How small. How vast. How if not boundless bounded. Whence the dim. Not now. Know better now. Unknow better now. Know only no out of. No knowing how know only out of. Into only. Hence another. Another place where none. Whither once whence no return. No. No place but the one. None but the one where none. Whence never once in. Somehow in. Beyondless. Thenceless there. Thitherless there. Thenceless thitherless there. (*WW* 92)

The text explicitly deals with causal relationships and hence with the linear passage of time. It consists, however, of a row of distinct, static observations, and Beckett goes to great lengths to keep them such. "A place whence none" would involve movement from one place to another, or from nothingness to thingness. To sever the connection and halt the movement Beckett inserts a full stop. As is familiar from apophatic texts, one observation will be displaced and corrected by a contradictory statement that directly follows it: "A place. Whence none." How can there be something where there was nothing? Or, more distinctly, "How small," followed directly by "How vast." Beckett repeats the exercise with distinctly apophatic vocabulary: "Know better now. Unknow better now." Throughout, games with similar-sounding words, internal rhymes, and alliterations ("whither once whence") set the mind reeling: "Not now. Know better now." And then: "None but the one where none." Finally, in a culmination of all the rhetorical strategies the passage has hitherto used, the point of a presence or a place without before and after is reiterated: "Thence less there. Thitherless there. Thenceless thitherless there." The differences between this and the breathless quest of *The Unnamable* are clear. The text does not lose its static quality although displacements occur.

The question is how to *write* a picture. In *Le Monde et le Pantalon*, Beckett observes in Bram van Velde a will to perceive in a way that is exclusively pictorial (*MP* 25), and then wonders how it would be possible to write the will to perceive in a purely visual fashion. He concludes that the only way is to write a sentence that "does not make sense," one in which the words cancel one another out or sublate one another (as they do in *Worstward Ho*), because only then will words begin to signify something beyond themselves (*MP* 25–26).[57] Only then can words be freed from time and thus become pictorial.

■ In 1988 Herta Schmid published an article on *Quad* with a very different trajectory. Hers pursues the convergences between *Quad* and Wassily Kandinsky's artistic theory, but at the beginning of her article she points out the similarities between a play by Bauhaus theater mastermind Oskar Schlemmer and *Quad*. Here I pursue this connection a little further, not to establish a case of direct influence between Bauhaus and Beckett, which would be inconsequential, but because the Bauhaus connection leads the way to a cluster of twentieth-century aestheticians and theorists of the theater and stretches further back in time to the Romanticism of Heinrich von Kleist. With these theorists we will return to "expressionless" art from a modern and a Romantic point of view. The group takes shape around Edward Gordon Craig's theorizations of the marionette and comprises Schlemmer himself, Craig, and Adolphe Appia. Kleist was an influence on this group and also on Beckett himself. It is known that Beckett was fascinated with Kleist's essay on the marionette theater, "Über das Marionettentheater," published in installments in the daily *Berliner Abendblätter* in 1810. He referred to it explicitly during rehearsals for the 1976 BBC version of *Ghost Trio*, although he had no interest in Kleist's other writings. Beckett had read the text in the original German, and James Knowlson and John Pilling are convinced that when Beckett referred to it during the rehearsals "[t]here was no doubt in the mind of anyone present that Kleist's essay also expressed memorably some of Beckett's own deepest aesthetic aspirations."[58]

Schlemmer conceived of a play in which three actors "dressed in the basic colors yellow, red and blue stride along a geometrical plane that is painted on the ground of the theatre, consisting of a square within a circle, the center of which is crossed by diagonal lines. The movements of the actors follow the geometry of the painted planes."[59] The play remained unproduced because of the architectural limitations of the space Schlemmer was working with. An audience member would have been unable to follow the figures' trajectories from where he or she was sitting or standing, a problem Beckett solved by tailoring the play to the medium of television. But *Quad* and the Bauhaus stage share further similarities. One is their concern with form. The Bauhaus dream of the completely mechanical stage leads to an extreme abstraction of the performance space. Theater becomes an exercise in form, color, and light— and this is precisely what *Quad* is, too.[60] The Bauhaus stage is an abstract space, a nonplace, a neutral space apparently suspended in nothingness and devoid of markers that would turn it into a definable place. In order to be consistent with this vision the actor must undergo an abstraction from his or her own specificity. Especially in the late drama, proper names for the characters, by tradition quirky and extravagant in Beckett's work, disappear in favor of phonemic variations ("Bim," "Bem," "Bam," "Bom" in *What Where*) or, following a related pattern, the inversion of letters that turns "May" into "Amy" in *Footfalls*. The actor is made to fit abstract space, rather than the space molded to be a fitting backdrop for the specific three-dimensionality of the actor. Knowlson emphasizes that Beckett's concern when directing his own work in the theater was never on emotional depth or character delineation in psychologically convincing terms.[61] Actors, like Jessica Tandy, would ask him for background-information on given characters in order to be able to portray them more convincingly, but he always refused to answer such questions—not out of spite, but because such questions did not interest him: for him a theatrical project was a formal exercise in "pace, tone and . . . rhythm."[62]

Such plays do not require plots. Theater is no exercise in verisimilitude. In both the Bauhaus and *Quad* there are no characters telling stories of the teleology of human existence, leading from birth to death, as a final occasion of taking stock of one's life. The actor becomes an art figure. As a result his or her own metaphysical implications are heightened. The art figure is an abstraction toward a universal and it becomes an entity more readily capable of conveying the universality of the human condition. The specificity of human experience and, likewise, of human embodiment recedes behind the universality of human experience. Instead of facial features and the like, which would single them out as individuals, the figures become distinguishable by formal markers: color (of the gown) and originally also light. Each figure was to be associated with a colored spotlight, but this plan proved impracticable as the different colors blurred into a muddled brown as soon as three or four figures populated the playing area. It should, however, be remembered that *Quad* was not Beckett's first attempt to use light as a formal force toward intrinsically dramatic ends. In *Play* the inquisitorial white spotlight triggers the characters' speeches and advances to the status of being a full-fledged "character" in its own right, and the one that holds the play together.

Instead of the specificities of individual human experience *Quad*, with its hooded figures in full-length robes, evokes the tradition of European monasticism, defined as it is by its efforts to transform the specificity of individual personality into the universality of Christ's nature.[63] This is the case especially in the second black-and-white version of the play in which the figures' graceful composure emerges more strongly. Stills from the first production of *Quad* (unfortunately the only form in which most people will encounter the play) show clearly why Beckett insists on "some ballet training" (*SP* 293) in the actors' backgrounds: the synchronicity in the figures' movements, the control with which they execute them, as well as their balanced positions in the playing area evoke a ballet. For the same reasons, however, they also evoke cloistered monks. Why this is so should become clear as we turn to Gordon Craig and the rationale that made him a champion of the marionette.

Craig was, of course, one of the foremost directors of so-called Symbolist theater; Beckett's stage, especially as I present it here, reveals quite a few parallels to the Symbolist aesthetic and was obviously influenced by it. The lack of depth and perspective in his stage images, their extreme reduction to essentials, and the dehumanization of the actor, all in an evocation of a "mystical" reality, are all Symbolist characteristics. And yet Beckett is no Symbolist. "At the centre of the Symbolist poetic is the notion of poetry as an evocation of a hidden reality through symbolic means," Frantisek Deak summarizes.[64] Symbolism is, in other words, ideatic: it aims to express an abstract idea by symbolic means. And Beckett tries this, too. His is also a philosophical theater of abstract ideas, but he does not assume any kind of translatability between the image and what it "stands for." Symbols suggest equivalence, which is especially problematic when such a one-to-one relationship is applied to the Ultimate. Any assumption that ultimate realities can be evoked by means of symbols will result in inevitable reductions and simplifications on both sides of the equation. The symbol will be unable to encompass the divine and the divine will not allow itself to be reduced to a symbol. As a result, many Symbolist productions were rather counterproductively one-dimensional instead of evoking the incomprehensible nature of ultimate reality. Beckett avoids the trap of equivalence. No single element straightforwardly *stands for* something else (in the way a rose stands for love), and in this respect Brater is right to suggest that "*Not I* . . . goes so far toward simplification and abstraction as to raise the question of whether it refers to anything outside of itself,"[65] but the inkling that the whole play is a metaphor for the human condition or that every element of the play is somehow charged with some metaphorical meaning is never far away. There are no straightforwardly "translatable" symbols, but rather a gesture toward meaning that cannot be pinned down. To put it succinctly, symbolism engages in a "simplification of means in order to evoke the essence of things."[66] Beckett engages in concentration rather than simplification and then is unsure of the nature of the essence. Instead he waits for it to show *itself* in the immediate experience of theater.

Beckett uses the theater to different ends than the Symbolists. The theater as a medium troubled the Symbolists because it seemed so rooted in its materiality. The "messy" physicality of the actor always destroyed the abstract conceptuality of the drama (on the page). Hence the appeal of the marionette or puppet to the Symbolist mind: puppets have a greater degree of abstraction (they are capable of only a limited range of movements) and therefore lend themselves more easily to conveying a conceptual universe. Beckett, on the other hand, never had issues with the pure materiality of theater. His reduction and abstraction of theatrical means work rather to focus the immediacy of the theatrical image— that is, to emphasize the peculiar nature of theater rather than to try to evade it.

What Craig objected to was the actors' dominating the play with their own or the characters' personalities, which he felt to be directly linked to perpetuating stage conventions that kept theater from coming into its own as a medium. The cult of personality with its dictum of consistent psychologically motivated characters locked the theater into the limiting role of being a mere copy of the real world. The tenacity of a "debased stage realism" kept the theater from unfolding its full potential as a medium: "Do away with the actor, and you do away with the means by which a debased stage realism is produced and flourishes. . . . The actor must go, and in his place comes the inanimate figure—the Über-marionette we may call him, until he has won for himself a better name."[67] Craig wanted to return the theater to its roots in ceremony and ritual— a return, in other words, to a fundamentally metaphoric rather than mimetic or metonymic relationship to the world. The marionette acquires symbolic value. It can represent the existential concerns of humankind as such because it is freed from the existential confinement of being human. Of course, Craig did not literally want to abandon the actor in favor of a puppet theater. The aesthetic limitations of the marionette would most likely have frustrated him. Rather, the marionette became for him the symbol of the ideal human actor. He trusted the creativity of the actor enough to envisage molding the dominant "psychological" acting style into one that would bring out in the human actor those characteristics that define the marionette.

Remarkably, Beckett's exhortations to Billie Whitelaw "not to act" are entirely consistent with Craig's vision. Like Craig, Beckett recognized that it is possible to abstract from the human actor so that she or he begins to resemble a puppet and become general. The reduction inherent in controlling one's emotions and fostering an emotionless acting style is thus not simply one that will transform his theater into its most essential, most pared down aesthetic incarnation. As a strategy it is essential to Beckett's artistic vision because it actively fosters his art's "religiosity," as it were, by emphasizing its essentially metaphorical nature. It becomes nonmimetic and nonrepresentational.

On the far side of Craig, Kleist is interested in how the artist might intuit the world of phenomena directly and he thinks to find the answer in a nondual fusion with it. The artist is to "become natural," or become one with nature, paradoxically by becoming more artificial: by approximating the unselfconsciousness of puppets. Kleist's essay takes the shape of a fictional encounter between the narrator and a certain Herr C, a dancer at the municipal opera house, in the course of which the latter enlightens the former on the virtues of the marionette theater, which the narrator had hitherto taken to be an artistically worthless diversion for the riffraff of society. According to Kleist's mouthpiece, Herr C, marionettes possess grace and harmony of movement and expression greater than that of any human actor because they lack the self-consciousness that makes humans lose their center of gravity. With this, Kleist offers a positive interpretation of the marionette that is rather unusual before as well as after him. The prevalent position is to see marionettes as mechanistic and soulless. Self-consciousness—the result of eating the fruit from the tree of knowledge—represents a very literal Fall from grace because it introduces a division within the individual herself. Self-consciousness means to perceive oneself as Other, and therefore also to perceive oneself in opposition to the world. The fruit from the tree of knowledge brings alienation from God, from world, as well as from self (that is, from the human being's divine nature). The person can no longer have a center of gravity, as it were, because she is constantly "beside herself," looking at herself from the outside. Beckett dramatizes this problem with the protagonist in *Film*, split into O (Object) and the onlooking eye (E), a character obviously off balance because in perpetual flight from himself. In Kleist's text we encounter the problem in the anecdote of the young man who spontaneously captures in his own body the grace and harmony of a statue previously seen in a museum, but who is unable to reproduce the same effect intentionally when he tries to do so in front of a mirror. The mirror image clearly is meant to stand for the split that the self-conscious intentional effort produces in the young man. The puppet's grace, on the other hand, derives from the fact that every limb, like a pendulum, subjects itself to and follows a single undivided center of gravity. Rather than control each limb, the puppeteer only needs to control this one center of gravity.

The real topic of Kleist's text goes a long way beyond "mere" aesthetic theory, then. Benno von Wiese observes that the subject of Kleist's text is, in fact, paradise lost and regained, human recovery of union with God and with oneself.[68] Implicit in the idea of the marionette is the notion of subjection to a higher will, the will of the divine puppeteer. In this case, Wiese points out, God, rather than the Herr C's of the world, would be the real dancer, present at the center of gravity of every human movement, and grace could only be attained if the split within the human as well as the split between human and God were healed. But these two trajectories are not mutually exclusive, for "when the divine puppeteer puts himself into the center of gravity of each of the puppet's movements, he simultaneously gives the puppet the freedom to be itself, and only itself."[69] This kind of "bilateral" movement is almost an analogy to the compatibility and complementarity of Christian theism and Buddhist nontheism. From a theist point of view the Buddhist tradition of illumination makes the human being receptive for divine grace, which overcomes all division and duality, while from the nontheist perspective the apparent dualism of Christian Revelation is subsumed in the nonduality of *sunyata*, founded as it is in a human (non-)effort.

True knowledge, then, knows no division of subject and object. It is connected, complete, and nondual. It is important that in Kleist's text paradise is neither regained by simple divine Revelation; nor is it regained by mere regression to a previous state of lost innocence, forsaking knowledge and consciousness. The development of his text is fully dialectical in that paradise is regained by taking consciousness further, as a third step, which is neither original innocence nor the duality inherent in the divisive step that separated humanity from its original innocence. Human beings have to eat from the tree of knowledge one more time, Kleist says.[70] This is to be imagined as a kind of circular movement (a "journey around the world," as Kleist puts it) that leads back to the origin, but this time from the other side: "[P]aradise is locked and the cherub behind us; we need to go on a journey around the world and see whether it may be open again through a backdoor somewhere."[71] It is the same innocence, but at the same time different because infused with a different history: that of knowledge.

While this overcoming of self-conscious duality does not happen through Revelation, neither does it happen through a long period of personal maturation. Kleist explicitly states that it happens "suddenly" and emphasizes this word by using it twice in close succession,[72] much like the grace of the statue personified suddenly by the young man when he did not try to engineer it. The appearance of nondual grace upsets patterns of linear temporality. In a moment of synchronicity the statue (seen in the past) and the young man, with whom the narrator shares the same space, are equally present. This kind of "eternal moment" in which the distinction between eternity and temporality is (temporarily) displaced is common in apophatic texts.

All similarities between Beckett and Kleist granted, one does well not to equate their ideas. Beckett is not a Romantic; his writings are thoroughly modernist. He finds in Kleist a kindred spirit who, from his own vantage point, articulates ideas that resonate with Beckett, but for Beckett what is at stake is not a question of recovering a lost original unity of, say, intuition. In Beckett, no lost origin can be reclaimed and thus no unity instituted. There can only be the nonduality of opposites. The aim is not to graduate from projecting "fake" depth to "genuine" depth of feeling radiating from the integrated person, but to do neither.

Because Beckett configures the problem differently than traditional apophaticism, the question why he does not find the traditional apophatic route compelling is moot. Apophaticism starts on a different premise, that adequacy to the divine need not be achieved in language, and therefore it can tolerate the endless succession of aporias its discourse produces; in fact, it embraces them as a viable strategy to produce the semantic equivalent of a nondual event. Beckett's language in *The Unnamable* is frequently indistinguishable from apophatic discourse, but because its premise is different in that it performs a quest, it had to ultimately frustrate him. The fact that he was unable, on abandoning the idea of the quest, to see the movement implicit in apophatic discourse as nonteleological and to adopt it as his own is also due to his original assumption. Continuing along the same route, but this time under a different premise, would have involved no artistic departure, would have constituted new territory only philosophically, and harbored the danger of lapsing into old patterns.

Therefore, Beckett's late prose texts also reveal a change in methodology in comparison to the earlier ones. They are constructed to keep the linear progression of discourse to a minimum. Beckett recognizes that a language-based apophaticism cannot function entirely without a strategy of displacement, but this strategy takes on a different form in his late prose. Daniel Albright poignantly observes that *The Unnamable* denies reference "semantically, by a strategy of perpetual contradiction of every proposition," while, in keeping with the image-centeredness of his late theater, "the method of *Worstward Ho* is to deny reference imagistically, by constructing a lapsed and incoherent thing, by displaying its deformity, its blight, its muteness from every angle, by letting it vanish into thinglessness."[73] In each case the sentences cancel each other out or stand in contradiction to one another, but in Beckett's late prose this strategy keeps the reader from forming conclusive, mimetic *images*, while *The Unnamable* questions the viability of its own *propositions*. It is Beckett's privilege as a literary artist to put his convictions in the starkest literary terms, where theology or philosophy as theoretically expository discourses would shy away from the ellipsis this involves. In this sense, Beckett's "literary apophaticism" is more uncompromisingly performative than theology or philosophy can be.

Chapter 6

The Reduction of *Film*

Film, first shown in 1965, was Beckett's first and remained his only excursion into the world of filmmaking. Not surprisingly, it is not the work of an accomplishe d filmmaker: it betrays Alan Schneider's inexperience at directing films (it was Schneider's first, too) as well as Beckett's in writing for the screen. But the film falls short not only in terms of execution. Thematically also, critics have found it less satisfying than Beckett's other work. Jane Alison Hale, for instance, thinks that it is less complex and hence less evocative than much of Beckett's work because in the film he limits himself to the illustration of one specific theme—*esse est percipi*. Hale goes so far as to claim that Beckett's central concern in *Film* is "to illustrate a philosophical 'truth.'"[1] Later in this chapter I return to this point of criticism by asking what precisely the relationship is between Beckett's film and Bishop Berkeley's famous dictum. Critics in general, and Hale in particular, have too readily assumed a straightforward and unproblematic relationship between the two.

One wonders to what extent the impression of single-minded, one-dimensionality is much rather due to the very different formal structure of *Film* in comparison with Beckett's other work. David Lodge observes that, in contrast with Beckett's work for the theater, the "plot" of *Film* follows a "logical space/time continuum."² In other words, as soon as Beckett switches to a metonymic medium his otherwise dominantly metaphoric work conforms to the horizontal and linear structures of metonymy. If this is the case, one has to ask to what extent *Film*, especially given its title, is a fundamental appraisal of the genre, since it obviously led Beckett in a direction he otherwise would not have taken. Beckett's tendency to explore the nature of a given genre and to take it to the limits of what it can do might find another manifestation here. This is one avenue criticism on *Film* has taken: Raymond Federman takes *Film* to be an investigation of "the essence of cinema, that is to say, visual expression of life and movement through photographic manipulation. If we accept this as the basic theme, we can then accept *Film* as a work of art which exploits its own substance so as to reveal its own limitations and failure."³ Enoch Brater, although oriented differently, also puts the emphasis on genre critique: "*Film* is, then, about the process of film-watching."⁴

Or, alternatively, does the critique of genre recede behind an illustration of Beckett's own artistic theory? Vincent Murphy is convinced that *Film* "condenses in it some of the most consistent and recurrent themes in the Beckett canon" and Brater agrees that it presents those central themes in specifically cinematic terms.⁵ One must ask, then, to what extent Beckett might have chosen film because its genre-specific characteristics gave him a unique opportunity to carve out central characteristics of his own artistic theory. *Film* does not merely illustrate a "philosophical truth," let alone one that defines a philosophical system quite different from Beckett's own (Berkeley's). While it does investigate a philosophical issue artistically, Beckett's emphasis, here as elsewhere, is the clarification of his own dilemmas and obsessions. As in his other works, Beckett tries to clarify his own relationship to visuality. *Film* is an allegorization of the process of seeing and, by extension, an allegorization of the failure of the phenomenological reduction: can a thing be identical with itself and is it hence possible to perceive it in its essence? *Film* answers "No." In the *Phenomenology of Perception* Merleau-Ponty teaches us that the phenomenological reduction is necessarily incomplete.⁶ We are no transcendental egos—pure intellect—but embodied, fallen beings inseparable from the natural world around us. Merleau-

Ponty questions the feasibility and spiritual desirability of the transcendental reduction à la Husserl. He stresses our original inherence in the world and our nondual inseparability from it. The transcendental ego becomes questionable.

If phenomena are to disclose themselves, it must be according to their own givenness, not the constitutive criteria of transcendental subjectivity. Jean-Luc Marion calls this the "third reduction" to givenness, which comes after Husserl's transcendental reduction to objectness and Heidegger's existential reduction to being. With the type of saturated phenomena he calls the "flesh," Marion's typology of saturated phenomena is able to account for the problematic Merleau-Ponty's phenomenology of the body addresses. When the category of relation is saturated, relation disappears in the nondual inseparability of the touch and the being touched, in the "feeler" and the feeling.

Whichever way one wants to interpret *Film*, one needs to answer the question why one suggests for contemplation a work that has been deemed one of Beckett's less successful ones. For one thing, the nature of Beckett's work emerges by way of contrast when it goes as far down the metonymic route as it can before it has to acknowledge its metaphoric nature on the most general level. More importantly, however, *Film* illustrates the two concomitant sides of Beckett's artistic theory as they present themselves in the *Three Dialogues:* the misguided quest for adequacy to the Unnamable and, on the other hand, the realization that only acceptance of aporetic structures offers a way "out of" the quest structure. Whatever one may think of the evocativeness of *Film*, for the phenomenological point that Beckett makes—the incompleteness of the transcendental reduction—the metonymic structure of deferral is ideally suited.

Knowledge, often of the highest order (as in "seeing" the light of God), has often been represented in visual terms.[7] In *Film* Beckett follows a long (and not always unproblematic) tradition based in Platonism and Neoplatonism, and continued throughout the history of Western philosophy, of equating vision with perception in general and with knowledge as such.[8] Everyday speech is permeated by reflections of this long tradition: we say "I see" when we mean "I understand." (See chapter 2.) St. Bonaventure's metaphysics of light, indebted as much to Plato, Plotinus, and the Pseudo-Dionysius as to St. Augustine, is an example of this tradition. In *On the Reduction of the Arts to Theology*, St. Bonaventure sees all of creation reflecting the light of God, at least as vestiges and sometimes as images or similitudes.[9] The light is reflected by creation and thus eventually returns to its origin: the arts eventually return to theology. If Bonaventure is right, this means that to ask questions about the nature of art separately from theological questions, as humanism is wont to do, fundamentally misses the point. If, on the other hand, one reads Bonaventure "ontotheologically," one will conclude that he dodges his own question by grounding his investigation in metaphysical assumptions (a metaphysics of light) he is not willing to question.

Beckett's investigations center around the dualism between O and E and the possibility of fusing it into a monistic unity, allowing the opposites to interpenetrate one another in a nondual way. Since the recent critique of occularcentrism has found "scopic regimes," more than other modes of perception, to be based on dualist assumptions and power structures, the visual mode lends itself especially well to Beckett's critique.[10] But Beckett leaves his viewer no safe place to stand. *Film* is no mere illustration of Berkeley's philosophy. Berkeley's monism enters the picture only as a foil that makes the peculiarly modern, atheological, and dualist assumptions put forward in *Film* emerge with particular force. The latter are in turn questioned by the film's comical, ironic tone. But even in ironizing the dualism Beckett does not present a nondual approach so much as insinuate it. *Film* is no manifesto.

The metonymic structure of (the) film reflects the plot's questlike structure. As in the "Three Dialogues" Beckett's point is twofold: given the dualistic assumptions of *Film* (the split of the protagonist into O[bject] and E[ye]) the quest structure is inevitable and this quest will of necessity remain an unfulfilled, failed one because the dualism cannot be transcended in an unproblematic effort for unity as was still possible in the Romantic imagination. The origin is always already split. We can never return to the hypothetical prereflective ground of experience Merleau-Ponty posits. The motivation that drives the quest for unity is the same one that produces the rift: the pursuit of unity is a teleologically motivated, linear endeavor that is by nature dualistic and thus in diametrical opposition to nonduality. Rather than the Romantic aspiration to be able, against all odds, to present the Unnamable in language, what is needed is a genuine apophaticism that will, as far as its discursive strategies go, not pretend to be able to present the unpresentable, but to present the unpresentable *as* unpresentable in language or conceptuality.

■ "To present the unpresentable as unpresentable" is, of course, Jean-François Lyotard's formulation of the sublime. But this does not mean that in postmodernity the apophatic inescapably turns into the sublime, or rather into an impoverished version of the sublime that makes no reference to transcendence. Laurence Hemming argues this point in *Postmodernity's Transcending: Devaluing God*. In Hemming's view postmodernity loses its sense of transcendence with its abandonment of concepts like substance because it no longer has a sense of where and what the immanent can be transcended *to*. First Kant splits the classical sublime into a separate analytic of the beautiful and the sublime in order to emphasize that one is a question of immanence and the other of transcendence, and then at Nietzsche's hands the sublime is turned into a version of sublimity that is entirely immanent. It is worth quoting Hemming at length:

> With the abandonment of substance, of the soul, and the unity of the cosmos is the rage to abandon upliftment itself, or rather to abandon that upliftment lifts up to some "where." Kant's distinction between beauty and upliftment was explicitly intended to demonstrate that beauty was an immanent, and upliftment a transcendent, value. For Nietzsche, however, all sublimity is immanent, such that all beauty becomes upliftment. All art, and so not only that which attains to substantiality, is sublime. . . . The term "uplifted" (*Erhabene, Aufgehobene*) has disappeared, now even Nietzsche's German speaks only of the sublime (*sublimer*). This is the devaluation of upliftment itself, as that which once superseded beauty in the transcendental analysis of aesthetical judgement, superseding beauty in order to indicate an infinite—a devaluation to a mere description of a psychological process, an activity—not even of the mind, but of the body (as the originary, causal, ground of mind).[11]

One can take issue with the view that postmodernity makes no reference to transcendence. Hemming's argument is based on the position, shared by David Harvey and Frederic Jameson, that all of postmodernism is nihilist. For Hemming nihilism is "the activity and manner of manifestation of postmodernity itself."[12]

It is pertinent here, I think, to invoke Graham Ward's distinction between radical and benign postmodernism. Ward counts Derrida, Irigaray, and Kristeva among the "benign poststructural philosophers"[13] and Barthes, Deleuze, and Baudrillard among those of a radically nihilist persuasion.[14] In the latter "strain," if such a grouping is permissible, difference loses meaning because in its play of surfaces all difference is equally nondescript. This is a type of postmodernism that revels in the ephemeral, the fragmented, the discontinuous, and the chaotic, to choose some of the adjectives with which David Harvey describes the postmodern.[15] The "other," "benign" postmodernism, on the other hand, can rather be seen to destabilize the power structures with which the radical version implicitly collaborates by going along with the play of surfaces that capitalism propagates and proliferates. The best benign postmodernism remains thoroughly phenomenological in that it attempts to cut through the baggage of so-called commonsensical assumptions and preconceptions, but no longer posits the "as such" of the transcendental ego. Rather, it guards from the pitfalls of human conceptuality a truth that is infinitely beyond what we are able to conceive. It saves this truth from idolatry, if one wants. As such it opens a door to a rethinking of theology and philosophy.

With this in mind I would like to return to the sublime and to another perspective on it. John Milbank also uses Kant's separation of the beautiful from the sublime as his starting point. He argues that because of this sundering of the realm of the transcendent and the realm of representation, postmodernity no longer works with a full-fledged sense of transcendence. Postmodernity cannot fill the transcendent with meaning because the realm of representation, within which we create meaning, is separate from it. "This means that all that persists of transcendence is sheer unknowability or its quality of non-representability and non-depictability."[16] In other words, there is a sense of transcendence in postmodernity—it is not merely immanent (as it is in Hemming's picture)—but this is an impoverished sense of transcendence in that it remains an empty transcendence. On this basis Milbank diagnoses in modernity a "yearning for the genuinely theological and for transcendence *rather than* sublimity."[17] Any attempt to recover this full-fledged transcendence will obviously try to reintegrate the beautiful and the sublime without trying to recover the unity of the classical worldview. I think that "benign" postmodernism is engaged in this project.

In his account of the shift to this modern sense of transcendence Milbank emphasizes the movement from classical poetics to modern aesthetics. In modernity the emphasis is no longer on the objective, but on the subjective—not on what it takes to make a good piece of art, but on what it means to experience art. What this also means, however, is that "[n]o longer is sublimity construed as something to which one gives voice: instead it is something one regards, or rather . . . endeavours to regard but cannot regard."[18] In other words, the movement involves a shift from actively producing the sublime in language to reacting to something one has seen.

If giving a voice to the transcendent is a way of reintegrating the beautiful and the sublime into full-fledged transcendence, then maybe the tendency in some postmodern texts, especially Derrida's, to evoke the transcendent by performing it can be seen as an attempt at such reintegration. Derrida reintroduces the poetic or the beautiful into a type of discourse that would otherwise be entirely analytical. Classical discourse used the beautiful to affirm God "as the eminent infinite reality of every harmonious proportion and value."[19] There was continuity between the relative and the absolute. For Derrida as a postmodern, the unpresentable transcendent cannot be an ultimate *value* because the concept of value belongs to the realm of representation and as such is subject to human fallibility. Nonetheless, there is the attempt to produce or perform, rather than describe or behold, the unpresentable in the realm of the beautiful, in language or representation. This endeavor remains distinctly modern insofar as what it aims to present in its performance is not the unpresentable as such, but the unpresentable in its affect for the one who experiences it. But it does grapple with something that is genuinely irreducible to the subjective horizon and as such transcendent.

The juxtaposition of the sublime and the apophatic is an uneasy and unequal one since the sublime is primarily an aesthetic category, while the apophatic is primarily an experiential category that is hardly reducible to its aesthetic and discursive dimension. Derrida's tendency to evoke the transcendent by performing it is a means of moving the sublime closer to the apophatic by making it experiential. For Jean-Luc Nancy the transcendent is neither aesthetical nor ethical, but rather defies such distinctions.[20] Nancy thinks of the sublime as that which moves always at the limit, "unlimiting" and "unbordering" in the process.[21] As a result it is necessary to rethink such concepts as "presence" (with its metaphysical overtones) and "the nonpresentable" that find their way into all the classic definitions of the sublime: "[O]ne (re)presents its nonpresentability, and one has thus aligned it, however negatively, with the order of presentable things."[22] The sublime "is presentation itself, but no longer presentation as the operation of a (re)presenter producing or exhibiting a (re)presented. It is presentation *itself* at the point where it can no longer be said to be 'itself' . . . and where it is consequently no longer a question of saying either that it presents itself or that it is nonpresentable."[23] As that which is always at the limit, the sublime makes necessary reference to the transcendent because it makes us aware of what is beyond the limit. But as an "unlimiting" force it questions even our conceptions of immanence and transcendence. It might be useful to remember the fully apophatic movements of Buddhism that do without the Christian dualism of immanence and transcendence. Nirvana is not elsewhere: the ontic range of nirvana and samsara is the same.

■ Presenting the unpresentable as unpresentable is possible only through the ambivalent, indeed aporetic, structures of apophatic discourse: the unpresentable is momentarily and experientially present as unpresentable (itself an aporia of the purest kind) in the fleeting moment of tension between two conceptually incompatible statements that transcends both and either of these statements. Seen in light of Merleau-Ponty, the split between O and E is a phenomenological necessity that has its roots in our existence as carnal beings. Because we are carnal beings, phenomena do not disclose themselves to us in all their radiance, or rather, they disclose themselves differently to us—namely, as counter-experience, as that which exceeds our cognitive limitations as carnal beings so that we continue futilely and thus endlessly to try to apply our hermeneutic blueprints to it. Only the disembodied transcendental ego (an impossibility, Merleau-Ponty says) would be able to apprehend phenomena in an unlimited way. We would be divine, not human. As it is, we are never fully grounded, never fully one with ourselves, so as to allow for such full disclosure. "[T]he perceiving subject," Kevin Hart says, "is unable . . . to coincide exactly with itself. I am never able to say 'I perceive,' only that an other subject, an impersonal 'one,' perceives in me. The subject of experience is divided, then, as is the object of experience."[24] The origin has always already slipped. Merleau-Ponty does not betray a longing for a lost origin. David Levin's 1989 work on "aurality" brilliantly demonstrates what Merleau-Ponty himself had indicated in the last chapter of the unfinished *The Visible and the Invisible*—namely, that his thought was moving in the direction of nonduality. Loss of unity or the prospect of unity does not foreclose on nonduality; in fact, it is the precondition for it.

In this sense, what appears as a limitation or failure (one has, after all, to give up on the idea of unity) is also the very condition that reminds us of the limitations of conceptuality and of what is beyond it. It is therefore this very split that reminds us of the precognitive, prediscursive element of experience: "Phenomenology," Kevin Hart reminds us, "does not attempt to render experience fully explicit to consciousness, but to make us aware of a pre-reflective dimension of experience."[25] But because we are embodied, temporal, thinking beings, this prereflective dimension can never be fully present: in order to allow for the possibility of *presence* of the prereflective dimension, one needs to allow for the hypothesis of the self-grounding, unified subject. At the moment in which the subject grounds itself in the cogito and then bases its experience of something on the certainty of the cogito (I cannot be sure of the existence of fire, but I can be sure of my own sensation of heat and light) the prereflective dimension evaporates. The experience of fire is turned instead into the thought of the experience of fire, into a representation of fire. There is a perpetual reflective reminder of the prereflective. In this sense Derrida is the prototypical phenomenologist.

I think it helpful to dwell here on the relationship between the "positive" and the "negative" interpretations of this rift in consciousness, which forms an aporia in Beckett's art: yes, there is the desire to present the unnamable, but only when we give up the quest and stop trying to present it does it finally allow itself to be presented (in Nancy's sense)— namely, as unpresentable. The "negative" rift is produced and maintained by the teleological quest to unify the subject with itself and with the object. This rift functions by virtue of the assumption that a fully grounded subjectivity or consciousness exists and that it only happens to be filtered through defective media: language or conceptuality. This is the Romantic quest that believes an undivided consciousness can be made fully present and recovered from behind the corrupted veils of language if only one tries hard enough. The assumption is that as soon as consciousness is fully grounded the subject will perceive no duality between itself and the surrounding world, while, in fact, it is this quest for groundedness that perpetuates the very split it seeks to abolish. Although this rift goes along with a rift in subjectivity itself, it is best imagined in spatial terms, as a division between subject and object, because that is where it manifests itself existentially and because the quest motif is also a spatial metaphor.

The (positive) acceptance of the rift, the nonwill that "enables" deification and enlightenment, stems from an awareness that the quest for unity is misguided. There is no fully grounded subjectivity, the grounding origin always out of reach, so that the only thing art can hope to accomplish is to hold the two sides—the pursuit of conceptual content and the preconceptual trace, the always receding origin of the fully grounded immediacy of experience—together in a passing aporia. It is out of an awareness of this impossibility of immediacy and groundedness that (expressionless) art must spring. The artist must give up the quest for groundedness and instead take the work of art to its own discursive, dialectical limits, so that from there it will open out into the possibility of thinking the impossible. Rather than trying to determine whether there is "something or nothing" behind the veil of language, Beckett's work generates the conditions for experiencing it. At this moment the subject/object duality produced by the quest falls away, not into a fusion of subject and object, but into the aporia of a full-fledged nonduality.

■   It needs to be shown that *Film* is, in fact, an exploration of Beckettian ideas, not an illustration of Bishop Berkeley's philosophy or its shortcomings. The premise of *Film* is *esse est percipi*, but the work is not a mere illustration of Berkeleian philosophy (as critics unanimously recognize), nor is it a critique or an artistic assessment of Berkeley's philosophy of perception, as Sylvie Debevec Henning seems to think. Henning knows that Beckett is not merely regurgitating Berkeley's ideas, but to her he is nonetheless trying systematically to work through Berkeley's main thesis: "I shall suggest, therefore, that Beckett is taking Berkeley seriously in *Film* in order to point up the weak spot in his generally fascinating work."[26] And in keeping with her thesis she concludes that Beckett's critique centers on Berkeley's failure to account for self-perception.[27]

There are two main reasons why I think that to assume such a straightforward relationship between Beckett and Berkeley is mistaken. First is the qualification with which Beckett presents *esse est percipi* as the governing principle of *Film:* "No truth value attaches to above, regarded as of merely structural and dramatic convenience" (*SP* 163). Henning fails to grasp the extent to which this disclaimer functions as a distancing device between Beckett and Berkeley. It does not merely mean that the dictum does not represent a philosophical truth and is thus open to critique. Rather, Beckett does not *necessarily* propose that Being resides in any way in being perceived—neither in Berkeley's understanding of the process nor in the interpretive variations it undergoes in Beckett's treatment of it. Rather, *esse est percipi* becomes a guiding line that is explored in a number of different directions. It yields insights precisely by allowing different approaches to coexist and fertilize one another: there is, for example, Berkeley's approach as well as the one dramatized in *Film*, which Beckett presents no more as philosophical truth than Berkeley's position, and finally the one that emerges as a result of the film's irony.

It is important to reckon with the film's comic atmosphere and ironic perspective. The notes to *Film* point out the climate of the film as "comic and unreal. O should invite laughter throughout by his way of moving" (*SP* 163). And then later: "[O] storms along in comic foundered precipitancy" (*SP* 164). It is thus impossible to expect O and E to dramatize a tenable philosophical position. They might well dramatize a perceptual (and lived) reality, but not a considered position that might seriously be put forth in response to a philosophical challenge—*esse est percipi*—unless Beckett were to descend into sarcasm; but sarcasm (apart from being out of character for Beckett) is not the tone of the film. We are encountering a familiar mechanism in Beckett's work: gentle humor and irony ask us to move beyond what the work shows to what it implies. Beckett's "disclaimer" asks the viewer to exercise critical judgment with respect to the form and content of the film before leaping to categories of philosophical truth.

Second, it makes little sense to criticize Berkeley for not having taken into account a category (self-perception) that is by virtue of his premise impossible in his system. For Berkeley the self is the underlying unity that perceives sense data. It cannot itself be an object of perception, and as such the self in Berkeley cannot be split into two halves. The reason for this indivisibility lies, of course, in the existence of God; indeed, Berkeley meant his theory to operate, among other things, as a proof of God's existence. God is the guarantor of the veracity of all sense ideas given in perception. God cannot be characterized as "extraneous" to the self's perception because it is on him that all of the self's perception fundamentally depends. Although Berkeley is a modern to whom the horizontal division of the world into perceiving subject and perceived object is familiar, he does not abandon the theological perspective.

The world of *Film*, however, is structured entirely secularly. It is only with this horizontal presupposition that God's perception of the self can be objectified and regarded as extraneous that O can rip the image of God the Father off the wall in order to reach a state in which "[a]ll extraneous perception [is] suppressed" (*SP* 163). It is as if Beckett wants deliberately to oppose to the verticality of Berkeley's perspective an exclusively horizontal one to show where the excesses of modern subjectivist philosophy will lead. Because there is no overarching, omniscient perspective to guarantee the subject's perceptions, the subject now has to provide this check itself and to find itself constantly beside itself, distancing itself from its own perceptions in order to dissect them.

In Berkeley, sense perception has truth value. Berkeley's is an immaterialism: an object's existence independent of perception has no meaning for him. But this does not open the door to a subject-centered free-for-all. Berkeley denies the dichotomy of perception and independent object, but he does not proclaim a subjectivism or idealism. This is rather what twenty-first-century subjectivists construct out of his theory because our subjectivism implies on the other side a transparent objective reality. For Berkeley, however, perception *is* truth, guaranteed by divine authority—there is no gap. Because this authority is missing in the picture *Film* presents, checks on the veracity of perception can never be conclusive because they are performed by a subjective, immanent, and limited agency. The self that in Berkeley was the indivisible ground of all perception is now split, constantly checking up on itself, constantly beside himself in an endless chase: "objectified in the form of a nervous fugitive."[28]

Self-perception, then, is possible only because the self is capable of perceiving itself as distinct from objects, and therefore to perceive itself as object. In the secular world, it has often been pointed out, the subject becomes the new reference point in the place of God, applying its own categories and measures to the world that lies objectified before it, so that even God ends up being made after its own image. The result can only be a gross caricature: a sloppy cartoon figure with bulging eyes carelessly plastered to a wall.

It is, of course, not unusual for human beings to make themselves images of their God, in an idolatrous way (by ignoring the apophatic moment) but also in an iconic way: icons are intrinsic parts especially of Orthodox worship. They depict scenes from Scripture, portraits of the saints, the Mother of God, or Christ himself, and they do so in a nonrepresentational way. What matters in iconography is the true, as it were, not the real. This truth does not reside in the materiality of the icon, in its wood or color or gold, if such is used. The icon does not materially participate in the holiness of the saints or the divine nature of Christ. Therefore, one does not worship icons, one venerates them; and one does not venerate the materiality of them, but the sanctity of the prototype depicted in them. In this sense, the icon remains an image, a copy of a prototype and not the "original."

And yet, as St. Theodore made clear, the icon as image is part and parcel of the thing itself: it is of the same order, not subservient or inferior to it. There is no copy and original, no logic of representation or mimesis. In iconography, one is always at the root of the other. There is the same originary doubling that we find in *Film* and at the basis of all of Beckett's art. As art (which it is not) iconography is *Darstellung*, not *Vorstellung*.[29] Icons of Christ, however nonrepresentational, are still depictions of God, but only of the incarnate God, that is of the shape in which God himself chose to enter the representational realm. The incarnation of Christ is the precondition for making icons, and, in fact, to deny the validity of icons would be to deny the incarnation of Christ. However, under no circumstances is it permissible to make an image of God the Father. Beckett makes his point by doing just that. The car- toonlike image on the wall in *Film* is an image of God the Father, but the caricature is not blasphemous. It is a statement of fact since any image of the transcendent God can only be a caricature and, second, the idola- trous image is implicit in the dualist premise *Film* investigates. We con- struct according to our own parameters what we see objectified be- fore us.

Thus, Henning is mistaken to assume that Beckett takes us along a Berkeleian trajectory and only moves into a world without God when the print of God the Father is torn from the wall.[30] *Film* was a godless universe all along; it is based on a thoroughly postmodern premise, the split of the subject. Similarly, Beckett never really takes "Berkeley at his word," as Henning suggests.[31] He does not explore the Berkeleian prem- ise until he can conclusively prove its weak spots. Rather, he starts from a premise that is diametrically opposed to Berkeley's and adopts Berke- ley's dictum so that he can explore the weak spots of the premise drama- tized by *Film*, which emerge with greater clarity when contrasted with Berkeley's position.

The postmodern premise of Beckett's endeavor in *Film* emerges with force when *Film* is seen foremost as genre critique: it is about "the essence of cinema," Federman thinks.[32] The identification of one of the characters (or half a character) with the eye of the camera emphasizes the role of the camera in both making and viewing films. Sidney Fesh- bach emphasizes that the working title of the film was, in fact, "The Eye."[33] By personalizing the camera Beckett makes it impossible for the viewer to slip into the engrained habit of treating it as an impersonal and impartial medium, a mere recording device. The presence of a cam- era actively alters a sequence of events. The camera becomes a character, whose doings and motivations are just as questionable as those of the other characters with whom the audience is accustomed to dealing in a detached way.

Film uses the eye of the camera for an allegorical thematization of the ontological and epistemological implications of a phenomenology of (visual) perception. Through its personification of the camera, *Film* makes the connection between a critique of seeing and a critique of the subject as ontological foundation unmistakably clear. In this way, the camera becomes less an instrument of filmmaking than a symbol of the splits and dualities that can lurk in visual perception. Indeed, *Film* seems to say, a truly "centered" subjectivity based on the dualist model of subject and object is an illusion.

But *Film* does not call for a simple resolution of the dualism into a fusion of subject and object. In the final "showdown" (when E finally emerges from behind O and leaves the "angle of immunity," that is, the 45° within which O is oblivious to E's presence) no merger between the two halves of the protagonist takes place. Instead, face-to-face with E, the characteristic look indicating acute "agony of perceivedness" comes over O before he covers his eyes with his hands because, ironically, not to see is the only way to evade the agony of being seen. "Agony of perceivedness" is not least the agony of perceiving oneself perceived.

At this point critics tend to say that eventually the split protagonist cannot evade self-perception and *Film* becomes yet another instance of what is seen as Beckett's all-pervasive "aesthetics of failure." Henning praises Beckett for not succumbing to the temptation of the uncorrupted space of union between O and E because the possibility of union would have, she thinks, aligned Beckett with a tradition of what she characterizes as "conventional" thought, and with that tradition Beckett is usually incompatible. Union of O and E "depends on the assumption that a realm of essential identity exists from which man is barred by his corrupted nature, a thoroughly traditional metaphysical assumption. If this were the case, then Beckett would appear to share some of the very conventional aspirations of those very conventional thinkers with whom he is usually completely at odds."[34] Henning takes the liberty of dismissing the wisdom of all religious traditions of spiritual illumination as utterly conventional. But let us not take issue with this facetious point. Henning reveals a rather conventional attitude toward theology. In the jaded world of nihilist postmodernism any positing of an uncorrupted space is seen as conventional. *Film* doesn't allow for union not because the uncorrupted, incorruptible space beyond the fallenness of human creatures does not exist (generally or in Beckett), but precisely because the emphasis of *Film* is on perception, that is, on the realm of representation, the very realm of human "corruption" in which essential identity is impossible.

For Henning, the failed union of E and O keeps Beckett reassuringly in the camp of secularism and nihilism. Yet against the majority of critical consensus it can be argued that it is Beckett's very preoccupation with failure that lifts him *out of* the realm of nihilism and secularism: he dramatizes not so much the failure of attempting to express the Ineffable in language, but rather the presentation of the unpresentable as unpresentable. He bids farewell to the Romantic idea of being able to say the Ineffable, and as such he is no longer concerned with the perpetual failure that this undertaking necessarily produces. In fact, Beckett no longer sees it as a failure. Failure in this sense becomes a prerequisite for success.

■ The idea of failure in Beckett's artistic theory needs reevaluation. "Failure" in its conventional teleological interpretation of not achieving a goal becomes meaningless. With its teleological implications the term "failure" belongs to the realm of rationality. What fails in Beckett's art, or, more to the point, what *explodes* in Beckett's art, are the rational categories incapable of containing the phenomenon, in this case the work of art. The failure Beckett tries to "perfect" ("No matter. Try again. Fail again. Fail better." [*WW* 89]) is the failure to conform to the teleological models that measure failure. "Failing better" is to devise a form of literary discourse that undermines itself increasingly successfully. It is a discourse that pushes oppositional structures to their limits until they are exhausted and forced into aporetic structures of undecidability. And through this aporetic process something is brought into "existence" that does not conform to rational categories, but exceeds them.

Marion grasps this paradox of aesthetic experience under the category of the "idol." He does not mean to suggest that all aesthetic experience is idolatrous. Rather, the name "idol" distinguishes the aesthetic from the icon, insofar as the aesthetic generates its radiance in itself and keeps it "to itself," without reference to a divine prototype. In other words, when we accept unfulfilled intention and limited intuition as basic phenomenological principles, we need to be aware that they are basic principles only from a subject-centered perspective. A shift to the saturated givenness of the aesthetic phenomenon, as Marion conceives of it, implies a reevaluation of subjectivity that acknowledges the sub-

ject's cognitive limitations. "With the name *witness*," which Marion substitutes for "subject," "we must understand a subjectivity stripped of the
characteristics that gave it transcendental rank. . . . Constituted and no
longer constituting, the witness no longer enacts synthesis or constitution."[35] Nonetheless, the saturated phenomenon remains entirely consistent with a phenomenological horizon because it does not alter the
epistemological limitations of the subject. The horizon remains in place.
The subject still does not experience these phenomena in their fullness,
but rather acknowledges the incomprehensible existence of something
that surpasses its deficient categories. The failure of rational thought
and subject-centered teleology in Beckett's work is hence a "success" insofar as it sees its limitations and opens the subject beyond them. The
subject becomes a "witness" or the "gifted."

Film is often seen as going round in circles. It begins and ends with
a close-up of what critics like to call "Keaton's reptilic eye" (recalling the
film's working title and its central theme of visual perception). Union
between O and E is never accomplished and therefore no resolution is
achieved: E is as far from his goal at the end as he was at the start. In
short, the film is, once again, about failure. There can be no doubt that
the frame of Keaton's reptilic eye introduces an element of circularity
into what has so far been an entirely linear structure of pursuit. But is
the image the reader encounters at the end really the same as the one at
the beginning? Critics have latched on too readily to a conventional idea
of failure and have proceeded to read Beckett's work as being single-
mindedly preoccupied with what appears as a notional cluster of the inevitability of suffering and failing. As a result, Beckett's work has been
seen as negative and pessimistic—an idea he has steadfastly rejected.[36]

It is likely that the character(s) in the film, O and E, would resume
their old routine on the next roll of film and plod along the same old
route in the quest for unity. But in the viewer's experience of the work
the final image has changed, although it is the same as the opening. If
the film has successfully gotten its "message" across, the viewer will
approach the opening images in a different frame of mind, aware of the
problematic nature of the quest—so, for the viewer at least, a learning
process and on that basis an exit from the circularity of the situation
is possible.

On his way to leading the reader to this realization, Beckett again
explores limits: of the respective genre in which he works, of language

and discourse, and of human conceptuality. An exploration of limits brings not only newfound freedom, but also an experience of one's own limits because it implies a point at which one's own subjectivity ends. In the exploration of limits one meets, implicitly, one's Other. The work of art itself becomes this Other that the subject turned witness or receiver encounters and experiences as a saturated phenomenon.

The word "experience" is itself an ambivalent term. In German there are two words for it: *Erfahrung* and the newer word *Erlebnis*, the first appearance of which Gadamer traces back to one of Hegel's letters.[37] If Gadamer is right, then the word *Erlebnis* would have risen to public consciousness (as a secondary formation of the older verb *erleben*) at the height of the apotheosis of the subject when one had not yet lost faith in all-encompassing philosophical systems. It is hardly a coincidence that *Erlebnis* denotes an inner experience of a specific person (the person who lived through the experience) and the content of the experience remains imprinted on his or her mind. *Erlebnis* is a stable affair: one lived through and referred back to as a concluded affair that *confirms* one's subjectivity. The central position of the subject in *Erlebnis* ensures that perceptions are integrated into a meaningful whole that is then available in the hermeneutic process of the production of meaning.

Erfahrung, on the other hand, is an experiential and experimental journey one undertakes: *fahren* means "to travel." Kevin Hart points out that this sense of experience preserves in its own way the Latin root of the English word "experience": *experiri*, which means "'to undertake', 'to attempt', 'to make trial of.'"[38] He also points out that *experiri* contains within it *peri*, "from which we get peril," and he concludes that *Erfahrung* "keeps in play a notion of experience as a setting at risk, a voyage that may well involve danger."[39] *Erfahrung* is not at all stable. It is experience that challenges a person's cherished beliefs and conceptions; it is a danger to the stability of the subject.

I cannot help but think of O here, who literally ventures out into the world of agony and peril, the unity and stability of his identity at stake. But the analogy fails because O is really on the run from *Erfahrung*. He is a panicked fugitive, not someone who confronts the challenges of his experience. The better image is the viewer's journey, the journey on which Beckett takes his audience, and, of course, Beckett's own in the perilous undertaking of creating an absolutely irreducible discourse—

an experiment (the French *expérience* means "experience" and "experiment") that upsets stable hermeneutic categories. The journeys one undertakes in experiencing Beckett's work are never journeys to a place a long way away. They are circular. We end up where we started out: with Didi and Gogo underneath the tree, in Moran's house, in Murphy's chair, or at the end of one cycle of Mouth's ramblings. The journey does not lead to a transcendent place, away from the brokenness of the world. And yet the place to which the reader or spectator returns is changed—*Erfahrung* ensures that it is not the same place though outwardly it is.

Beckett's art is an art of *Erfahrung*. It embarks on the perilous journey of an exploration of limits. Beckett's journey, therefore, is not primarily inward. It is, of course, intensely inward, but it is not *Erlebnis*, that is, it is not subject centered. Rather it contests a conventionally centered subjectivity. It is a meeting or a confrontation with an Other in which it explores and exhausts that opposition dialectically in a process of reduction until the opposition turns into an undecidability. With regard to death as the ultimate, defining experience we encounter again the Blanchotian aporia of between death as possibility and as impossibility, or of that which generates meaning and that which continuously evades any meaning. In writing or in literature the subject (as constituted meaningfully by the world of possibility) encounters the neutral, which has no meaning as possibility, but contests such meaning and finds itself outside the distinction of possibility and impossibility.[40]

Such a conception of *Erfahrung* as undoing *Erlebnis* is a significant reinterpretation of the philosophical tradition in which the objective externality of *Erfahrung* has dominantly been seen as deferential to the direct immediacy of *Erlebnis*. Kant's conception of *Erfahrung*, in the throes of the Enlightenment, focuses so much on the objectivity of the categories of experience that the human being is reduced merely to synthesizing this objectivity. Human experience becomes a scientific processor. "The categories, with the help of their underlying basis, 'the transcendental unity of apperception,' mechanistically synthesize sensations received from a mechanistic natural world to produce a concept of experience which is predictably mechanistic in turn," Richard Wolin observes.[41] Notably the early Walter Benjamin took issue with this underappreciated idea of *Erfahrung* and developed out of it a conception of "total experience," not the particularized ideal of scientific experience. To him the exercise of categorizing experience makes a unified, higher conception of experience, which would also allow for religious experience, impossible. In fact, religious experience holds a privileged position for Benjamin because it is able to transcend the dichotomy of subject and object that is implicit in subjective *Erlebnis* and objective *Erfahrung*. Total experience approaches counter-experience.

What, then, does the encounter with the Other in *Erfahrung* mean for the status of transcendence in Beckett's art? Beckett's analysis is immanent, but it retains the structures of transcendence. Beckett's observations on language and on the nature of the dire human condition always evoke a limit and a beyond. Even his German letter to Axel Kaun, in which he speaks of language as a veil to be torn to reach the things (or the nothing) behind it, evokes a boundary beyond which there is something else. He is uncertain merely of what he will find there, but the basic pattern of transcendence is unaffected by this. A notion of transcendence is also implicit in what Beckett told Tom Driver about the extent of human misery and confusion: "The only chance of renovation is to open our eyes and see the mess. It is not a mess you can make sense of."[42] "The mess," in other words, can be transcended—there is hope of renovation—but in order to do so we need first to acknowledge its existence and, second, see it as being of our own production. This is a central aspect of Beckett's outlook on human misery and suffering that the (pseudo) existentialist critics prefer to ignore, but one that Driver articulates fully as early as 1961. Esslin and his followers liked to stress what they saw as the inescapability of suffering: Godot never comes; Didi and Gogo will continue their monotonous existence of empty hours and night-time beatings and are indeed never delivered from their suffering by an external power. However, they will continue only for as long as they agree to play their parts in the play, for as long as they do not acknowledge themselves as creators, perpetrators, and perpetuators of their own situations. Then they give their salvation a chance. Driver poignantly concludes his reflections on his meeting with Beckett: "The walls that surround the characters of Beckett's plays are not walls that nature and history have built irrespective of the decisions of men. They are the walls of one's own attitude towards his situation. The plays are themselves evidence of a human capacity to see one's situation and by that very fact to transcend it."[43]

Beckett's position with respect to transcendence is comparable to Derrida's, who also insists on an immanent point of view but does so within a frame of reference that is structured toward a transcendent. His evocation of the "closure of metaphysics" itself implies another space that opens up beyond metaphysics or that takes its place. Deconstruction is structured like a messianic religion around a longing for the transcendent that is never fulfilled. Even Christianity, where the Messiah has already arrived, does not let go of it but instead invokes a Second Coming. *Différance*, as semi-transcendent, is situated "outside" the cycle of deconstructions, but in a peculiar way. It cannot be deconstructed because it does not present conceptual knowledge, so one cannot say that *différance* is "inside" because everything that exists is potentially subject to deconstruction. It does not come with a context that would allow us to fit it into our cognitive patterns. It is never really present. So, is *différance* immanent or transcendent? It is, of course, both and neither, but it nonetheless shares an important characteristic with transcendence, its unattainability. Humans can never "have" God because "owning" him would mean containing him, at which point he would cease to be God and become a human concept. Transcendence is by definition elusive—it is a trace. Indeed, Derrida adopts the idea of the messianic as a further "incarnation" of the aporetic structure of *différance*. Messianic religions expect their members to live in vigilance, as if the Messiah were to come tomorrow, but without *expecting* Him to come. Their lives are spent in anticipation of and preparation for the coming of the Messiah, but at the same time that defining orientation disappears with his coming. Structurally, the Messiah must not come, hence the Second Coming. It is paradoxically transcendence that keeps the cycle of deconstructions moving.

But the messianic or apocalyptic impulse in deconstruction, as in Beckett, is no license to wallow in expectant passivity. Deconstruction is always motivated by the desire to go where one cannot go, to disarm the powers of instrumentalist reason by exposing its dualisms as aporias, and, once "the way of knowledge has been blocked," to follow "the imperative of *doing* the truth, *facere veritatem*, which is what deconstruction is all about. To put it all in a very condensed formulation, in deconstruction, the very conditions under which something is impossible, is declared impossible by what calls itself 'the light of reason' or 'philosophy,' are likewise and especially the conditions of possibility. Being impossible is what ignites our passion, gets us off dead center, and drives our desire to make it happen."[44] In this sense, deconstruction is indeed, as John Caputo and Michael Scanlon say, structured like a religion.[45] Both are structured toward something just out of reach of the rational mind. Faith begins where knowledge fails. Because *différance* transcends the structures of the rational mind, refuses to be compartmentalized and to remain a purely intellectual idea, Derrida, like Adorno, resorts to the rhetoric of experience—*doing* the truth—to elucidate its impact. "For Derrida," Caputo and Scanlon write, "the experience of the impossible represents the least bad definition of deconstruction."[46] This experience does not amount to anything more clear than the confusing, boundary and definition shattering tumble into an aporia, but this tumble means that at this moment the boundaries of intellectual cognition are transgressed into the experiential. It is necessary to *live* the aporia. Likewise, once Beckett has exposed the dead ends and absurdities into which his characters' blind adherence to reason (Watt, Murphy, Molloy) or their inability to awaken to the impact of their own decisions (Didi and Gogo) has lead them, the imperative for us as audience is not to assume the horizon of human suffering and blindness to be insurmountable, untranscendable (and thus to limit our insight to that of the characters'), but to use our privileged insight and live accordingly.

If, then, art as *Erfahrung* is an exploration of limits and if the latter necessarily involves danger because it breaks the horizons of that place we have come to expect and in which we feel comfortable, then one would expect that it also, sometimes, involves failure. This is especially so since from the Derridean point of view "failure" is written into the picture because it is what maintains the longing for the "wholly other," the basic structure of religion. Within the horizon of instrumental, teleological reason this "failure" remains a failure, not least because it is the failure *of* instrumental reason. Otherwise, it is a success. Failure as failure of instrumental reason is central not only for Beckett and Derrida, but also for Adorno. And for Adorno, as for Beckett, aesthetic experience is a matter of *Erfahrung*, not *Erlebnis*. Aesthetic experience is the encounter of something separate and different from the experiencing subject. The subject encounters its Other, and thereby its own finitude. But what happens in this encounter? The central term in Adorno's aesthetic theory is *Erschütterung*: an upheaval that rocks the subject to its foundations because the Other—in this case the work of art—will overwhelmingly refuse to be pigeonholed by the categories according to which a human being in the grip of the dialectic of Enlightenment will structure her world, the categories of reason. This upheaval is the only hope of freedom from the dialectic of Enlightenment because in it the subject has to give in to nature rather than to dominate it. (Adorno tends to use the term "nature" for anything that defies instrumental reason.) *Erschütterung*, Adorno emphasizes, is thus diametrically opposed to *Erlebnis* because it is not based on satisfaction of the ego. Rather, it is an instance of the "liquidation of the ego."[47] An emotional response to art is hence not *Erschütterung* because what breaks through in the emotional response is not the objectivity, or truth, of the work of art, but an otherwise suppressed subjectivity. Emotion is a confirmation of subjectivity, not its demise.[48]

However, although the subject encounters something beyond itself and is thoroughly rattled by it, *Erschütterung* remains an entirely subjective category. *Erschütterung* is not the breakthrough of an objectivity into the subjective realm against the subject's will, as it were. Rather, the subject actively invites something into its realm that it then cannot process. In other words, the beginnings for aesthetic experience are always made in the subject, and no one but the subject can experience its own *Erschütterung*: aesthetic experience, according to Adorno, is firmly rooted in the subject.

For Adorno, this must be the case because there is no escape from the dialectic of Enlightenment. There can be no transcending its corkscrew mechanism and hence no positive experience of an Other, or of a transcendent reality. As a result, the experience of the Other in aesthetic experience is solely that of "a border and a beyond."[49] The subject in *Erschütterung* has only a *negative* experience of an objectivity that in its quiddity remains beyond the subject's grasp. And this failure to grasp the object in its essence is the very definition of aesthetic *Erfahrung*— without it there would be no *Erschütterung*. Gunnar Hindrichs saliently points out that failure to grasp the object does not imply that any *attempt* to grasp it becomes pointless and superfluous. The attempt to grasp and define is a necessary precondition for aesthetic experience because it is

precisely the failure to grasp and define the aesthetic object that constitutes its experience.[50] Marion's counter-experience also involves an endless hermeneutic circle. There is no aesthetic experience without failure.
Aesthetic experience *is* failure. While the idea of *Erschütterung* is very
useful with a view to Beckett's critique of reason, Marion's phenomenology is more rigorously able to explain how one is to imagine such an
erschüttertes subject—namely, as witness or receiver.

Adorno makes clear that failure need not be seen as the seal to the
misery of everlasting sameness beyond hope of salvation. Indeed, for
him, it is failure that orients us toward the transcendent. It makes us
aware of a transcendent without giving us the ability to say what it is. It
is true that there is no transcendence in Adorno, just as there is none
in Derrida. But Adorno, like Derrida, holds on to the idea of transcendence, although as a stance it does not exist for him.[51] Otherwise, as Hindrichs points out and Adorno knows, philosophy would become a socially
irresponsible endeavor. It would abandon human beings to the quagmire
of their own existences without offering any incentive for responsible
living. If the dialectic of Enlightenment is an inescapable, escalating spiral anyway, why bother to try and make a difference? (Here I find Adorno's position implausible. Either the dialectic is inescapable—then why
bother with an idea of transcendence, however "negatively" defined; or
it is not—in which case the ability to analyze the dialectic rationally, as
Adorno is doing, would mean that by rational means we can situate ourselves sufficiently outside the dialectic to be able to see it clearly. Thus it
should be possible to defeat the dialectic by its own means, and this, in
turn, would mean that positive experience of the transcendent must be
possible because the dialectic would cease to be the only horizon.) Aesthetic experience is transcendence without transcendence for Adorno
because in it transcendence is exclusively negative and does not offer a
positive ground outside the subjectivity.

Beckett's worldview is a thoroughly immanent one; there is no certainty of the transcendent dimension. But at the same time his work is
permeated by an insistent gesture toward the transcendent. Its fundamentally metaphoric structure, the aporetic nature of its prose, the
Zen-inspired balance of his stage compositions all point toward a transcendence—an "immanent transcendence," as in the case of Zen, that is
never reached, possessed, let alone represented. "Immanent transcen-

dence" is not to imply the modern sense of transcendent subjectivity, but
to evoke linguistically the nondual aporetic moment in which the duality
between transcendence and immanence disappears. Jean Wahl's distinction between transascendence and transdescendence is a useful one. At
the level of the transcendental, in the depths of the text rather than
above it, Beckett performs a similarly irreducible, aporetic space as fully
apophatic discourse for which the theological transcendent is a given.

■   Eventually, Beckett, like Derrida and Adorno, resorts to the immediacy of experience, or rather counter-experience, as a purveyor of that
which cannot be represented in language. Beckett holds painting in especially high regard for its ability to bypass the mediation of language.
In an homage to Jack Yeats, for example, he says: "In images of such
breathless immediacy as these there is no occasion, no time given, no
room left, for the lenitive of comment" (*D* 149). The immediacy of painting is able to rock—*erschüttern*—the subject's rational constitution in
language, to overwhelm the dichotomy of constituting subject and alienated object on which the subject ordinarily builds its interactions with
the world. The inadequate term "immediacy of experience" must not be
seen as part of a rhetoric of a centered, constituting subject. The center
of gravity shifts from the subject to phenomenal givenness. It can appear as if Beckett ascribes greater proximity to an origin to painting.
Painting lacks the mediation of language and is thus able to convey a
more immediate reality. In *The Painted Word*, Lois Oppenheim argues
that Beckett ascribes an ontological value to painting and to seeing
itself. At a crucial yet superficially argued stage in her argument she
draws parallels between Beckett's attitude to painting and Heidegger's
argument in "The Origin of the Work of Art," in which he argues the
unveiling of Being at the moment of the apprehension of the work of art.
She hastily concludes that "[s]o, too, Beckett situates art on the level of
the primordial apprehension of the real."[52]

There are at least two problems with equating Beckett's position
with Heidegger's in this way. First, Heidegger argues that the truth of
the thing itself is imparted in the work of art. This can be construed as
a metaphysical argument for which Beckett would have little patience:
Oppenheim herself assumes that Beckett's point of view on aesthetics is

not so much aesthetical as anaesthetical insofar as Beckett will not allow himself to be pinned down to a coherent set of aesthetic assumptions. Second, Heidegger's argument is not specific or limited to the visual. For him poetry, too, has the potential to open our thinking to the unconcealment of Being. For Beckett painting is closer to an origin only insofar as the painting as Idol in Marion's sense facilitates a shift to givenness so that the self-giving phenomenon becomes *its own* origin, as givenness, without the transcendental determinations of objectness or being. Counter-experience itself warrants the existence of saturated phenomena as a new non-Husserlian class of phenomena.

In this sense, Oppenheim's point cannot be dismissed. The philosophical assumptions implicit (at least in the Western tradition) in the perceptual process of seeing clearly pose the most important problem for Beckett—one that, could it be resolved, would configure the human condition differently. Unresolved, it might even itself be the cause of the human condition. Again and again he struggles to overcome the Cartesian dualisms epitomized most poignantly by the process of seeing: *Catastrophe* deals most explicitly with the objectification and the power relations that can be implicit in seeing. *Film* continues this investigation on more of a philosophical than political level. With the wordless *Quad* Beckett's intensely visual art reaches its zenith, and in the "Three Dialogues" he attempts to lay the theoretical foundations for an entirely "objectless" and "expressionless" (visual) art, one not based on the autonomy of the work of art as an object of artistic expression, that is, a work of art not determined by a constituting subject. Interestingly, for Beckett the visual paradigm at once illustrates the dualism to be overcome and harbors the possibility of overcoming it. The work of art lies objectified before the beholder, but the immediate intensity of the visual image as givenness has the power to melt the dualism. Oppenheim summarizes that "[Beckett] cannot endure the defining relation of critic to art any more than he could 'the definition of the artist as one who never ceases to be *in front of.*'"[53]

In *Le Monde et le Pantalon* Beckett again speaks of the immediacy of painting, which again he sees ideally realized in the art of Bram van Velde. In van Velde he encounters a will to perceive that is so exclusively and overwhelmingly pictorial that we with our "murmuring reflections" (*MP* 25), our whispering rational thought, have trouble comprehending it, which is only possible by drawing it back into a syntactic succession, a "ronde syntaxique" (*MP* 25)—by, in other words, pulling it back into time (*MP* 25), from which it had already freed itself. The immediacy of van Velde's art manages to free the object—the painting—from the constraints of the subject–object duality in which it is commonly regarded, so that in its immediacy it is possible to see "the thing for itself," to see the thing "strictly as it is" (*MP* 28)—the "pure object" (*MP* 28), yet not really an object because not reified by the beholder or by its context. Van Velde, according to Beckett, presents "the immobile thing in emptiness" (*MP* 28), and he does so not merely by "wanting to stop time through representing it" (*MP* 27), as the rest of painting throughout the history of art has tried to do, but by doing more: by lifting it "out of time," as it were, insofar as our perception of time as a teleological arrow depends on a perceptional dualism. In order for our conventional perception of time as a syntactic succession to disappear, the dualism has to disappear. And yet we are still fallen beings. The reduction is necessarily incomplete because of our inherence in the world, in nature, and nirvana does not last. After the enlightenment of nonduality we have to continue our embodied existence and return to the world to teach others. In other words, the motionless moment van Velde depicts is still a moment in time, we are still fallen and thus still inside time . . . we just went *into* Sacré-Coeur in order not to see it anymore.[54]

Beckett compares and contrasts this favored approach of Bram van Velde with that of Geer van Velde, the artist's brother. He argues that although the approaches of the two brothers are in antithetical opposition to each other—so much so that Beckett thinks it best not to expose oneself to both in one day (*MP* 33)—they nonetheless have their roots in the same experience, namely, that of nonduality (*MP* 37). But while Bram van Velde presents the motionless thing in emptiness so immediately as not to allow for the dualism that enables rational thought and "the lenitive of comment," thus presents a moment of no-time, Geer van Velde presents *only* the flow of time. His art is, Beckett surmises, the representation of "the river into which no one steps twice" (*MP* 34). It is nondual because it abolishes the notion of time as a container. David Loy points out that the nondual solution is to realize that objects are not *in* time, but rather *are* time, which consequently implies that they are free from time and in that sense *truly* eternal.[55] There are no unchanging objects caught in time, but rather objects are necessarily temporal. Like-wise, they are not *in* (temporal) space, but they are "what space is doing in that place," as Loy puts it.[56] As a result, there is no dualism and hence no concept of time as reified, teleological flux because there is *only* flux, and therefore no flux, in the same sense in which the color green has no meaning if everything is green. Geer van Velde presents, then, an atti-tude of detachment from the attachments to and reifications of self.

Geer van Velde's approach Beckett likens to literature ("C'est ça, la litérature" [*MP 33*]). If one associates Bram van Velde's approach with the stillness of metaphor and Geer van Velde's approach with the flux of metonymy, one can say that Beckett knows that the two poles, metaphor and metonymy, complement each other toward the same nondual end. Beckett's own preference for Bram's approach would then be due pri-marily to his own artistic development and predilections and hence to the fundamentally metaphorical nature of his art. Whether the flux of metonymy is perceived as nondual flux or as teleological linearity is a matter of perception.

The importance of *Film* lies less in its being a film and more in the opportunity it provides for Beckett to allegorize seeing and knowing it-self. Classical phenomenology and negative theology are based on op-posing principles insofar as phenomenology is in pursuit of knowledge, whereas negative theology aims to guard God's absolute transcendence from the tentacles of human knowledge. But they meet as soon as phe-nomenology has to acknowledge a remainder that consistently evades human knowledge. Adequation remains an ideal. The Ineffable, Hyppo-lite says, is the absolutely singular whose singularity dissolves and turns into the trace at the moment one tries to say it, at the moment of inscrip-tion. No thing, least of all the Ineffable, ever coincides with itself. It is doubled as soon as it enters discourse. And yet the nondual Absolute will not be absent from language, or else it would not be absolute. If lit-erature is the adventure of creating an absolutely irreducible space, as Beckett, Blanchot, and Derrida suggest, and God is unsayable because he is *a se*, and hence absolutely singular, then talking about God and about literature must be apophatic. But negative theology practices this with regard to the transcendent while "apophatic" criticism of literature does so with regard to the transcendental.

Strikingly, there is no indication in *Film* of the enormous saving grace the visual possesses for Beckett. This is precisely where *Film* fails (here in the conventional sense) at its own task of "failing better" by destroying teleological models. It remains a "theoretical" or "analytical" work in the sense that it appeals primarily to the rational faculties. This is also why it falls short in comparison with the majority of Beckett's other works. *Not I* and *Quad* emphasize, in addition to the intellectual challenges they pose, the prerational element or work deliberately at wearing down the audience's rational shield—Beckett, one recalls, wanted *Not I* to work primarily on the audience's nerves, and it is impossible to evade a sense of annoyance at *Quad*. Moreover, the visual images of these plays have the very immediacy Beckett observes in Jack Yeats's pictures.

If *Film* is first of all an analytical work (even if it is extremely self-conscious about being analytical), this is not least due to its metonymic structure. In what way is an audience's reaction to it different from the reaction to Beckett's "more typical," that is, more dominantly metaphorical work? As one would expect, the difference is due largely to its metonymic character. The world of *Film*, its setting, though distorted through O's "comic foundered precipitancy" and his bizarre obsession with eliminating all potential sources of external perception, remains recognizable in its elements. *Film*, like all film, remains in principle imitative of reality: based on previous experience with the world, the viewer is to recognize a street, "about 1929," in a "small factory district" (*SP* 164). Likewise, the house and room that O enters later in the film have a similarly recognizable quality: the viewer has seen hundreds of buildings like it and similar rooms. To increase this sense of recognition, Beckett adds the entirely unwarranted and unnecessary piece of information that the room is that of O's mother (maybe to make sure that the mimetic firmly overrides the bizarre). As if in an awareness that film calls for linearly motivated narrative, Beckett adds this piece of homey detail to help the reader make sense of the proceedings: in the familiar world people generally visit their mother's rooms, never mind that those usually have the mother in them and look rather different from the one Beckett presents to us. Importantly, the reader/viewer can now ascribe a motivation to O's visit to the room; it is possible to fill the recognizable exterior with motivation and hence with metonymic progression.

Beckett's *plays* function the other way around: the settings are antimimetic while at the metaphorical level the characters' predicaments are utterly familiar. (The Voice's loneliness and anger at an alienated world, for instance.)

Throughout *Film*, a mixture of recognizable elements and bizarre elements of alienation spurs the viewer on to generate meaning. These elements are presented metonymically and therefore in such a way as to invite the construction of a cohesive, linear narrative: the street in which the camera first encounters O is recognizable; odd is why the protagonist behaves in such a strange manner. He obviously fears observation or pursuit, but by whom and why? There is no one in sight but the camera. Could he be fleeing from the camera itself? On the sidewalk and in the vestibule, O encounters an elderly couple and an old woman, respectively. Both are recognizable and maybe even familiar types: the couple is "of shabby genteel aspect" (*SP* 165), and the old woman is a small-scale flower seller with a vendor's tray slung around her neck. But both respond to O's, or maybe the camera's, presence with a reaction that is clearly extraordinary: they faint with a look of horror on their faces. Again, the viewer is urged to advance tentative hypotheses as to why this is. Either what the characters see is of such horrible aspect as to induce fainting, or else the mere fact of being the object of perception has that effect on them. If the latter, then what is it about being looked at that is so objectionable? Here the viewer enters into the whole philosophical complex of inquiry surrounding perception and visuality, while using the rest of the film to test their hypotheses: how does *Film* as a narrative try to advance its thesis regarding these questions?

It has often been observed that *Film* is a rediscovery of the roots of the filmic medium: it is a black-and-white minimalist effort that reminds critics of the mood and substance of the experimental films of the 1920s, when film was just emerging and arguably represents the genre in its most genuine form.[57] As a conscious alignment with the aesthetic of the early films Beckett's film is playfully, self-referentially, silent: the only "word" spoken is the admonishing "ssshh" that escapes the woman in the street in her effort to keep her husband from breaking into an even more substantially decorum-breaking scream upon encountering E head-on. The film, then, is silent by choice, not technological limitation, and it makes a point of drawing the viewer's attention to this fact.

Beckett aligns his own project with an effort to return to the essence of the medium. He had read Rudolf Arnheim's writings on film, whose conviction it was that film is "a unique experiment in the visual arts that took place in the first three decades of this century."[58] Thus Raymond Federman concludes that "*Film*, consistent with the Beckettian aesthetic system of destruction and purification, represents an attempt to expose one of the cinema's most flagrant failings today: the exploitation of sound, action, plot, and message to the detriment of the visual image."[59]

As a conscious divergence from the aesthetic of the early filmmakers, however, Beckett does not make extensive use of metaphoric techniques, especially montage.[60] On the level of technique, rather than style, *Film* adopts the extremely metonymic narrative structure of Hollywood and it does this although it is common for experimental films to break up the metonymic, narrative, mimetic nature of film with self-referential devices such as showing the camera on screen to expose the constructed nature of the film, or metaphoric techniques like montage. In this sense, *Film* is not so much a return to an earlier film aesthetic, but more fundamentally a crystallization of those aspects that define the medium: a strong visuality best expressed in the contrastive patterns of black and white and emphasized by the lack of dialogue, as well as a metonymic structure.

Finally, though, *Film*, like any other of Beckett's works, has to be read abstractly in metaphorical terms. No one would take the world that *Film* portrays to be a copy of the reality they inhabit. At the highest level of abstraction *Film* is most obviously not "about" a "chase" in the same way in which a car chase defines an action movie (namely, mimetically), but rather it invites viewers to read it metaphorically as being an allegorization of seeing and, by extension, of phenomenological apprehension. Beckett resisted allegory, "that glorious double-entry, with every credit in the said account a debit in the meant, and inversely" (*D* 90): "[N]o symbols where none intended," it says at the end of *Watt* (*W* 255). And he discouraged philosophical readings of his works, emphasizing that if his work were reducible to philosophy that is what he would have written. But both of these objections have their roots in something other than a fundamental aversion to allegory. The first is an ironic stab at Beckett's many readers who labor to find significance in even the most insignificant detail—an attempt to combat hero worship. And it is also an effort to retain authorial control, something consistently high on Beckett's list of priorities. The second objection is born out of a concern to preserve the inherent multivalence of literary language: it is no coincidence that Beckett did not choose the univocity of the philosophical text as his venue, but turns rather to a mode of discourse that is, as Derrida recognizes, inherently multivalent, always already under erasure. Derrida's concern is primarily philosophical and therefore he has to situate himself within philosophy and write deconstructively from within metaphysics, while Beckett's priority is not to pick a bone with the philosophical tradition. His is not a stringently argued, linear argument, while at the same time it has consequences for the type(s) of discourse (such as the philosophical) with which it chooses not to interfere. "In the beginning was the pun," says *Murphy* (*M* 65). Beckett situates multivalence and the lack of stable signification and origins at the "center" of what it means to be human. Hence there can be no one-to-one correspondence in Beckett between the allegorical text and what it "stands for"—that would be reductive. Any allegorical reading of Beckett can only be one attempt of many to make sense of a notoriously elusive text.

In the end, then, those critics who criticize *Film* for illustrating a "philosophical truth" have a point. While *Film* is not philosophical discourse—it shares with Beckett's literary works the fact that its points are made in a work of fiction that is automatically under erasure—it departs from Beckett's other work in that it does not appeal to a precognitive element in an experiential way. It posits the existence of this precognitive element analytically, but it does not make it an immediate experiential reality for the viewing audience.[61]

Chapter 7

Conclusion

O does not fuse with E, Mouth's ramblings do not cease, and Beckett's scurrying monks continue methodically along their imaginary paths. The classical phenomenological reduction cannot be complete because of our inherence in the world. We are incarnate, embodied (and fallen) beings, rather than pure spirit or transcendental ego, and hence irrevocably part of the realm of representation. Reflection (by way of thought and language) will always be a secondary activity. Therefore it is equally impossible for us to see a worldly phenomenon in its essence as it is to see the divine in all its radiance—but should that be our aim? We are fabricating a problem, Beckett might say, that has its roots in our need to impose our will on the world and proclaim ourselves to be at its center. When we shift the focus of the reduction from transcendental subjectivity to phenomenological givenness, the subject's intention no longer sets the criteria for what is to give itself and the impossible task disappears.

The subject and the object never coincide with themselves or with each other. As soon as a phenomenon appears to us in experience or in language it is already doubled. It harbors the potential to become a representation, an image of itself. It becomes an object in the observer's gaze and ceases to be the singular thing in and of itself. As soon as we, as subjects, begin to reflect on our experience, as soon as experience becomes the experience of a particular subject, which means that as long as we apply substantialist categories to the content of experience, it, like language, turns into a representation. In counter-experience (as that which is irreducible to the subjective categories of experience) the (objectified) content of experience dissolves together with the subject. It is possible to approach experience from a nonsubstantialist perspective if one allows for a "decentered" subjectivity after the transcendental ego: the witness or the gifted of phenomenological givenness. Then subject and object do not need to coincide with themselves or each other. In counter-experience neither position holds. Rather, counter-experience revels in iconic nonduality.

Likewise, language can become counter-experiential. Merleau-Ponty points out that there is no thought (no reflection) without language. Thought does not exist separately from language and by extension thought is necessarily embodied. Language is the body, not the clothes of thought. Language, thought, or conceptuality cannot be irrevocably dualist because its grammatical building blocks are dualist, because language is always already embodied. Language is like a snake, Nagarjuna suggests: if one grabs it at the wrong end it will bite, become dualist and destructive, and further our spiritual alienation. But this is not necessarily so. Toby Foshay proposes, through Nagarjuna, that language is inherently empty (*sunya*). It will not be harmful if we treat it iconically through a frame of mind that is also *sunya:* "Everything depends on grasping language rightly."[1] Only then can thinker and thought be grasped nondually, as inhabiting one another, rather than as being distinct and separate from one another.

The prereflective origin of cognition, at which the subject would be one with itself, is always already gone and there cannot be any hope of reinstating it in the place of the representation or image. Rather, one is to embrace the originary doubling of language and experience in literature—to run with the challenge of creating, through the double-voicedness of literature, an absolutely irreducible discourse. And to find the way "out" of the dilemma of having to express yet being unable to express adequately by this much more direct and only apparently circuitous route. Apparently it is *The Unnamable* that hammers away relentlessly at the problem of not being able to (re-)present the un(re-)-presentable while simple acceptance of the dilemma seems to avoid the problem. Indeed, Beckett's post-*Unnamable* approach addresses a more fundamental point that tends to go unnoticed because we are too busy hammering away at the dilemma: the dilemma itself is of our own making.

David Loy points out that the Buddhist doctrine of dependent origination would more accurately be described as "nondependent nonorigination" because it describes "not the interaction of realities, but the sequence and juxtaposition of 'appearances'—or what could be called appearances if there were some nonappearance to be contrasted with. What is perhaps the most famous of all Mahayana scriptures, The Diamond Sutra, concludes with a statement that 'all phenomena are like a dream, an illusion, a bubble and a shadow, like dew and lightning.' . . . As soon as we abolish the 'real' world, 'appearance' becomes the only reality."[2] This is no nihilistic, "postmodern" embrace of mere images or simulacra. Rather, the image is shown to be of the same order as the real and our valorization of the real is useless. Thus Loy goes on to explain that for Buddhism "our way of trying to solve a problem turns out to be what maintains the problem. We try to 'peel away' the apparent world to get at the real one [Beckett formulates this tendency in the letter to Axel Kaun], but that dualism between the two is our problematic delusion, which leaves, as the only remaining candidate for the real world, the apparent one—a world whose nature has not been noticed because we have been so concerned to transcend it."[3] The real does not disappear in favor of the apparent or the image. Rather, Buddhism realizes that the very idea of the real maintains a fatal dualism between real and apparent. It does not matter whether that we perceive is "real." The dualism between real and apparent is deconstructed into a nonduality, and nonduality is not unity. The real and the apparent are not the same but whether that nonsameness is dualist or iconic depends on our attitude to it.

In not attempting to transcend the imaginary for the real Beckett foregrounds the decisive characteristic of literature. Literature is by definition doubled. It is always the real and the imaginary at the same time; it says and unsays at the same time, but not every work is as single-minded about foregrounding this aspect as Beckett's. The task is to allow literature to become "real" in the sense of elevating it from the degrading position of the book as social pastime or status symbol and granting it its inherent capacity to question comprehensively and existentially, not of speaking authoritatively within the discourse of the real, the function it has in the utilitarian, result-oriented framework of business. This implies formalism, or rather counterformalism. Beckett empties the book of its content, while Beckett criticism has for the most part busied itself with doggedly reinstating it in one form or another. He becomes more interested in the shape ideas take in language than in their content, but the focus on language must not turn into a reification of the literary object, as it did in formalism. Writing subverts itself and encounters the Outside. Then we—literary practitioners, authors and critics—can become "real" at the very moment we realize that in the semitranscendent Outside the very distinction between the real and the fake does not hold. In Beckett's hands literature becomes a spiritual practice of sorts.

For the late Beckett in particular the image is no longer derivative, as it had been throughout most of Western philosophical and theological history. An image is not to be understood as the copy of an original or the representation of an object. When understood iconically, the original and the image are of the same order, as St. Theodore the Studite pointed out as early as the ninth century in his contribution to the iconoclastic debate. The difference is one of quantity, not of quality. Beckett embraces the image, both painted and theatrical, because he believes in its capacity to give itself immediately, bypassing the mediation and the temporal and linear discursiveness of language. The necessary conclusion for him as a writer is to reproduce this stark immediacy of the image as closely as possible poetically in his late prose, which also proceeds imagistically or pictorially rather than narratively or discursively. Language is to present, not to represent.

The image as idol in the Marionian sense of visual aesthetic saturation dethrones the subject that has hitherto constituted the phenomenon. One could suspect a mere reversal of the conventional scenario here in which the image would stand for immediacy and originality—presentation—and language would find itself on the sidelines of "mere" representation. But this is not at all what occurs in Beckett's art. Reduced to givenness, the image undermines the usual distinction between presentation and representation, original and copy, subject and object.

As something that has long been repressed and subjugated to the rule of the real, the image is also a potent reminder of the elusive power of the prereflective dimension of cognition that is always out of reach yet fundamentally fuels our interest in art. Pursuing a point through writing that owes its elusive existence to the process of writing itself must be understood in its complete aporetic sense. No causality is implicit here: the pursuit is no *result* of the unattainability and it does not seek its own termination.

Allowing literature to unleash its potential and to come into its own by acknowledging and cultivating this originary doubling as the "essence" of literature means to allow for a "fundamentally" open space for the radical contestation of all received concepts. Literature is emptied of everything that conventionally, and one might say idolatrously, defines it. The nonduality of this empty space is absolutely irreducible, as is the aseity of the divine, and as soon as we try to grasp this space critically the vocabulary we use, the verbal acrobatics we resort to, become indistinguishable from the discursive forms of apophatic theology. Beckett performs a literary apophaticism by making the nature of writing both his subject and his object—and thereby neither; literature as doubled is irreducible to objectivity and subjectivity. Primary and secondary discourse interpenetrate each other. Beckett both produces and describes absolute irreducibility. His is both a mysticism and a theology of language. At the transcendental level of the literary Beckett creates a dark icon of the transcendent divine. Yet he is not able to affirm God . . . not yet: not God and not no God, but an open space in which he may give himself.

Notes

Chapter 1   Introduction

1. Beckett qtd. in Knowlson, *Damned to Fame*, 352.
2. Beckett qtd. in Knowlson, *Damned to Fame*, 677.
3. McKnight, *Sacralizing the Secular*, 41.
4. Hart, *The Dark Gaze*, 6.
5. Blanchot, *Faux Pas*, 3.
6. Blanchot, *Book to Come*, 7.
7. Beckett qtd. in Driver, *Madeleine*, 23–24.
8. Heidegger, *Thing*, 184.
9. Heidegger, *Thing*, 184.
10. Nancy, *Nom de Dieu*, 67.
11. Bair, *Biography*, 26.
12. Knowlson, *Damned to Fame*, 61.
13. Driver, *Madeleine*, 24.
14. "'In six days, do you hear me, six days, God made the world. . . . And you are not bloody well capable of making me a pair of trousers in three months.' [*Tailor's voice, scandalized.*] 'But my dear Sir, my dear Sir, look—[*disdainful gesture, disgustedly*]—at the world—[*pause*]—and look—[*loving gesture, proudly*]—at my TROUSERS!'" (*E* 21–22).
15. Loy, "Deconstruction of Buddhism," 232.
16. Loy, "Deconstruction of Buddhism," 232.

Chapter 2   Visuality and Iconicity in Samuel Beckett's *Catastrophe*

1. For this purpose the Protagonist's stare back at the audience need not be one of defiance. Other ways of performing this crucial moment are

conceivable: an expression of pleading, for instance, would lend the play an entirely different tone.

2. Gussow, *Conversations*, 88.

3. Gussow, *Conversations*, 85.

4. Ben-Zvi, "Through a Tube Starkly," 24.

5. States, "Laboratory," 14.

6. "Noch das äußerste Bewußtsein vom Verhängnis droht zum Geschwätz zu entarten. Kulturkritik findet sich der letzten Stufe der Dialektik von Kultur und Barbarei gegenüber: nach Auschwitz ein Gedicht zu schreiben, ist barbarisch, und das frißt auch die Erkenntnis an, die ausspricht, warum es unmöglich ward, heute Gedichte zu schreiben. [Even the most extreme consciousness of the calamity threatens to degenerate into blabber. Cultural critique is confronted with the final stage of the dialectic of culture and barbarism: to write a poem after Auschwitz is barbaric, and that even nags away at the realization that articulates why it became impossible to write poems today.]" Adorno, *Gesammelte Schriften*, 30. Translation mine.

7. Beckett qtd. in Harvey, *Poet and Critic*, 249–50.

8. Hegel, *Aesthetics*, 38.

9. Levin, *Opening of Vision*, 7.

10. Virilio, *Art of the Motor*, 19.

11. Levin, *Opening of Vision*, 194.

12. Jay, *Downcast Eyes*, 28.

13. Jay, *Downcast Eyes*, 29.

14. See Hayes, *On the Reduction*.

15. Jay, *Downcast Eyes*, 44.

16. Jay, *Downcast Eyes*, 54.

17. Jay, *Downcast Eyes*, 69.

18. States, "Laboratory," 21.

19. Abe, *Kenosis*, 20.

20. This argument has been made particularly from Buddhist points of view (cf. Loy, *Nonduality*, and Coward, *Indian Philosophy*). What makes Derrida's deconstruction incomplete for these authors is the fact that in order to avoid reification the cycle of deconstructions has to be endless. It remains within the system of textual difference (in Derrida's usual broad understanding of this term), thus privileging and reifying language, instead of opening onto a third space that is fully nondual and does not require the movement of the trace.

21. Loy, "Deconstruction of Buddhism," 239.

22. Loy, "Deconstruction of Buddhism," 246.

23. Candrakirti, *Lucid Exposition*, 262. While it is true that the term "perception" refers to all the senses, not just the visual, at the same time most sense perception in the Western world is of a dualist kind (cf. Loy, *Nonduality*, 39). In this sense the visual, because of its cultural-historical prevalence, merely exem-

plifies in the most conspicuous way what is the case with all the senses. Although moments of nonduality occur readily in the aural realm, especially during listening to music, nondual listening is, as Loy points out, by no means the norm (Loy, *Nonduality*, 70). Compare, in this respect, the following quote from contemporary Zen master Yasutani Hakuun: "Usually when I hear a bell ringing you think, consciously or unconsciously, 'I am hearing a bell.' Three things are involved: I, a bell, and hearing. But when the mind is ripe, that is, as free of discursive thought as a sheet of pure white paper is unmarred by a blemish, there is just the sound of the bell ringing" (Yasutani qtd in Loy, *Nonduality*, 71). David Levin, then, it seems to me, posits listening as an alternative mode of perception primarily because of the greater propensity of the aural to lend itself to nondual perception, not because it is by nature nondual.

24. Loy, "Deconstruction of Buddhism," 249.

25. There are other instances in Beckett's work of characters looking directly into the audience, notably in *Endgame*, when Clov turns his telescope on the audience and says: "I see . . . a multitude . . . in transports . . . of joy" (*E* 25). Similar to the moment in *Catastrophe*, here also the gaze indicates a moment in which the play steps outside its fictional horizon and self-referentially acknowledges its metaphorical character as a play on stage. In an ironically self-deprecating manner Beckett turns Clov's comment into a verdict on the entertainment value of his play: the audience, it is implied, is less than riveted by it.

26. Cf. McAuley, *Space in Performance*, 39: "The behavior of actors onstage is marked; spectators know that it is to be interpreted differently from apparently identical behaviors occurring in other places. Spectators in the theatre both believe and disbelieve."

27. Freedman, *Staging the Gaze*, 1.

28. Paris, *Painting and Linguistics*, 39.

29. Paris, *Painting and Linguistics*, 43.

30. Paris, *Painting and Linguistics*, 66.

31. Garner, "(Dis)figuring Space," 64.

32. Marion, *Crossing of the Visible*, 232.

33. Cf. Lévinas, *Of God Who Comes to Mind*.

34. Marion, *God without Being*, 21.

35. Marion, *Crossing of the Visible*, 78.

36. Theodore, *Holy Icons*, 110.

37. Matoba, "Religious Overtones," 40. Interpolation mine.

38. Bryson, "Gaze," 100.

39. Bryson, "Gaze," 103.

40. Sprung, *Lucid Exposition*, 7.

41. Loy, *Nonduality*, 153.

42. Bryson, "Gaze," 103.

43. Marion, *Being Given*, 217.
44. Marion, *In Excess*, 63.
45. Marion, *In Excess*, 64.

Chapter 3   "Three Dialogues" and the Economy of Art

1. Kant, *Critique of Judgment*, 182.
2. The nature of God is meta-metaphysical and meta-ontological. The danger is for negative theology to insist on this status so that it becomes ontological. Derrida is acutely aware of this problem.
3. It also talks in the awareness that to fulfill its soteriological goal its own discourse will not suffice. It has to become experiential.
4. Beckett seems to have adapted the formulation from Blanchot, who writes in *Faux Pas* that "[t]he writer finds himself in the increasingly ludicrous condition of having nothing to write, of having no means with which to write it, and of being constrained by the utter necessity of always writing it. Having nothing to express must be taken in the most literal way" (Blanchot, *Faux Pas*, 3). Given the closeness of the two formulations the question of influence arises: *Faux Pas* was first published in French in 1943, while the issue of *Transition* that contains the "Three Dialogues" first appeared in 1949. It seems atypical for Beckett to be indebted to one of his contemporaries. He quotes and borrows widely, but usually not from contemporary sources. If this is indeed a question of influence of Blanchot on Beckett it is further proof of the closeness in sentiment between these two thinkers. Blanchot himself often demonstrates the affinity he feels to Beckett's thought by quoting from Beckett's work to illustrate his own (as in "Who now? Where now?" [*Book to Come*]).
5. Hyppolite, "Ineffable," 13.
6. Nancy, "Le nom de Dieu," 68.
7. Nancy, "Le nom de Dieu," 67.
8. Nancy, "Le nom de Dieu," 67.
9. Nancy, "Le nom de Dieu," 67.
10. Nancy, "Le nom de Dieu," 68. Translation mine.
11. Nancy, "Le nom de Dieu," 68. Translation mine.
12. Nancy, "Le nom de Dieu," 68.
13. Nancy, "Le nom de Dieu," 68.
14. Cf. Marion, *Being Given*, 282.
15. Thomas Trezise, in *Into the Breach*, diagnosed Beckett's "sustained interest in a 'general economy'" (Trezise, *Breach*, 6), especially in the "Three Dialogues."
16. For a discussion of *Darstellung* and *Vorstellung* in modern aesthetics, cf. Seyhan, *Representation and Its Discontents*.

17. Barthes, *Neutral*, 199.

18. Barthes, *Neutral*, 199.

19. Hart, *Trespass*, 201.

20. See, e.g., Coward, *Derrida*; Loy, "Deconstruction."

21. Duthuit tries to present Masson as an "improvement" on Tal-Coat's methodology, but precisely by presenting his project as a quest in search of a solution he "re-metaphysizes" him.

22. Dionysius, *Complete Works*, 136.

23. Derrida, "How to Avoid Speaking," 135.

24. Derrida, *Given Time*, 40.

25. Obligation is the aporia of answering to the general (which for Derrida is synonymous with the ethical) while doing so in one's singularity, thus finding oneself in each responsible decision "skewered on the ferocious dilemma," as Beckett would say, of alleviating misery in a specific case while necessarily allowing it to continue in countless others—therefore we wriggle.

Beckett's artist fortunately does not face an ethical problem (or only insofar as he chooses to create art rather than be a political activist), but is concerned with the same split between general and specific, or universal and singular. The expressions of artistic vision are necessarily conceptual, socially negotiated manifestations, while the acute awareness of their inadequacy comes out of a singular encounter with the absolute that points out the inadequacy of the relative. Without this inkling of the absolute the artist would have no idea of the inadequacy of her creation. Not wanting to stretch the specific parallels between Beckettian and Derridean obligation too far, the general parallels are clear. In both cases the aporia is between the general and/or conceptual ("the ethical involves one in substitution, as does speaking" [Derrida, *Gift of Death*, 61]) and the nonsubstitutable call of the absolute that manifests itself in multiple guises. Obligation is a double bind: one is positioned between irreconcilable moral precepts that could lock one into inactivity if one did not accept the impossibility of one's situation and acted in it anyway, however inadequately. This leads Derrida to think that "absolute responsibility could not be described from a *concept* of responsibility and therefore, in order for it to be what it must be it must remain inconceivable, indeed unthinkable: it must therefore be irresponsible in order to be absolutely responsible" (Derrida, *Gift of Death*, 61). Like any aporia, the aporia of responsibility is "nothing other than sacrifice, the revelation of conceptual thinking at its limit, at its death and finitude" (Derrida, *Gift of Death*, 68).

26. Derrida in Caputo, *God, Gift, Postmodernism*, 59.

27. Derrida in Caputo, *God, Gift, Postmodernism*, 59.

28. Derrida in Caputo, *God, Gift, Postmodernism*, 66.

29. Marion, *God without Being*, 21.

30. Derrida in Caputo, *God, Gift, Postmodernism*, 66.

31. Derrida, *"Différance,"* 6.

32. Derrida, *On the Name*, 67, 68.

33. Cf. A. H. Armstrong, "Escape of the One."

34. Aquinas, *Summa Theologiae*, 32.

35. Hart, *Trespass*, 191.

36. Cf. A. H. Armstrong, "Escape of the One" and "Negative Theology"; Turner, *Darkness*, 257.

37. Marion, "In the Name," 25.

38. Hart, *Trespass*, 186.

39. Hart, *Trespass*, 202.

40. Marion, *In Excess*, 140.

41. Hart, *Trespass*, 192. It seems to be the case that all negative theology can achieve is to save discourse from lapsing into idolatry. It can only be "about" God in the sense of this endless vigilance.

42. See Turner, *Darkness*, 178.

43. Loy, *Nonduality*, 219.

44. Loy, *Nonduality*, 220.

45. Heidegger, *Basic Writings*, 431.

46. Beckett qtd. in Harvey, *Poet and Critic*, 248.

47. Miller, *Expressive Dilemma*. Miller gives one of his chapters this title.

48. Derrida, *Acts*, 47.

49. Miller, *Expressive Dilemma*, 9.

50. Pilling, *Notebook*, 100.

51. Turner, *Darkness*, 176.

52. Ben-Zvi, "Limits," 192.

53. Caputo, "Heidegger and Theology," 282.

54. Heidegger, *Gelassenheit*, 32. Translation mine.

> G – Insofern wir uns wenigstens des Wollens entwöhnen können, helfen wir mit beim Erwachen der Gelassenheit.
> L – Eher beim Wachbleiben für die Gelassenheit.
> G – Weshalb nicht beim Erwachen?
> L – Weil wir die Gelassenheit nicht von uns aus bei uns erwecken.

55. *Mulamadhyamakakarika*, chap. 25, verse 20, qtd. in Loy, "Deconstruction of Buddhism," 246.

56. Loy, "Deconstruction of Buddhism," 247.

57. Sprung, *Lucid Exposition*, 17, 18.

58. "The Nature of Language." Heidegger, *Unterwegs zur Sprache*.

59. Heidegger, *Unterwegs zur Sprache*, 159.

60. Heidegger, *Way to Language*, 57.

61. Heidegger, *Unterwegs zur Sprache*, 241.

62. Heidegger, *Basic Writings*, 398.

63. Heidegger, *Unterwegs zur Sprache*, 166.

64. Heidegger, *Unterwegs zur Sprache*, 164.

Chapter 4   Metaphor and Metonymy in *Not I*

1. Whitelaw, *Who He?*, 120.
2. Barthes, *Neutral*, 6.
3. Barthes, *Neutral*, 49.
4. Barthes, *Neutral*, 51.
5. Lodge, *Modes*, 76.
6. Lodge, *Modes*, 77.
7. Stephen Ullman qtd. in Lodge, *Modes*, 75.
8. "In England the true successors of Dickens and Trollope were Gissing, Bennett, Wells, and Galsworthy; just as the true successors of James were Virginia Woolf, Ford Madox Ford and E. M. Forster. Neither line of succession is Christian, but surely there is no doubt which of the two is the more 'religious'? The concept of sin is at the heart of Ford's best work; *A Passage to India* is full of the longing for transcendence, even if it is ultimately unfulfilled; and was it not for their 'materialism' that Virginia Woolf condemned Bennett, Wells and Galsworthy?" (Lodge, *Modes*, 51). Compare the following from Virginia Woolf's essay "Modern Fiction," which Lodge quotes: "Life is not a series of gig-lamps symmetrically arranged: life is a luminous halo, a semi-transparent envelope surrounding us from the beginning of consciousness to the end. Is it not the task of the novelist to convey this varying, this unknown and uncircumscribed spirit, whatever aberration or complexity it may display?" (Woolf qtd. in Lodge, *Modes*, 44).
9. Essif, "Concentrated (Empty) Image," 19.
10. Essif, "Concentrated (Empty) Image," 21.
11. Essif, "Concentrated (Empty) Image," 21–22.
12. Lodge, *Modes*, 83.
13. Butler, *Meaning of Being* approaches Beckett primarily through the lenses of various continental philosophers, and tests the ground for a theological reading in only a few pages at the end of the book. He arrives there after what seems to be a continuous progression toward the divine from Sartre, through Heidegger, to Hegel.
14. Bair, *Biography*, 622. The same incident is reported by Knowlson, *Damned to Fame*, 589. Regarding the stage image of *Not I* Beckett wrote to Knowlson: "Image of *Not I* in part suggested by Caravaggio's *Decollation of St. John the Baptist*" (Knowlson, *Damned to Fame*, 588).
15. Beckett qtd. in Armstrong, *Images and Words*, 69.
16. Brater, *Beyond Minimalism*, 24.
17. Beckett qtd. in Armstrong, *Images and Words*, 70.
18. Artaud, *Double*, 71. Ellipsis mine.
19. Essif, "Concentrated (Empty) Image," 20.

20. "In those days came John the Baptist, preaching in the wilderness of Judea, 'Repent, for the kingdom of heaven is at hand.' For this is he who was spoken of by the prophet Isaiah when he said, 'The voice of one crying in the wilderness: Prepare the way of the Lord, make his paths straight'" (Matt. 3:1–3).

21. Whitelaw qtd. in Brater, *Beyond Minimalism*, 31.

22. Brater, *Beyond Minimalism*, 34.

23. Qtd. in Brater, *Beyond Minimalism*, 74. Cf. also Bair, *Biography*, 625.

24. Lawley, "Counterpoint," 407.

25. Brater, *Beyond Minimalism*, 24.

26. Garner, "(Dis)figuring Space," 72.

27. Garner, "(Dis)figuring Space," 74.

28. Interestingly in all his questioning and pushing of boundaries in the theater, Beckett never actually transgressed the boundaries of the proscenium stage.

29. Reading Archive MS 1639. Qtd. in Knowlson and Pilling, *Frescoes*, 219.

30. Brater, *Beyond Minimalism*, 35.

31. Brater, *Beyond Minimalism*, 31.

32. Brater, *Beyond Minimalism*, 18.

33. Garner, "(Dis)figuring Space," 65–66, 66.

34. Garner, "(Dis)figuring Space," 62.

35. Bryson, *Gaze*, 101.

36. Bryson, *Gaze*, 103.

37. At the highest level of generality a metonymic text is, of course, itself metaphorical because it is unable to postpone its "metaphorization" indefinitely. Any work of literature, Lodge points out, is metaphorical by virtue of being an artistic construct that stands for something that it is about: "[T]he text is the vehicle, the world is the tenor" (Lodge, *Modes*, 109). Even at this level of generality, however, it is easier, Lodge points out, to read the metaphoric text as a "total metaphor" than the metonymic text. This ultimate metaphoricity of metonymy must not blur the valid and valuable distinction between the metaphoric and metonymic modes.

38. I quote at length the beginning of MS 1227/7/12/3 to illustrate this process of paring down. Words that appear in brackets are crossed out in the manuscript and comparison with the familiar published version reveals further reduction and excision in subsequent versions.

39. Lodge, *Modes*, 146.

40. Cf. Lodge, *Modes*, 151–52.

41. Lodge, "Modernist Fiction," 489.

42. Lodge, *Modes*, 230.

43. Lodge, *Modes*, 147–48.

44. Garner, "(Dis)figuring Space," 79.

45. Lodge, *Modes*, 83.

46. Lodge, *Modes*, 81.

47. Lodge, *Modes*, 83.

48. Brater, *Beyond Minimalism*, 256.

49. "If there is no essence of literature—i.e., self-identity of the literary thing—if what is announced or promised as literature never gives itself as such, that means, among other things, that a literature that talked only about literature or a work that was completely self-referential would immediately be annulled" (Derrida, *Acts*, 47).

50. Acheson, "Madness," 92.

51. Bair, *Biography*, 624; Knowlson, *Damned to Fame*, 591.

52. Howard, "Not Mercies," 316.

53. Zeifman, "Being and Non-Being," 43.

54. Brater, *Beyond Minimalism*, 23.

55. Buning, "Negative Way," 138–39.

56. Politi, "'Not (Not I),'" 353, 354.

57. Politi, "'Not (Not I),'" 345.

58. Derrida, *On the Name*, 69.

59. Blanchot, *Book to Come*, 213.

60. Blanchot, *Book to Come*, 212.

61. Blanchot, *Space of Literature*, 22.

62. Blanchot, *Book to Come*, 213.

63. Cf. Hart, *Dark Gaze*, 130.

64. Blanchot, *Book to Come*, 386.

65. Blanchot, *Book to Come*, 387.

66. In so doing Beckett's *Worstward Ho*, with its still iconicity, ironically contrasts with the linearity of Kingsley's story of adventure, exploration, power, and conquest. *Westward Ho!* is about individual and imperial exploits in a world of action and possibility while *Worstward Ho* dramatizes repetition and inaction and the concomitant dissolution of centered subjectivity, as well as aporetic states of impossibility.

Chapter 5   The Empty Space of *Quad*

1. Marion, *Being Given*, 215.

2. I see language as a "questlike structure" because its movement from subject to verb and object can be seen as inherently linear and sequential. I am not attempting to insinuate that poststructuralist deferral, nonteleological as it is, betrays questlike structures or that language is necessarily dualist.

3. Cf. Schmid, "Abstract Synthesis," 263, where *Quad* is seen as "the culmination of the author's minimal art" and "the quintessence of theater."

4. Translations from Beckett's German letter mine throughout. "Es wird mir tatsächlich immer schwieriger, ja sinnloser, ein offizielles Englisch zu schreiben. Und immer mehr wie ein Schleier kommt mir meine Sprache vor, den man

zerreissen muss, um an die dahinterliegenden Dinge (oder das dahinterliegende Nichts) zu kommen" (*D* 52).

5. "Jene fürchterlich willkürliche Materialität der Wortfläche" (*D* 52).

6. "Selbstverständlich muss man sich vorläufig mit Wenigem begnügen. Zuerst kann es nur darauf ankommen, irgendwie eine Methode zu erfinden, um diese höhnische Haltung dem Worte gegenüber wörtlich darzustellen" (*D* 53).

7. "Das Sprachgewebe ist wenigstens porös geworden" (*D* 53).

8. "Die unglückliche Dame (lebt sie noch?) ist ja ohne Zweifel immer noch in ihr Vehikel verliebt" (*D* 53).

9. Garner, "(Dis)figuring Space," 53.

10. Deleuze, "L'épuisé," 57. Translations from Deleuze's text mine throughout.

11. Deleuze, "L'épuisé," 66.

12. Deleuze, "L'épuisé," 70.

13. Deleuze, "L'épuisé," 71.

14. Deleuze, "L'épuisé," 93

15. Deleuze, "L'épuisé," 94.

16. Deleuze does not differentiate between "visual" and "acoustic" images, but I wish to argue the case of visual theatrical images and hence confine myself to those, without trying to suggest that the visual is the only dimension of theatrical images.

17. Chatman, *Rhetoric of Narrative*, 110.

18. Chatman, *Rhetoric of Narrative*, 7–8.

19. Chatman, *Rhetoric of Narrative*, 7–8.

20. Gontarski, "Introduction," vii.

21. Gontarski, "Introduction," xxvi.

22. Abbott, "Arts of Time," 14.

23. Abbott, "Arts of Time," 16.

24. Cf. Glasmeier, "Stillstand," 149.

25. Kenner, *Critical Study*, 111.

26. "Watt's way of advancing due east, for example, was to turn his bust as far as possible towards the north and at the same time to fling out his right leg as far as possible towards the south, and then to turn his bust as far as possible towards the south and at the same time to fling out his left leg as far as possible towards the north, and then again to turn his bust as far as possible towards the north and to fling out his right leg as far as possible to the south . . . and so on, over and over again, many many times, until he reached his destination and could sit down" (*W* 28).

27. Kenner, *Critical Study*, 119.

28. Under the heading "Music if any" in one of the drafts of the *Quad* manuscript held at the Reading Beckett Archive (MS 2189), it reads: "4 types of concussion corresponding to four players." The slip perfectly summarizes the impact the percussion accompaniment has on the listener.

29. Brater, *Beyond Minimalism*, 109.

30. Deleuze, "L'épuisé," 55.

31. Deleuze, "L'épuisé," 56.

32. Glasmeier, "Stillstand," 156–58. Translation mine. "Beckett hat hier das Literarische endgültig abgestreift. Er ist, wie in seinem ganzen Spätwerk zu beobachten, zum Bilderfinder auf der Basis von Bilderfahrung geworden. Seine Ekphrasis beschreibt nicht, sie kreiert."

33. Translation mine. "Bilder ohne Vorher und Nachher, Bilder in nackter Präsenz" (Glasmeier, "Stillstand," 154).

34. Glasmeier, "Stillstand," 156. Translation mine. "Denn hier wurde das Theater des Stillstands, der eingefrorenen Gesten zelebriert. Hier wurden Szenen im Atelier aufgebaut. . . . inszenierte Realität in diffusen Räumen, gemalte Bühne, totale Künstlichkeit."

35. Cf. Arnheim, *Visual Perception*, 412–15.

36. Garner, "(Dis)figuring Space," 62.

37. Arnheim, *Visual Perception*, 26. Arnheim looks at drama in terms of the composition of its visual forces. Therefore he treats drama and painting/sculpture as obeying the same basic principles: there are "similar, though often less sharply manifest, phenomena in the photographic and performing arts" (Arnheim, *Visual Perception*, 4) as there are in painting and sculpture.

38. Garner, "(Dis)figuring Space," 77.

39. Arnheim, *Visual Perception*, 16.

40. Arnheim, *Visual Perception*, 33.

41. Arnheim, *Visual Perception*, 30.

42. Niten is the pseudonym of Miyamoto Musashi, who was born in the Harima Province of Japan in 1584.

43. In the Reading Beckett Archive MS 2189 the center is called "O." In MS 2198, "O" is crossed out and changed to "E," obviously to continue the sequence established by calling the four corners of the square "A," "B," "C," and "D." But then, in MS 2199, Beckett reverts to "O" on the first page and then continues with "E" from the second page onward. Obviously, the idea of calling the center "O" has a strange tenacity.

44. Deleuze, "L'épuisé," 77.

45. Qtd. in Duckworth, *Angels*, 18.

46. Bryden, "Figures of Golgotha," 46. The chapter in *Samuel Beckett and the Idea of God* is a rewritten version of this earlier article.

47. Bryden, *Idea of God*, 140.

48. Bryden, "Figures of Golgotha," 53.

49. Ward, "Kenosis and Naming," 236.

50. Bryden, "Figures of Golgotha," 46.

51. Ackerley, *Demented Particulars*, 169.

52. Ackerley, *Demented Particulars*, 169.

53. "Deleuze, "L'épuisé," 83. "Epuiser l'espace, c'est en exténuer la potenti-alité, en rendant toute rencontrer impossible." Translation mine.

54. Garner, "(Dis)figuring Space," 73.

55. Loy, *Nonduality*, 220.

56. Cf. Schubert, *Plotin*, 44.

57. "Ecrire aperception purement visuelle, c'est écrire une phrase dénuée de sens. Comme de bien entendu. Car chaque fois qu'on veut faire aux mots un véritable travail de transbordement, chaque fois qu'on veut leur faire exprimer autre chose que des mots, ils s'alignent de façon à s'annuler mutuellement. C'est sans doute, ce qui donne à la vie tout son charme" (*MP* 25–26).

58. Knowlson and Pilling, *Frescoes*, 277.

59. Schmid, "Abstract Synthesis," 164. The play is without title, unless one wants to use the generic description *Gestentanz* as a title. Schlemmer's *Gesten-tanz* (or gesture dance) experiments comprise more than just this one play.

60. Cf. Gropius, *Bauhaus*, 88.

61. Knowlson, *Damned to Fame*, 502.

62. Knowlson, *Damned to Fame*, 502.

63. Glasmeier sees in the hoods an evocation of the seventeenth-century Dutch masters. Figures in their paintings often wear hooded items of clothing of various descriptions. This is, however, a very specific connotation, which, in all likelihood, would not be at the forefront of the spectator's mind.

64. Deak, *Symbolist Theater*, 23.

65. Brater, "Noah," 256.

66. Deak, *Symbolist Theater*, 174.

67. Craig in Kirby, *Total Theatre*, 49.

68. von Wiese, "Paradies," 206.

69. von Wiese, "Paradies," 209. Translation mine. "Wenn nämlich der gött-liche Maschinist sich in den Schwerpunkt der Bewegung der Puppe hineinver-setzt, so gibt er damit der Puppe zugleich die Freiheit, sie selbst, und nur sie selbst zu sein."

70. von Kleist, "Marionettentheather," 16.

71. von Kleist, "Marionettentheather," 12. Translation mine. "Doch das Paradies ist verriegelt und der Cherub hinter uns; wir müssen die Reise um die Welt machen, und sehen, ob es von hinten irgendwo wieder offen ist."

72. von Kleist, "Marionettentheather," 16.

73. Albright, *Beckett and Aesthetics*, 14.

Chapter 6   **The Reduction of** *Film*

1. Hale, *Broken Window*, 92.

2. Lodge, *Modes*, 86.

3. Federman, "Agony," 366.

4. Brater, "Thinking Eye," 171.

5. Murphy, "Being and Perception," 43; Brater, "Thinking Eye," 166.

6. Merleau-Ponty, *Phenomenology*, xiv.

7. Cf. Martin Jay's work on occularcentrism, especially "Scopic Regimes of Modernity" and *Downcast Eyes*.

8. In (Neo-)Platonism, of course, occularcentrism is not just a question of taking vision to represent or symbolize all of perception, but of following a kind of natural hierarchy of perception in which the visual sense is the least embodied and hence the one most suited to carrying the spiritual aspirations of the tradition.

9. Hayes, *Introduction*, 49.

10. In *The Listening Self* David Levin develops an alternative, aural, nondual model of perception.

11. Hemming, *Devaluing God*, 209.

12. Hemming, *Devaluing God*, 210.

13. Ward, "Kenosis and Naming," 235.

14. Ward, "Kenosis and Naming," 254 n.2.

15. Harvey, *Condition of Postmodernity*, 44.

16. Milbank, "Modern Transcendent," 259.

17. Milbank, "Modern Transcendent," 272.

18. Milbank, "Modern Transcendent," 263.

19. Milbank, "Modern Transcendent," 259.

20. Nancy, "Sublime Offering," 49.

21. Nancy, "Sublime Offering," 37, 43.

22. Nancy, "Sublime Offering," 41.

23. Nancy, "Sublime Offering," 43.

24. Hart, "Experience," 8.

25. Hart, "Experience," 8.

26. Henning, "Dialogue," 89.

27. Henning, "Dialogue," 92.

28. Murphy, "Being and Perception," 45.

29. To approach them as art is to move them perilously close to being ends in themselves and as such to being idols.

30. Henning, "Dialogue," 92.

31. Henning, "Dialogue," 91.

32. Federman, "Agony," 366.

33. Feshbach, "Unswamping a Backwater," 336.

34. Henning, "Dialogue," 98–99.

35. Marion, *Being Given*, 217.

36. In his collaboration with theater photographer, John Haynes, James Knowlson relates the following episode: "I remember writing to [Beckett] shortly after Saul Bellow had won the Nobel Prize for Literature. At the end of

the letter, somewhat misguidedly, I wrote: 'Another Nobel prize-winning pessimist'. Beckett wrote back wryly asking: 'Where did you get the idea I was a pessimist?'" (Haynes and Knowlson 2003, 19).

37. Gadamer, *Truth and Method*, 55.

38. Hart, "Experience," 12.

39. Hart, "Experience," 12.

40. Cf. Hart, *Dark Gaze*, 139.

41. Wolin, *Walter Benjamin*, 33.

42. Driver, "Madeleine," 21.

43. Driver, "Madeleine," 24.

44. Caputo and Scanlon, *God, Gift, Postmodernism*, 3–4.

45. Caputo and Scanlon, *God, Gift, Postmodernism*, 4.

46. Caputo and Scanlon, *God, Gift, Postmodernism*, 3.

47. Adorno, *Ästhetische Theorie*, 364.

48. Cf. Adorno, *Ästhetische Theorie*, 365. The question then is to what extent experience without a subject to ground it is possible, especially given that the subject is a relatively recent concept in the history of philosophy. Cf. Jay, "Experience," in which Jay investigates the convention of free indirect speech as an example of experience without a subject. Free indirect speech is not unequivocally rooted in either the author's or the character's experience. Also interesting with regard to Beckett's linguistic pursuits is that, for Jay, *language* becomes the locus of such nondual experience.

49. Hindrichs, "Scheitern als Rettung," 140.

50. Hindrichs, "Scheitern als Rettung," 149.

51. Cf. Gunnar Hindrichs: "Während Benjamin an der Idee eines entrückten Standortes festhält, eines Standortes, der außergeschichtlich am Himmel zu suchen ist, gibt Adorno diese Idee auf. Der Standpunkt der Erlösung ist zu suchen, obgleich er als Standpunkt unmöglich geworden ist. Er muß innerhalb der Katastrophe gegen diese gefunden werden. Adorno behält sozusagen die Idee der Rettung bei, nachdem sich die Englein (und der Messias) vom Himmel auf die Erde totgefallen haben (Hindrichs, "Scheitern als Rettung," 169) [While Benjamin holds on to the idea of a remote position, a position to be sought in the heavens outside of history, Adorno abandons this idea. One is to try for salvation, although as a position it has become impossible. It needs to be found within the catastrophe against the latter. Adorno holds on to the Idea of salvation after the angels (and the Messiah) have plunged down to earth and into their death, as it were]." Translation mine.

52. Oppenheim, *Painted Word*, 78.

53. Oppenheim, *Painted Word*, 88. The snippet Oppenheim quotes is from a letter Beckett wrote to Georges Duthuit.

54. "Espace et corps, achevés, inaltérables, arrachés au temps par le faiseur de temps, à l'abri du temps dans l'usine à temps (qui passait sa journée dans le Sacré-Coeur pour ne plus avoir à le voir?)" (*MP* 26).

55. Loy, *Nonduality*, 319.

56. Loy, *Nonduality*, 220–21.

57. Cf. Brater, "Thinking Eye," 167.

58. Arnheim, *Film as Art*, 11.

59. Federman, "Agony," 363.

60. Montage is metaphoric because it combines elements on the basis of contrast, not on the basis of natural contiguity. But even when it deliberately foregrounds montage, film has a hard time establishing a counterweight to its metonymic predisposition because montage uses the same editing techniques (cut and splice) as are generally used in film editing (cf. Lodge, *Modes*, 84).

61. I am indebted to Kevin Hart's "The Experience of Poetry" in my conceiving and working out the themes of this chapter.

Chapter 7   Conclusion

1. Foshay, "Denegation," 555.

2. Loy, "Deconstruction of Buddhism," 248.

3. Loy, "Deconstruction of Buddhism," 248.

Bibliography

Beckett Primary

Beckett, Samuel. *Proust*. London: Chatto and Windus, 1931.

———. *Waiting for Godot*. New York: Grove, 1954.

———. *Endgame*. London: Faber, 1964.

———. *Film*. New York: Grove, 1969.

———. *Watt*. London: Calder, 1976.

———. *Ill Seen Ill Said*. *Nohow On*. New York: Grove, 1981. 47–86.

———. *Disjecta*. London: Calder, 1983.

———. "Three Dialogues." *Disjecta*. London: Calder, 1983. 138–45.

———. *Worstward Ho*. *Nohow On*. New York: Grove, 1983. 87–116.

———. *Collected Shorter Plays*. New York: Grove, 1984.

———. *Le Monde et le Pantalon*. Paris: Les Editions Minuit, 1989.

———. *The Trilogy: Molloy, Malone Dies, The Unnamable*. London: Calder, 1994.

———. John Pilling, ed. *Beckett's "Dream" Notebook*. Reading: Beckett International Foundation, 1999.

Beckett on Film. 2001. Blue Angel Films/Tyrone Productions for Radio Telefís Éireann and Channel 4.

Beckett Secondary

Abbott, H. Porter. "Samuel Beckett and the Arts of Time: Painting, Music, Narrative." *Samuel Beckett and the Arts: Music, Visual Arts, and Non-Print Media*. Ed. Lois Oppenheim New York: Garland, 1999. 7–24.

Ackerley, Chris. *Demented Particulars: The Annotated* Murphy. Tallahassee: Journal of Beckett Studies Books, 1998.

Acheson, James. "Madness and Mysticism in Beckett's *Not I.*" *AUMLA* 55 (May 1981): 91–101.

Albright, Daniel. *Beckett and Aesthetics.* Cambridge: Cambridge University Press, 2003.

Armstrong, Gordon. *Samuel Beckett, W. B. Yeats, and Jack Yeats: Images and Words.* Lewisburg: Bucknell University Press, 1990.

Bair, Deirdre. *Samuel Beckett: A Biography.* London: Cape, 1978.

Baldwin, Hélène. *Samuel Beckett's Real Silence.* University Park: Pennsylvania State University Press, 1981.

Barge, Laura. *God, the Quest, the Hero: Thematic Structures in Beckett's Fiction.* Chapel Hill: North Carolina Studies in the Romance Languages and Literatures, University of North Carolina, Department of Romance Languages, 1988.

Begam, Richard. "Splitting the *Différance:* Beckett, Derrida and the Unnamable." *Modern Fiction Studies* 38.4 (1992): 873–92.

Ben-Zvi, Linda. "Samuel Beckett, Fritz Mauthner, and the Limits of Language." *PMLA* 95 (1980): 183–200.

———. *Samuel Beckett.* Boston: Twayne, 1986.

———. "*Not I:* Through a Tube Starkly." *Samuel Beckett: Teleplays.* Vancouver Art Gallery, 1988. 21–27.

Birkett, Jennifer, and Kate Ince, eds. *Samuel Beckett.* London: Longman, 2000.

Blau, Herbert. *Sails of the Herring Fleet.* Ann Arbor: University of Michigan Press, 2000.

Brater, Enoch. "Noah, *Not I,* and Beckett's Incomprehensibly Sublime." *Comparative Drama* 8.3 (1974): 254–63.

———. "The Thinking Eye in Beckett's *Film.*" *Modern Language Quarterly* 36 (1975): 166–76.

———. *Beyond Minimalism: Beckett's Late Style in the Theatre.* Oxford: Oxford University Press, 1987.

Breuer, Rolf. *Die Kunst der Paradoxie: Sinnsuche und Scheitern bei Samuel Beckett.* Munich: Fink, 1976.

Brienza, Susan. *Samuel Beckett's New Worlds: Style in Metafiction.* Norman: University of Oklahoma Press, 1987.

Bryden, Mary. "Figures of Golgotha: Beckett's Pinioned People." *The Ideal Core of the Onion: Reading Beckett Archives.* Ed. John Pilling and Mary Bryden. Reading: Beckett International Foundation, 1992. 45–62.

———. *Women in Samuel Beckett's Prose and Drama: Her Own Other.* Lanham: Barnes and Noble, 1993.

———. *Samuel Beckett and the Idea of God.* Houndmills: Macmillan, 1998.

Butler, Lance St. John. *Samuel Beckett and the Meaning of Being: A Study in Ontological Parable.* London: Macmillan, 1984.

Buning, Marius. "Samuel Beckett's Negative Way: Intimations of the 'Via Negativa' in his Late Plays." *European Literature and Theology in the Twentieth*

Century: Ends of Time. Ed. D. Jaspers and C. Crowden. London: Macmillan, 1990. 129–42.

Burkman, Katherine, ed. *Myth and Ritual in the Plays of Samuel Beckett.* Rutherford: Fairleigh Dickinson University Press, 1987.

Calder, John, ed. *Beckett at Sixty: A Festschrift.* London: Calder, 1967.

———. *The Philosophy of Samuel Beckett.* London: Calder, 2001.

Cavell, Stanley. "Ending the Waiting Game." *Must We Mean What We Say? A Book of Essays.* Cambridge: Cambridge University Press, 1969. 117–37.

Clurman, Harold. *The Divine Pastime; Theatre Essays.* New York: Macmillan, 1974.

Coe, Richard. *Beckett.* Edinburgh: Oliver and Boyd, 1964.

———. "God and Samuel Beckett." *Twentieth-century Interpretations of Molloy, Malone Dies, The Unnamable.* Ed. J. D. O'Hara. Englewood Cliffs: Prentice-Hall, 1970. 91–113.

Cohn, Ruby. *Just Play: Beckett's Theatre.* Princeton: Princeton University Press, 1980.

Cohn, Ruby, ed. *Disjecta: Miscellaneous Writings and a Dramatic Fragment by Samuel Beckett.* London: Calder, 1983.

Connor, Steven. *Samuel Beckett: Repetition, Theory and Text.* Oxford: Blackwell, 1988.

Deleuze, Gilles. "L'épuisé." Samuel Beckett. *Quad et Trio du Fantôme. . . . que nuages . . . , Nacht und Träume, L'épuisé par Gilles Deleuze.* Paris: Minuit, 1992. 57–106.

Dobbs, Michael. "Waiting for the Author of 'Waiting for Godot.'" *Mexico City News,* January 20, 1987. Arts and Leisure 18 (interview with Avigdor Arikha).

Doll, Mary Aswell. *Beckett and Myth: An Archetypal Approach.* Syracuse: Syracuse University Press, 1988.

Driver, Tom F. "Beckett by the Madeleine." *Columbia University Forum* 4.3 (1961): 21–25.

Duckworth, Colin. *Angels of Darkness: Dramatic Effect in Samuel Beckett with Special Reference to Eugène Ionesco.* New York: Barnes and Noble, 1972.

Essif, Les. "The Concentrated (Empty) Image Behind the Fragmented Story in Beckett's Late Plays." *Essays in Theatre/Études théâtrales* 17.1 (1998): 15–32.

Esslin, Martin. *Das Theater des Absurden.* Reinbek: Rowohlt, 1965.

Federman, Raymond. "Samuel Beckett's Film on the Agony of Perceivedness." *James Joyce Quarterly* 8 (1971): 363–71.

Feshbach, Sidney. 1999. "Unswamping a Backwater: On Samuel Beckett's *Film.*" *Samuel Beckett and the Arts: Music, Visual Arts, and Non-Print Media.* Ed. Lois Oppenheim. New York: Garland. 333–63.

Fletcher, John, and John Spurling. *Beckett: A Study of His Plays.* London: Eyre Methuen, 1972.

Foster, Paul. *Beckett and Zen.* London: Wisdom Publications, 1989.

Garner, Stanton. "(Dis)figuring Space: Visual Field in Beckett's Late Plays." *Bodied Spaces: Phenomenology and Performance in Contemporary Drama.* Ithaca: Cornell University Press, 1994: 52–86.

Glasmeier, Michael. "Bewegter Stillstand: Alte Meister im Quadrat." *Samuel Beckett. Bruce Nauman.* Kunsthalle Wien, 2000. 149–60.

Gontarski, S. E. *The Intent of Undoing in Samuel Beckett's Dramatic Texts.* Bloomington: Indiana University Press, 1985.

———. "Introduction" (vii–xxviii). *Nohow On.* New York: Grove, 1996.

Gontarski, S. E., ed. *The Beckett Studies Reader.* Gainesville: University Press of Florida, 1993.

Gussow, Mel. *Conversations with (and about) Beckett.* London: Nick Hern, 1996.

Hale, Jane Alison. *The Broken Window: Beckett's Dramatic Perspective.* West Lafayette: Purdue University Press, 1987.

Harmon, Maurice, ed. *No Author Better Served: The Correspondence of Samuel Beckett and Alan Schneider.* Cambridge, Mass.: Harvard University Press, 1998.

Harvey, Lawrence. *Samuel Beckett: Poet and Critic.* Princeton: Princeton University Press, 1970.

Haynes, John, and James Knowlson. *Images of Beckett.* Cambridge: Cambridge University Press, 2003.

Henning, Sylvie Debevec. "Film: A Dialogue between Beckett and Berkeley." *Journal of Beckett Studies* 7 (Spring 1982): 89–99.

Hobson, Harold. "Samuel Beckett: Dramatist of the Year." *International Theatre Annual* 1. London: Calder, 1956. 153.

Howard, Patricia. "Not Mercies/Not I." *Samuel Beckett Today/Aujourd'hui* 2 (1993): 311–20.

Juliet, Charles. *Conversations with Samuel Beckett and Bram van Velde.* Leiden: Academic Press, 1995.

Kalb, Jonathan. *Beckett in Performance.* Cambridge: Cambridge University Press, 1989.

Katz, Daniel. *Saying I No More: Subjectivity and Consciousness in the Prose of Samuel Beckett.* Evanston: Northwestern University Press, 1999.

Kawin, Bruce. "On Not Having the Last Word: Beckett, Wittgenstein, and the Limits of Language." *Ineffability: Naming the Unnamable from Dante to Beckett.* New York: AMS, 1984. 189–202.

Kenner, Hugh. *Samuel Beckett: A Critical Study.* London: Calder, 1961.

Knowlson, James. *Damned to Fame. The Life of Samuel Beckett.* London: Bloomsbury, 1996.

Knowlson, James, and John Pilling. *Frescoes of the Skull: The Recent Prose and Drama of Samuel Beckett.* London: Calder, 1979.

Lawley, Paul. "Counterpoint, Absence and the Medium in Beckett's *Not I.*" *Modern Drama* 26.4 (1983): 407–14.

Levi, Shimon. *Samuel Beckett's Self-Referential Drama: The Three I's.* Basingstoke: Macmillan, 1990.

Locatelli, Carla. *Unwording the World: Samuel Beckett's Prose Works after the Nobel Prize.* Philadelphia: University of Pennsylvania Press, 1990.

Matoba, Junko. "Religious Overtones in the Darkened Area of Beckett's Later Short Plays." *Samuel Beckett Today: Beckett and Religion* 9. Amsterdam: Rodopi, 2000. 31–41.

McMullen, Anna. *Theatre on Trial: Samuel Beckett's Later Drama.* New York: Routledge, 1993.

Mercier, Vivian. *Beckett/Beckett.* New York: Oxford University Press, 1977.

Miller, Lawrence. *Samuel Beckett: The Expressive Dilemma.* Houndmills: Macmillan, 1992.

Murphy, Vincent. "Being and Perception: Beckett's *Film.*" *Modern Drama* 18 (1975): 43–48.

O'Hara, James Donald. *Samuel Beckett's Hidden Drives: Structural Uses of Depth Psychology.* Gainesville: University Press of Florida, 1997.

Oppenheim, Lois. *The Painted Word: Samuel Beckett's Dialogue with Art.* Ann Arbor: University of Michigan Press, 2000.

Pilling, John. *Samuel Beckett.* London: Routledge, 1976.

Pilling, John, ed. *The Cambridge Companion to Beckett.* Cambridge: University Press, 1994.

———. *Beckett's "Dream" Notebook.* Reading: Beckett International Foundation, 1999.

Politi, Jina. "'Not (Not I).'" *Journal of Literature and Theology* 6.4 (1992): 345–55.

Pountney, Rosemary. *Theatre of Shadows.* Gerrards Cross: Colin Smythe, 1988.

Read, David. "Artistic Theory in the Work of Samuel Beckett." *Journal of Beckett Studies* 8 (Autumn 1982): 7–22.

Ricks, Christopher. *Beckett's Dying Words.* Oxford: Clarendon Press, 1990.

Rosen, Steven. *Samuel Beckett and the Pessimistic Tradition.* New Brunswick: Rutgers University Press, 1976.

Schmid, Herta. "Samuel Beckett's Play, *Quad:* An Abstract Synthesis of the Theater." *Canadian-American Slavic Studies* 22.1–4 (1988): 263–87.

States, Bert. *The Shape of Paradox: An Essay on Waiting for Godot.* Berkeley: University of California Press, 1978.

———. "Beckett's Laboratory/Theatre." *Modern Drama* 30.1 (1987): 14–22.

Trezise, Thomas. *Into the Breach: Samuel Beckett and the Ends of Literature.* Princeton: University Press, 1990.

Vancouver Art Gallery. *Samuel Beckett: Teleplays,* 1988.

Whitelaw, Billie. *Who He?* London: Hodder and Stoughton, 1995.

Wolosky, Shira. *Language Mysticism: The Negative Way of Language in Eliot, Beckett, and Celan.* Stanford: Stanford University Press, 1995.

Worth, Katherine. *Samuel Beckett's Theatre: Life Journeys*. Oxford: Clarendon, 2001.

Zeifman, Hersh. "Being and Non-Being: Samuel Beckett's *Not I*." *Modern Drama* 19 (1976): 35–46.

Zilliacus, Clas. *Beckett and Broadcasting: A Study of the Works of Samuel Beckett for and in Radio and Television*. Abo: Akademi, 1976.

Theology, Philosophy, Literary Theory, Performance Theory

Abe, Masao. "*Kenosis* and Emptiness." *Buddhist Emptiness and Christian Trinity*. Ed. Roger Corless and Paul Knitter. New York: Paulist, 1990. 5–25.

———. "Kenotic God and Dynamic Sunyata." *The Emptying God*. Ed. John Cobb and Christopher Ives. Maryknoll: Orbis, 1990. 3–65.

Adorno, Theodor W. *Ästhetische Theorie*. Frankfurt: Suhrkamp, 1970.

———. *Gesammelte Schriften: Kulturkritik und Gesellschaft I*. (Bd. 10). Frankfurt: Suhrkamp, 1977.

Aquinas, St. Thomas. *Summa Theologiae: A Concise Translation*. Ed. Timothy McDermott. London: Eyre and Spottiswoode, 1989.

Armstrong, A. Hilary. "The Escape of the One." *Plotinian and Christian Studies*. London: Variorum Reprints, 1979. 77–89.

———. "Negative Theology." *Plotinian and Christian Studies*. London: Variorum Reprints, 1979. 176–89.

Arnheim, Rudolf. *Film as Art*. London: Faber, 1958.

———. *Art and Visual Perception: A Psychology of the Creative Eye*. Berkeley: University of California Press, 1974.

Artaud, Antonin. *The Theater and Its Double*. New York: Grove, 1958.

Auslander, Phillip. *Liveness: Performance in a Mediatized Culture*. London: Routledge, 1999.

Barthes, Roland. *The Neutral*. New York: Columbia University Press, 2005.

Benjamin, Walter. *Das Kunstwerk im Zeitalter seiner technischen Reproduzierbarkeit*. Frankfurt: Suhrkamp, 1977.

Blanchot, Maurice. *The Space of Literature*. Trans. Ann Smock. Lincoln: University of Nebraska Press, 1982.

———. *The Infinite Conversation*. Trans. Susan Hanson. Minneapolis: University of Minnesota Press, 1993.

———. *Faux Pas*. Trans. Charlotte Mandell. Stanford: Stanford University Press, 2001.

———. *The Book to Come*. Trans. Charlotte Mandell. Stanford: Stanford University Press, 2003.

Bloom, Harold. "The Internalization of Quest-Romance." *Romanticism and Consciousness: Essays in Criticism*. Ed. Harold Bloom. New York: Norton, 1970. 3–24.

Bradley, Arthur. "God *Sans* Being: Derrida, Marion and 'A Paradoxical Writing of the Word *Without*.'" *Literature and Theology* 14.3 (2000): 299–312.

von Brück, Michael, and Whalen Lai. *Buddhismus und Christentum: Geschichte, Konfrontation, Dialog.* Munich: Beck, 1997.

Bryson, Norman. "The Gaze in the Expanded Field." *Vision and Visuality.* Ed. Hal Foster. Seattle: Bay, 1988. 87–113.

Candrakirti. *Lucid Exposition of the Middle Way.* Trans. Mervyn Sprung. Boulder: Prajna, 1979.

Caputo, John. "Heidegger and Theology." *The Cambridge Companion to Heidegger.* Ed. Charles Guignon. Cambridge: University Press, 1993. 270–88.

———. *The Prayers and Tears of Jacques Derrida.* Bloomington: Indiana University Press, 1997.

Caputo, John, and Michael Scanlon, eds. *God, the Gift, and Postmodernism.* Bloomington: Indiana University Press, 1999.

Carlson, Thomas A. *Indiscretion: Finitude and the Naming of God.* Chicago: University of Chicago Press, 1999.

Chatman, Seymour. *Coming to Terms: The Rhetoric of Narrative in Fiction and Film.* Ithaca: Cornell University Press, 1990.

Clément, Olivier. *The Roots of Christian Mysticism.* New York: New City, 1993.

Corless, Roger, and Paul Knitter, eds. *Buddhist Emptiness and Christian Trinity: Essays and Explorations.* New York: Paulist, 1990.

Coward, Harold. *Derrida and Indian Philosophy.* Albany: State University of New York Press, 1990.

Coward, Harold, and Toby Foshay, eds. *Derrida and Negative Theology.* Albany: State University of New York, 1992.

Deak, Frantisek. *Symbolist Theater: The Formation of an Avant-Garde.* Baltimore: Johns Hopkins University Press, 1993.

Derrida, Jacques. *Writing and Difference.* Trans. Alan Bass. Chicago: University of Chicago Press, 1978.

———. "*Différance.*" *Margins of Philosophy.* Trans. Alan Bass. Chicago: University of Chicago Press, 1982. 1–27.

———. "How to Avoid Speaking: Denials." *Derrida and Negative Theology.* Ed. Harold Coward and Toby Foshay. Albany: State University of New York, 1992. 73–142.

———. *Given Time: Counterfeit Money.* Trans. Peggy Kamuf. Chicago: University of Chicago Press, 1992.

———. *Acts of Literature.* Ed. Derek Attridge. London: Routledge, 1992.

———. *On the Name.* Stanford: Stanford University Press, 1993.

———. *The Gift of Death.* Trans. David Wills. Chicago: University of Chicago Press, 1995.

———. *Archive Fever.* Trans. Eric Prenowitz. Chicago: University of Chicago Press, 1996.

Dionysius the Areopagite. *On the Divine Names and the Mystical Theology.* Trans. C. E. Rolt. London: Macmillan, 1920.

———. (Pseudo-Dionysius). *The Complete Works.* Trans. Colm Luibheid. New York: Paulist, 1987.

Eckhart, Meister. *The Essential Sermons, Commentaries, Treatises, and Defense.* New York: Paulist, 1981.

———. *Selected Writings.* London: Penguin, 1994.

———. *Deutsche Predigten: Eine Auswahl.* Stuttgart: Reclam, 2001.

Foshay, Toby Avard. "Denegation, Nonduality, and Language in Derrida and Dogen." *Philosophy East and West* 44 (July 1994): 543–58.

Freedman, Barbara. *Staging the Gaze: Postmodernism, Psychoanalysis, and Shakespearean Comedy.* Ithaca: Cornell University Press, 1991.

Gadamer, Hans Georg. *Truth and Method.* New York: Seabury, 1975.

———. "Thinking as Redemption: Plotinus between Plato and Augustine." *Hermeneutics, Religion, and Ethics.* New Haven: Yale University Press, 1999. 76–90.

Gropius, Walter, et al., eds. *The Theater of the Bauhaus.* Baltimore: Johns Hopkins University Press, 1996.

Hadot, Pierre. *Plotinus or the Simplicity of Vision.* Chicago: University of Chicago Press, 1993.

Hart, Kevin. *The Trespass of the Sign.* Cambridge: Cambridge University Press, 1989.

———. "The Experience of Poetry." http//:www.arts.monash.edu.au/cclcs/about/staff_info/hart.html. *Boxkite* 2 (1998): 285–304. My references are to the online version, the link to which has since disappeared.

———. "Jacques Derrida: The God Effect." *Post-Secular Philosophy: Between Philosophy and Theology.* Ed. Phillip Blond. London: Routledge, 1998. 259–80.

———. *The Dark Gaze: Maurice Blanchot and the Sacred.* Chicago: University of Chicago Press, 2004.

Harvey, David. *The Condition of Postmodernity: An Enquiry into the Origins of Cultural Change.* Oxford: Blackwell, 1989.

Hayes, Zachary. *St. Bonaventure's on the Reduction of the Arts to Theology: Translation with Introduction and Commentary.* St. Bonaventure: Franciscan Institute, St. Bonaventure University, 1996.

Hegel, G. W. F. *Aesthetics: Lectures on Fine Art,* vol. 1. Trans. T. M. Knox. Oxford: Clarendon Press, 1975.

Heidegger, Martin. *Gelassenheit.* Pfullingen: Neske, 1959.

———. *Unterwegs zur Sprache.* Pfullingen: Neske 1959.

———. "The Thing." *Poetry, Language, Thought.* Trans. Albert Hofstadter. New York: Harper and Row, 1971. 163–86.

———. *On the Way to Language.* Trans. Peter Hertz. San Francisco: Harper and Row, 1971.

———. *The Question concerning Technology.* Trans. William Lovitt. New York: Harper, 1977.

———. "The Nature of Language." *Critical Theory since Plato.* Ed. Hazard Adams. Fort Worth: Harcourt Brace, 1992. 1091–97.

———. *Basic Writings.* San Francisco: Harper, 1993.

Hemming, Laurence Paul. *Postmodernity's Transcending: Devaluing God.* London: SCM Press, 2005.

Hindrichs, Gunnar. "Scheitern als Rettung: Ästhetische Erfahrung nach Adorno." *Deutsche Vierteljahrsschrift für Literaturwissenschaft und Geistesgeschichte.* March 2000, 74.1. 146–75.

Horkheimer, Max, and Theodor W. Adorno. *Dialectic of Enlightenment.* Trans. John Cumming. New York: Continuum, 1982.

Hughes, Kevin L. "Remember Bonaventure? (Onto)theology and Ecstasy." *Modern Theology* 19.4 (October 2003): 529–45.

Hyppolite, Jean. "The Ineffable." *Logic and Existence.* Albany: State University of New York Press, 1997. 7–21.

Jay, Martin. "Scopic Regimes of Modernity." *Vision and Visuality.* Ed. Hal Foster. Seattle: Bay, 1988. 3–23.

———. *Downcast Eyes.* Berkeley: University of California Press, 1993.

———. "Experience without a Subject: Walter Benjamin and the Novel." *Cultural Semantics: Keywords of our Time.* Amherst: University of Massachusetts Press, 1998. 47–61.

Kant, Immanuel. *Critique of Judgment.* Trans. Werner Pluhar. Indianapolis: Hackett, 1987.

Katz, Steven. *Mysticism and Philosophical Analysis.* London: Sheldon, 1978.

Kirby, E. T. *Total Theatre: A Critical Anthology.* New York: Dutton, 1969.

Kleist, Heinrich von. "Ueber das Marionettentheater." *Kleists Aufsatz über das Marionettentheater: Studien und Interpretationen.* Hg. Walter Müller-Seidel. Berlin: Erich Schmidt, 1967. 9–16.

Lacoste, Jean-Yves. *Experience and the Absolute: Disputed Questions on the Humanity of Man.* New York: Fordham University Press, 2004.

Levin, David M. *The Opening of Vision: Nihilism and the Postmodern Situation.* New York: Routledge, 1988.

———. *The Listening Self: Personal Growth, Social Change and the Closure of Metaphysics.* London: Routledge, 1989.

Levin, David M., ed. *Modernity and the Hegemony of Vision.* Berkeley: University of California Press, 1993.

Lévinas, Emmanuel. *Of God Who Comes to Mind.* Stanford: Stanford University Press, 1998.

Lodge, David. "The Language of Modernist Fiction: Metaphor and Metonymy." *Modernism 1890–1930.* Ed. Malcolm Bradbury et al. Harmondworth: Penguin, 1976. 481–96.

———. *The Modes of Modern Writing: Metaphor, Metonymy, and the Typology of Modern Literature.* Ithaca: Cornell University Press, 1977.

Lossky, Vladimir. *The Mystical Theology of the Eastern Church.* Crestwood: St. Vladimir's Seminary Press, 1998.

Loy, David. *Nonduality: A Study in Comparative Philosophy.* New Haven: Yale University Press, 1988.

———. "The Deconstruction of Buddhism." *Derrida and Negative Theology.* Ed. Harold Coward et al. Albany: State University of New York Press, 1992. 225–53.

———. *Healing Deconstruction: Postmodern Thought in Buddhism and Christianity.* Atlanta: Scholars, 1996.

Marion, Jean-Luc. *God without Being: Hors-Texte.* Trans. Thomas Carlson. Chicago: University of Chicago Press, 1991.

———. "The Saturated Phenomenon." *Philosophy Today* 40.1–4 (Spring 1996): 103–24.

———. "In the Name: How to Avoid Speaking of Negative Theology." *God, the Gift, and Postmodernism.* Ed. John Caputo and Michael Scanlon. Bloomington: Indiana University Press, 1999. 20–53.

———. *Being Given: Toward a Phenomenology of Givenness.* Trans. Jeffrey L. Kosky. Stanford: University Press, 2002.

———. *In Excess: Studies of Saturated Phenomena.* New York: Fordham University Press, 2002.

———. *The Crossing of the Visible.* Trans. James K. A. Smith. Stanford: Stanford University Press, 2004.

———. *Le visible et le révélé.* Paris: Cerf, 2005.

McAuley, Gay. *Space in Performance: Making Meaning in the Theatre.* Ann Arbor: University of Michigan Press, 1999.

McKnight, Stephen A. 1989. *Sacralizing the Secular: The Renaissance Origins of Modernity.* Baton Rouge: Louisiana State University Press.

Merleau-Ponty, Maurice. *Phenomenology of Perception.* Trans. Colin Smith. London: Routledge, 1962.

Milbank, John. "Sublimity: the Modern Transcendent." *Religion, Modernity and Postmodernity.* Ed. Paul Heelas. Oxford: Blackwell, 1998. 258–84.

Nagarjuna. *The Fundamental Wisdom of the Middle Way: Nagarjuna's Mulamadhyamakakarika.* Trans. Jay L. Garfield. Oxford: Oxford University Press, 1995.

Nancy, Jean-Luc. "The Sublime Offering." *Of the Sublime: Presence in Question.* Ed. Jean-Francois Courtine. Albany: State University of New York Press, 1993. 25–53.

———. "Le nom de Dieu chez Blanchot." *Magazine Littéraire* 424 (2003): 66–68.

Nishitani, Keiji. *Religion and Nothingness.* Berkeley: University of California Press, 1982.

Ouspensky, Leonid, and Vladimir Lossky. *The Meaning of Icons.* Crestwood: St. Vladimir's Seminary Press, 1999.

Pandit, Moti Lal. *Sunyata: The Essence of Mahayana Spirituality.* New Delhi: Munshiram Manharlal, 1998.

Paris, Jean. *Painting and Linguistics.* Pittsburgh: Carnegie-Mellon University, 1975.

Phelan, Peggy. "The Ontology of Performance: Representation without Reproduction." *Unmarked: The Politics of Performance.* London: Routledge, 1993. 146–66.

Prokurat, Michael, et al. *Historical Dictionary of the Orthodox Church.* Lanham: Scarecrow, 1996.

Scharfstein, Ben-Ami. *Ineffability: The Failure of Words in Philosophy and Religion.* New York: State University of New York Press, 1993.

Schubert, Vernanz. *Plotin: Einführung in sein Philosophieren.* Munich: Karl Alber, 1973.

Sells, Michael. *Mystical Languages of Unsaying.* Chicago: University of Chicago Press, 1994.

Seubold, Günter. *Heideggers Analyse der neuzeitlichen Technik.* Freiburg: Alber, 1986.

Seyhan, Asade. *Representation and Its Discontents: The Critical Legacy of German Romanticism.* Berkeley: University of California Press, 1992.

Sprung, Mervyn. Trans. Candrakirti. *Lucid Exposition of the Middle Way.* Boulder: Prajna, 1979.

Suzuki, Daisetz Teitaro. *Mysticism: Christian and Buddhist.* New York: Allen and Unwin, 1979.

Theodore, St. the Studite. *On the Holy Icons.* Crestwood: St. Vladimir's Seminary Press, 2001.

Turner, Denys. *The Darkness of God: Negativity in Christian Mysticism.* Cambridge: University Press, 1995.

Virilio, Paul. *The Art of the Motor.* Minneapolis: University of Minnesota Press, 1995.

de Vries, Hent. *Philosophy and the Turn to Religion.* Baltimore: Johns Hopkins University Press, 1999.

Waldenfels, Hans. *Absolutes Nichts.* Freiburg: Herder, 1976.

Ward, Graham. "Kenosis and Naming: Beyond Analogy and Towards *Allegoria Amoris.*" *Religion, Modernity, and Postmodernity.* Ed. Paul Heelas et al. Oxford: Blackwell, 1998. 233–57.

Ward, Graham, ed. *The Postmodern God.* Oxford: Blackwell, 1997.

Wiese, Benno von. "Das verlorene und wieder zu findende Paradies: Eine Studie über den Begriff der Anmut bei Goethe, Kleist und Schiller." *Kleists Aufsatz über das Marionettentheater: Studien und Interpretationen.* Hg. Walter Müller-Seidel. Berlin: Erich Schmidt, 1967. 196–220.

Williams, A. N. *The Ground of Union: Deification in Aquinas and Palamas.* New York: Oxford University Press, 1999.

Williams, J. P. *Denying Divinity: Apophasis in the Patristic Christian and Soto Zen Buddhist Traditions.* Oxford: Oxford University Press, 2000.

Wolin, Richard. *Walter Benjamin: An Aesthetic of Redemption.* New York: Columbia University Press, 1982.

Wolosky, Shira. "An 'Other' Negative Theology: On Derrida's 'How to Avoid Speaking: Denials.'" *Poetics Today* 19.2 (1998): 261–80.

Index

ICONIC SPACES